TREATING THE PUBLIC

TREATING THE PUBLIC

CHARITABLE THEATER AND CIVIC HEALTH IN THE EARLY MODERN ATLANTIC WORLD

RACHAEL BALL

LOUISIANA STATE UNIVERSITY PRESS
BATON ROUGE

Published by Louisiana State University Press

Manufactured in the United States of America
First printing

Designer: Barbara Neely Bourgoyne
Typeface: MillerText
Printer and binder: Maple Press (digital)

Map by Mary Lee Eggart

Library of Congress Cataloging-in-Publication Data
Names: Ball, Rachael, 1980– author.
Title: Treating the public : charitable theater and civic health in the early modern Atlantic world / Rachael Ball.
Description: Baton Rouge : Louisiana State University Press, [2016] | Includes bibliographical references and index.
Identifiers: LCCN 2016027052| ISBN 978-0-8071-6508-9 (cloth : alk. paper) | ISBN 978-0-8071-6509-6 (pdf) | ISBN 978-0-8071-6510-2 (epub) | ISBN 978-0-8071-6511-9 (mobi)
Subjects: LCSH: English drama—Early modern and Elizabethan, 1500–1600—History and criticism. | English drama—17th century—History and criticism. | Theater—Great Britain—History—16th century. | Theater—Great Britain—History—17th century. | Spanish drama—Classical period, 1500–1700—History and criticism. | Theater—Spain—History—16th century. | Theater—Spain—History—17th century. | Latin American drama—16th century—History and criticism. | Latin American drama—17th century—History and criticism. | Theater—Latin America—History—16th century. | Theater—Latin America—History—17th century. | Theater and society.
Classification: LCC PR651 .B25 2016 | DDC 792.09/031—dc23
LC record available at https://lccn.loc.gov/2016027052

The paper in this book meets the guidelines for permanence and durability of the Committee on Production Guidelines for Book Longevity of the Council on Library Resources. ♾

CONTENTS

ACKNOWLEDGMENTS

I initially began this project while in graduate school at the Ohio State University. I was lucky enough to be supported by generous colleagues and mentors in the Departments of History, Theater, Spanish and Portuguese, and English. I thank my graduate school colleagues Katy Becker, Jim Bennett, David Dennis, Laura Michele Diener, Gina DiSalvo, John Hunt, Steven Hyland, Cameron Jones, Lizzie Nixon, Andrea Smidt, and Dustin Walcher. For their time, guidance, and generous feedback in the early stages of this project, I owe debts to Kenneth Andrien, John Brooke, David Cressy, Elizabeth Davis, Richard Dutton, Richard Gordon, Donald Larson, Kittiya Lee, Thomas Postlewait, Dale van Kley, and Lisa Voigt.

I'm particularly grateful to Geoffrey Parker, who was my dissertation supervisor. Geoffrey has been my mentor, my collaborator on other projects, and my friend. I can never thank him enough for his continued support and kindness.

This book could not have been completed without funding from the Ohio State University Department of History, the US Fulbright Commission, the Spanish Ministry of Culture, and the University of Alaska Anchorage College of Arts and Sciences. During my Fulbright year, I had the good fortune to work with Jim Amelang, whose guidance was invaluable at a crucial time. The friendships that I formed with other Fulbrighters, especially Mayte Green-Mercado and Patrick O'Banion, enriched my research and my life. Ángel Bernardos, Maria Cruz de Carlos, José Luis Manso, Maribel Porras, Carlos Rodriguez, and Javier Varela helped make Madrid my home back then and continue to do so every time I return.

As the project progressed, I racked up a number of debts. This book could not have been completed without the gracious help of a number of librarians and archivists who assisted me during the course of my research on *corrales de comedias* over the past decade. Special thanks go to the Interlibrary Loan department at UAA and to the many archivists at the Biblioteca Nacional de España, the Archivo de la Villa de Madrid, the Archivo Histórico Nacional de España, the Archivo General de Simancas, the Archivo General de las Indias, the Archivo General de la Nación de México, the Archivo Histórico del Distrito Federal de México, the Archivo del Ayuntamiento de Puebla, and the Hispanic Society of America.

My colleagues in the History Departments at Kenyon College, Minnesota State University–Mankato, and finally, the University of Alaska Anchorage supported me with good cheer. I'm particularly indebted to Eliza Ablovatski, Jeff Bowman, and Glenn McNair at Kenyon; to Chris Corley, Lori Lahlum, and Matt Loayza at MNSU; and to Elizabeth Dennison, Paul Dunscomb, Songho Ha, Ian Hartman, and Bill Myers at UAA. My write on site compatriots, Heather Adams, Dayna Defeo, Sharon Emmerichs, Kurt Johnson, Zeynep Kilic, Rebeca Maseda, Amanda Murphy, Curtis Murphy, and Jennifer Stone, gently peer-pressured me to write when I felt unmotivated and helped me celebrate milestones. Kelly Shannon and I went through much of the process of writing our book manuscripts together. I am so grateful for her friendship and solidarity. I tested out some of my ideas in the classroom and am obliged to Khafani Amundson, Anthony Davis, Celeste Earley, David Reamer, Jen Ruckle, and Kailyn Vaughan, whose questions and comments pushed me to think about my material in new ways. Heather Caldwell, Annie Dubois, Josh Grabel, Kyle Hampton, Kae Hartman, Solveig Pedersen, Jekka Roder, Eliza Salvo, and Caroline Wilson have helped me to make the forty-ninth state my home.

I presented parts of various chapters of this work at several conferences, and I appreciate the feedback colleagues gave me at these venues. I'm also thankful to the editors and anonymous readers at *Comedia Performance* and *The Sixteenth Century Journal*. Some colleagues deserve special debts of gratitude for their feedback and support and for reading parts of the manuscript at various stages. In particular,

Rayne Allinson, Michelle Armstrong-Partida, Jodi Campbell, Kaja Cook, Anne Cruz, Meg Greer, Ian Hartman, Liz Lehfeldt, Meg Pearson, and Betsy Wright helped make this book a reality. Alisa Plant and then Rand Dotson at LSU Press have worked patiently with me through the process. Gary Von Euer's copyediting work in preparing this manuscript for publication has exceeded all expectations. Without them this project would never have come to fruition.

My family has been a great source of comfort and inspiration. My late father Robert Ball, who was an educator and researcher, instilled in me a lifelong desire to learn. My mother Nan Ball is probably the reason that I'm an early modernist. I have been buoyed through hard times and able to appreciate the good ones more because of my relationships with Hilary and Toby Winkler, Wally and Gitta Rice, and Jodi Rice and David Kruger. I thank my nieces Norah, Isla, Lily, and Charlotte. Finally, I owe a special debt of gratitude to my husband Mark Rice. With graciousness, good humor, and a sense of adventure, he has followed me across the country in my pursuit of academic employment. Mark has read countless drafts of chapters and constantly cheered me on toward the finish line. I could not have completed this book without him as its champion and as mine. I dedicate this book to him.

TREATING THE PUBLIC

Introduction

PUBLIC THEATER AND PUBLIC HEALTH IN THE EARLY MODERN ATLANTIC WORLD

Over the course of his career, the Golden Age Spanish playwright Lope de Vega (1562–1635) became an incredibly famous celebrity. This prodigious and prolific "monster of nature" produced hundreds of works for the stage. Although at times the playwright disparaged his own plays as "mercantile verses," their popularity was remarkable.[1] In the later stages of his career, Lope worked to deliver corrected originals of his *comedias* to the book printers who published them and thereby increased their readership as written texts and extended their lives as theatrical ones.[2] Performances of the dramatist's works took place in front of large urban audiences at the *corrales de comedias,* or inn-yard theaters, in cities throughout Spain and parts of colonial Latin America. Lope's portrait hung in the homes of many early modern Spaniards. When he died, his funeral rites in the court and capital of Madrid lasted nine days. The success of Lope de Vega during the Golden Age—a period in Spanish history that includes the last decades of the sixteenth century and the first half of the seventeenth century and that corresponds with the tremendous output of many other brilliant literary and visual artists, such as Miguel de Cervantes, Tirso de Molina, Pedro Calderón de la Barca, Diego Velázquez, Francisco de Quevedo, and Sor Juana Inés de la Cruz—highlights the visibility and importance of theater in urban daily life in early modern Spain and its global empire.

In the sixteenth and seventeenth centuries large playgoing audiences and significant readerships existed for Spanish *comedias* in Castile and beyond. In New Spain, colonial subjects and authors staged or imitated the plays of Tirso. Some, such as Bartolomé de Alva Ixtlixóchitl, were busy translating plays by Lope de Vega and Calderón into Nahuatl.[3] Yet in spite of the tremendous output and contemporary fame of Spanish playwrights and performers, it is William Shakespeare (1564–1616) and the Globe Theatre of London that have come to epitomize Renaissance drama throughout much of the English-speaking world.

The "upstart Crow" was less internationally famous and less prolific during his lifetime than the "Spanish Phoenix of Wits," but this seems a near-blasphemous statement from an English speaker on the four hundredth anniversary of Shakespeare's death. For a myriad of reasons, the Bard and his plays have continued to dominate the literary canon and classrooms of many English and Theater departments across the United States.[4] Shakespeare has been and, undoubtedly, will continue to be the subject of countless popular biographies and academic studies. Many digital humanities projects and numerous scholarly journals are devoted solely to the study of Shakespeare's poetry and the nearly forty plays attributed to him.

This book is not a study of Lope de Vega or of Shakespeare or of their dramatic works, but this discussion of their early modern fame and continued influence serves as an entry point into this comparative study of theater as an urban phenomenon and as a political, social, and cultural institution in the early modern Spanish and Anglo Atlantic Worlds from approximately 1560 to 1660. In both Catholic and Protestant polities in Europe, troupes of approximately twelve to eighteen actors formed to perform plays, which were increasingly written by professional dramatists. By the second half of the sixteenth century, performances had become regular at many European courts, and permanent structures to accommodate actors and audiences began to be built. In Elizabethan England, the court at Westminster began to patronize the best of the acting troupes based in the wider London metropolis.[5] This patronage took place in spite of the concerns about disorder, disease, and sanitation felt by some city authorities in London. By 1598 only monarchs and great nobles had the authority to authorize acting companies in England.

In Spain, the Council of Castile and the Council of Aragon licensed acting companies, which quickly came to include not only men but also women. Because of decrees that forbade more than one troupe of actors to be resident in or to perform in most Spanish cities at a given time, acting companies had to travel with relative frequency.[6] Consequently, public theaters developed as important social sites in urban locations throughout the kingdoms of Spain in the sixteenth and seventeenth centuries. These same companies of actors and actresses also competed for the contracts to perform the *autos sacramentales,* or religious one-act plays, during important Catholic festivals such as Corpus Christi. Literary scholars and theater historians have demonstrated that during the second half of the sixteenth century, Spanish theater and playwriting underwent a series of significant changes. In the 1540s and 1550s, companies of actors, like those created by Lope de Rueda and Alonso de la Vega, began to form in order to meet the growing appetite for performed drama in Spanish cities, particularly Seville, Valencia, and Valladolid. Another crucial series of developments were the visits of companies of Italian actors, who toured both peninsulas and helped to make the comedy of intrigue and witty dialogue popular in Spain. Their style of performance had a marked effect on Lope de Vega's dramatic writing and the development of the *comedia nueva.*[7]

The *comedia nueva* that developed in the late 1570s and 1580s and that Lope de Vega adopted, adapted, and popularized has a particular—though not rigidly set—form of three acts, and polymetric verse.[8] *Comedias* vary tremendously in subject matter, but many of these plays are tragicomedies that feature a pair of lovers, comic servants, complicating characters, and representatives of authority and order. Although many of these lovers, buffoons, and rulers might easily be seen as generic or stock characters, others have forcible personalities and idiosyncratic tendencies and moved audiences to laughter and tears then and now. *Comedias* tend to fall into one of two thematic varieties: the nationalistic history play or the cloak and sword drama. Both of these types of drama appealed to Spanish audiences that included men and women, nobles, middling merchants, artisans, and servants and other day laborers.

During the early modern period, it was the theater of Lope, not the theater of Shakespeare, that dominated the daily lives of the people who watched it. The commercial theater of the kingdoms of the universal Spanish monarchy was the greatest hit of its day. Deep and significant influences that fostered the integration of theater into daily life in cities were largely the products of the important connections that developed between the evolving theater of the *comedia* and charitable funds devoted to the care of patients in the hospitals and orphanages of early modern Spanish cities. These financial ties aided and abetted the production of commercial drama and created a protected and integrated space for theaters to operate within the urban frameworks of the cities whose populaces they entertained and whose opinions they sometimes overtly influenced. The English theater of Shakespeare, while undeniably influential, did not have the same reach and impact because it did not have these same deep connections to the charitable institutions that became so important to understandings of urbanism in the Spanish Empire.

Medieval monasteries had undertaken charitable endeavors by founding hospitals to care for the sick, wounded, and needy of Western Europe.[9] These hospitals had flourished during the Crusading Era, and during the thirteenth century many urban centers began to create and utilize these institutions as well. From the fourteenth century on, municipalities as well as urban religious brotherhoods and wealthy individual patrons began to take over the role of establishing hospitals in cities. These institutions both cared for the most marginalized—the sick, the poor, the orphaned, the abandoned—and, from a late medieval and early modern perspective, cared for society by removing a large segment of its most allegedly disreputable individuals from the public view. Hospitals aimed to heal both the physical body and the soul of patients; in Catholic lands they continued to employ priests, as well as university-educated physicians, licensed phlebotomists, apothecaries, and many other staff both before and after the Council of Trent (1545–1563).

Early modern hospitals varied greatly in their size and focus: there were military hospitals founded for troops; plague hospitals; small hospitals that specifically catered to the elderly members of certain guilds and professions; and large hospitals, which treated a variety of maladies, served as practical training grounds for young physicians, and developed anatomy theaters for instruction. Hospitals in Renaissance Spain and England also fought homelessness and hunger, two problems that plagued early modern cities. They were institutions that combined the qualities of the clinic, the poorhouse, and the nursing home. Some, such as Madrid's Hospital General, which Philip II founded in 1566 by combining three older hospitals, took in hundreds of patients with curable diseases in any given year.[10] Others like Bethlem, or Bedlem as it was commonly known in early modern London, housed the severest cases of destitute persons suffering from mental illnesses yet deemed curable by the institution's governors.

The hospitals of Spanish cities received significant financial aid in these endeavors from the proceeds of the *corrales de comedias*. This relationship between the Spanish theaters and the hospitals had some ironic complications: the centrally located theaters were places where playgoers of all social ranks and walks of life mingled and potentially spread disease as they sought entertainment. Yet it was this relationship and the mass production, both literary and theatrical, of the national Spanish drama, or *comedia,* that allowed theater to provide a social service for Spaniards, and this financial relationship made it extremely difficult to shut down the playhouses of Spain for any great length of time.

Several scholars have examined the connections between the *corrales* and charitable institutions, but their work lacks the chronological and conceptual focus of this study. Carmen Sanz Ayán and Bernardo García García have examined the financial and institutional relationship between Madrid's *corrales de comedias* and hospitals during the reign of Philip II in their study, *Teatros y comediantes en el Madrid de Felipe II.*[11] They compellingly demonstrated the influence that social welfare in Madrid had on the production of public theater in the court and capital during the last decades of the sixteenth century. Their study, however, focuses solely on the court city and ends with the changes in administration of the *corrales de comedias* that I discuss at length in the first chapter of this book. Golden Age theater historians N. D. Shergold, Charles Davis, and J. E. Varey have made many of the archived documents regarding the *corrales de comedias* of Madrid available to readers of Spanish in valuable document collections.[12] However, they do not comparatively analyze the relationship between theaters, city hospitals, and charitable organizations.

This study contends that the institutional relationships between the playhouses and acting companies and hospitals in England and the Anglo-Atlantic world played a less significant role in funding pious and charitable works of health care than they did in the Spanish Atlantic. This was in part because the Protestant emphasis on scripture and grace had reconceptualized charity and good works as less important to social life. Additionally, outside of London and its immediate environs, the populations and urban infrastructures of the early modern Anglo Atlantic could not and did not fully support such endeavors to the same degree until over a century later.

Although English acting companies did pay parish poor rates, thereby establishing a legal connection between theater and charity, these connections were largely limited to specific neighborhoods and had a more limited impact on social welfare. Scholars of early modern English drama have thus been more interested in metaphorical connections between playhouses and hospitals. They have noted the use of hospital scenes in some plays, and both historians and literary scholars have noted the ways that encouraging public visitation to hospitals like Bedlem mirrored the practice of playgoing as it put mentally ill patients onstage as a spectacle for entertainment.[13] Kenneth Jackson's work explores not only the ways that Bedlem was both a charity and an entertainment but also the ways that charity's meaning was contested in early modern London and the ways playwrights understood their own art.[14]

In the following chapters, I will explore the relationships between commercial drama and public health and urbanism, including issues of public opinion, in important cities of the Spanish and Anglo Atlantic in the sixteenth and seventeenth centuries. While this study compares the *corrales de comedias*, or inn-yard theaters, of Spanish cities with their English counterparts, it is fundamentally a work of asymmetrical comparative history: the heart of the study is Spain and the Spanish Atlantic World rather than England and the Anglo Atlantic, which is generally better known to English-speaking scholars. Such a juxtaposition of the two helps to reveal what is distinctive and significant about the lesser-studied Spanish case, and allows us to debunk reified notions of what is normative about early modern theater and its connection to urban and other social institutions. Thus, each of the first four chapters contains case studies that comparatively examine the early modern development of public theater in important cities. These comparisons—between Madrid and London, Seville and Bristol, Mexico City and Dublin, and Puebla de los Angeles and colonial British North American locations, particularly Williamsburg, Virginia—establish the uniqueness and importance of the system of public theater and charitable hospitals that developed in Castile and that Spaniards exported to their American colonies during the early modern period.

Actors, directors, and playwrights, who were looking to make a living, and administrators, who were looking to fund social services in the Spanish Atlantic, created an inn-yard empire of sorts, treating the public as they entertained it. Theaters became regular and central features of cities, and the production of plays helped to finance the physical and spiritual care of the marginalized sick and impoverished. Acting troupes fanned out from the court and capital of Madrid, performing in other major centers of the Hapsburg realms, such as Seville, Mexico City, Puebla, and Lima, and also in numerous other cities, including Valladolid, Toledo, Cordóba, and Saña, a colonial city in Peru abandoned in the eighteenth century after pirate raids and a severe flood. Many of those who made up early modern audiences welcomed the diversion, and municipal authorities and religious brotherhoods welcomed the chance to provide financial assistance to their hospitals, even if they wanted to exert greater authority over the often unruly and occasionally riotous audiences whose admission fees they so desired to collect.

It should come as no surprise that such a popular and influential cultural form has fostered a variety of scholarly interpretations. For many years, the dominant narrative in the history of the Renaissance theater in Spain was the one established by scholars such as José Antonio Maravall and José María Díez Borque. According to this view, Spanish theater was a mechanism for political and religious control used by absolutist authorities and a monolithic Church.[15] Díez Borque contended that the Golden Age *comedia* enabled its audience members to escape from the drudgery of their lives and their political and social troubles. While in his analysis the escapist spectacle of the *comedia* was a more democratized one than that put forward by Maravall, this was a limited democracy due to the marked separations in the playhouses and the price variations between sitting in a box and standing. In this view, while the *corrales de comedias* were a microcosm of early modern urban society, the dramas performed in them and the physical space of the playhouses still upheld rigid social structures promoted by the monarchy and Church.[16]

Such understandings of the theater as hegemonically representing the view of a monolithic Church or royal officials have been substantially undermined by scholarly works that examine the ways many authorities regarded theater with suspicion or ambivalence and that demonstrate the various positions held by the clergy and the widespread debate among promoters of reform, known as *arbitristas,* and officials about how to deal with social, political, and economic problems faced by the Spanish government.[17] While there are some elements of truth to the contentions of Maravall and Díez Borque, Golden Age Spanish theater could also subvert such conventions, and much more complex interactions took place between authorities, actors, and audiences than Maravall and Díez Borque allowed.

Melveena McKendrick, Elizabeth Wright, and Jodi Campbell, among others, have pushed against this older dominant narrative of the Spanish *comedia* as a baroque hegemon. McKendrick has posited that Spanish drama had a dual identity—national institution and artistic expression—and she argues that the relationships between society, politics, and drama were much more complex than the Maravall thesis allowed. In her study of Lope de Vega, Wright explores the complexity of the obstacles that Lope's success as a writer of *comedias* presented along his path of becoming a royal chronicler under the patronage of Philip III. Campbell has argued that numerous Golden Age playwrights examined political issues in their *comedias.* She contends that Tirso de Molina, whom scholars of Spanish drama have long assumed to be an exception for his marked political stances, was merely one of many who wrote plays with a critical edge to them, and that these plays can be used, not only by literary scholars but also by historians to consider early modern understandings of political events and contexts.[18]

For England, there is a large and ever-growing body of scholarship of literary analyses of various dramatic works and literary biographies of Shakespeare and other playwrights. There are also numerous histories of the early modern English theater and studies of acting companies and the audiences they drew, especially in London.[19] This extensive scholarship is in part the natural result of the reality that far more plays were performed in the playhouses of London than anywhere else in the Anglo Atlantic World. Many playwrights and actors were resident there or spent months or years resident there even if they came from elsewhere.[20]

As in the historiography of Spanish theater, there has been significant scholarly debate about the ways that theater in early modern England reflected court tastes—and was subject to censorship by the office of the Master of the Revels when it did not. Whiggish historical and literary traditions often viewed such censorship as heavy-handed and representative of an oppressive monarchy.[21] More recently the work of theater historians and literary critics has complicated this older view. As literary scholar Richard Dutton has perceptively argued, restrictions on the theater and actors in London and its suburbs stemmed from issues of having to deal with a growing, unclean, and often plague-ridden city as much as from partisan political censorship.[22] Similarly, shifting political and social attitudes of London and its audience meant that plays with subversive aspects made it past the censors and onto the stages for performance.[23]

Most scholars of Renaissance drama, including all those discussed above, have tended to situate their studies within national frameworks. None of the comparative studies of Spanish and English theater has extensively examined the differing relationships that theater had to public health in their respective environments in spite of the fundamental connection between hospitals, ideas about care for the poor, and the financing of public theaters. Although some have examined public opinion or urbanism, none of these comparative studies has taken an Atlantic World approach. Additionally, most of these previous studies, such as those by Walter Cohen, John Loftis, and Ivan Cañadas, have focused on the similarities between English and Spanish drama from a literary rather than a historical standpoint.[24] These studies, as undertaken by Loftis and Cohen, have done a great deal to foster our understandings of drama beyond national boundaries as they have examined the ways that English and Spanish drama independently developed from medieval literature and in parallel with the development of early modern capitalist structures. Most recently, Cañadas has insightfully analyzed the discourses of rank, gender, and hierarchy in the text of plays to discuss the polyphonic nature of public drama in these early modern societies. However, more historically grounded work would greatly contribute to our understanding of these processes and how they actually operated on the ground.

Margaret Greer has offered an entry point into this type of scholarship in her essay "A Tale of Three Cities: The Place of the Theatre in Early Modern Madrid, Paris, and London," in which she compares the Renaissance public drama of these three important urban locations. She observes that many of the similarities developed because of cross-fertilization across boundaries and cites the particular example of court spectacle, which originated in Italy and began to spread across Europe in the late fifteenth century, and humanist interest in the revival of classical works of drama. Greer's research has shown that public theaters were built more centrally in Madrid and Paris than they were in London. However, a 1548 ban on religious plays, the turmoil of the French Wars of Religion, and the early monopoly on performance by the Confrérie de la Passion stunted the development of theater in Paris.[25] While the early modern French theater also developed out of relationships with a religious brotherhood, the continued court influence on the theater made it less exportable to the provincial and colonial cities of seventeenth-century France.

Although there have been some broad comparative surveys of drama in the Americas, these works have been synthetic in nature. Scholars of colonial Mexican and Latin American theater have paid little attention to comparative issues in part because they have no direct, chronological analogues in the English colonies, which were founded later and often developed infrastructure more slowly, and in part because of the dominance of national frameworks of historiography. Instead, a number of

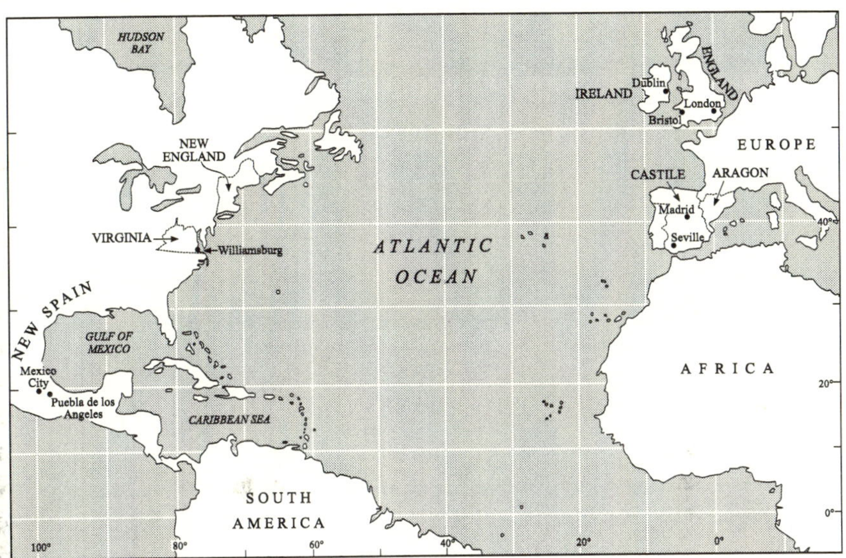

Some Key Theatrical Cities in the Spanish and Anglo Atlantic Worlds

scholars of Latin American drama have focused on the evangelical nature of religious theater in the Americas. For example, Adam Versényi, who largely follows Maravall's understanding of Golden Age Spanish theater as an oppressive, aristocratic, social force, argues that Cortés used theater as a tool to imitate the Aztec emperor and to reinforce the power of Franciscan friars. He argues that this was successful because evangelical and indigenous ritual spectacles blurred the lines between actor and audience.[26]

This book builds on the work of literary scholars, such as those discussed above, but it does so from a historical rather than literary perspective. It also draws on the foundations provided by theater historians and social and cultural historians, who have used theater as a lens for looking at history. However, this project employs a more Atlantic World rather than national perspective in its asymmetrical comparative analysis of the ways that urban dwellers experienced and used theater as a social, cultural, and economic institution. I draw on a rich variety of sources that includes royal decrees, town council minutes, contracts for the leases on playhouses, the contracts negotiated by acting companies, petitions from actors and actresses, hospital visitation records, polemical tracts and sermons written in opposition to the stage, letters and diaries, and the printed texts of some representative performed plays. Drawing these sources together reveals not only that the *corrales de comedias* became an integral part of urban daily life in the early modern Spanish Atlantic but also that they did so by providing significant aid to charitable endeavors and public health.

Chapter one, "'The Money That Comes from the Plays': Comedies and Charitable Urban Public Health Institutions in Madrid and London," examines the development of the theater and its relationship to the hospitals in the capital and court city of Spain in the sixteenth and seventeenth centuries. It compares the development of the centrally located theaters of the Spanish capital to that of the public theaters of London, which were outside the city's jurisdiction, and the private theaters, which emerged within the jurisdiction of the city but served a more elite set of playgoers. The permanent playhouses of Madrid were constructed during a period of rapid urban growth and in central neighborhoods that drew audiences of men and women from a number of different ranks and backgrounds.

This urban integration was reinforced as the *corrales de comedias* of Madrid emerged out of relationships between the hospitals and charitable confraternities that sponsored theater as a means of charitable funding for hospitals and orphanages, and then evolved into a mechanism for funding the city's efforts at public health and welfare. Madrid's playhouses thus faced regulation and scrutiny from both the court and the municipality. However, men and women involved in the business and those involved in hospital administration played up theater's charitable function and helped mitigate this regulation. As a result, the playhouses and the activities that took place in them became integrated into daily life in the rapidly growing court of Castile to an extent that was unmatched in any other European capital during the Renaissance.

This chapter also explores the development of audiences, playgoing publics, and theater's potential to influence public opinion in these two early modern urban centers. Playwrights, the characters they created in their plays, and the audiences who watched them all had an intimate working knowledge of the cities in which they operated. This knowledge led to the emergence of a genre of city comedies that catered to rather different types of audiences in Madrid and in London and that provide humorous, but nonetheless insightful, takes on a number of issues of urbanism. Playwrights and actors made reference to city institutions and public spaces; they exploited their audiences' knowledge of its streets and architecture; and at times they referenced specific events that had cultural currency and influenced opinion beyond the space of the playhouse.

In the second chapter, "Playing in the Port: Theater in Early Modern Seville and Bristol," I trace the development of commercial theater in the important port cities of Seville and Bristol. As home of the Indies trade and an important port, Seville was not only a city constantly in flux but it was also a microcosm of an early modern theater society. This was so even when it underwent population decline during the seventeenth century, as a result of the expulsion of the *moriscos,* flooding, and outbreaks of plague. Although there was ambivalence about theater on the part of civil and ecclesiastical authorities in Seville, and the port city's numerous early modern theaters did not develop out of any regular relationships with the religious brotherhoods, the municipal government of Seville decided to use theater to augment its coffers and to help fund institutions of charity. Acting company directors and performers frequently came to Seville to perform in the public theaters and to participate in the city's lavish Corpus Christi festivals that fostered urban pride and religious devotion.

This reality and the importance of urban institutions such as playhouses become strikingly clear when the early modern theaters of Seville are compared to the emerging playhouses of Bristol. By the seventeenth century, Bristol was second only to London in trade. Like Seville, Bristol played a key role in linking the metropole to wider Atlantic communities and economies. In both of these important provincial cities, commercial drama developed quite centrally in their respective urban topographies and landscapes. Both provided important funds that assisted hospitals and poor relief in these port cities, which were frequently in a state of flux and demographic change. Nonetheless, in spite of these parallels in economic roles and between theatrical activity and public health in these two cities, the comparison between them is ultimately asymmetrical because of the differences in their sizes, in the levels of documented commercial theatrical activity, and in the ways religious confessionalization shaped poor relief.

Chapter three, "Comedies in Colonial Contexts: Theater in Early Modern Mexico City and Dublin," outlines the way in which theater emerged as a thriving institution in Castile's overseas realms by the beginning of the seventeenth century, whereas this was less true of English colonial holdings in the Atlantic. Looking particularly at the cases of Mexico City and Dublin, it becomes clear that the Spanish colonists of the New World transported the symbiotic arrangement between the *corrales de comedias* and the hospitals to their new urban environments. The theater in Mexico, while strikingly similar to that in Castile, had new uses in the colonial setting, as dramatic performance became a tool for missionary activity and the conversion of the Native American population during the sixteenth century. It also became a potential tool for reasserting Spanish identity for peninsular Spaniards and for expressing wider identity as subjects of the universal Spanish monarchy for creole subjects in the Viceroyalty of New Spain. While theater could be a tool for colonial agendas, it was still one whose use was often blunted by competing interests and the necessary negotiation of jurisdictions and ambivalent authorities. By the mid-seventeenth century theatrical activity was a regular feature of urban life in Mexico City in spite of setbacks caused by catastrophic floods.

This development is especially striking when compared to the more halting development of commercial drama in the Anglo North Atlantic through an examination of the case of Dublin, a colonial city in many ways and the viceregal center of Tudor-Stuart power in Ireland. Public performances of plays in Dublin remained reliant on court patronage late into the seventeenth century. And although Dublin's playhouse was more centrally located than many of the theaters were in London, commercial drama in Dublin remained a less crucial factor in the public life of the city than it was in Mexico City. Even so, in both locations playwrights, actors, and some members of audiences were agents engaged in Atlantic crossings of the ocean seas.

In the fourth chapter, "'Aware That It Is a Public Work': Commercial Drama in Puebla and Williamsburg," I contend that the case of Puebla demonstrates that the public theater had become a desirable commodity in the early modern Spanish Atlantic World as well as a regular—if still contested—institution of urbanism in New Spain. The histories of Puebla and Williamsburg as parts of an Atlantic World context of European empires are separated by about a century, and the differences in their sizes and urban institutions make for what is a strikingly asymmetrical comparison. However, these two colonial cities were both new urban foundations. In Puebla the *corrales* served charitable functions that helped to facilitate its integration into daily life for migrant peninsular Spaniards, creoles, and *casta* colonists. Such connections also helped to subvert the antitheatrical efforts of some authorities, such as those of Bishop Palafox in the 1640s. Because urban growth in the British mainland colonies of North America was slower, the first playhouses in colonial Virginia could not draw playgoers with enough frequency to be profitable or permanent fixtures in the topography of the city.

Chapter five, "'The Plague of the Republic': Antitheatrical Sentiment and Its Limits in the Atlantic World," discusses the ways that discourses of opposition to the playhouses and performed drama operated in these early modern empires. At the heart of the concerns of antitheatrical polemicists were issues of the sinful nature of mimesis, gendered anxieties about damaged masculinity and national and imperial virility, and the conception of the body politic as an organism that could become subject to disease. Although both Spain and England closed their theaters and issued long-term bans on theater during the 1640s, the reasons behind these closures were different, as were the audiences of readers whom antitheatrical polemicists sought to reach and influence. For one, there were more antitheatrical writers publishing tracts and sermons opposing the theater in Spain and its transatlantic colonies, but because of the relationship between the theaters and hospitals, the impact of this opposition was ultimately diluted. There were also significant differences in not only the availability of theater, but in the ways in which antitheatrical writings emerged in general, traditional, and humanistic contexts as well as locally specific and topical ones in the Spanish and Anglo Atlantic Worlds.

In the following pages, I historically analyze some specific theater events, and I consider the content and contexts of a few select plays and the ways early modern audiences reacted to them. Mainly, though, I attempt to more fully demonstrate the important social, cultural, and political roles theater played in early modern urban environments. Apart from London, these crucial urban roles were especially true of the Spanish *corrales* where *comedias* became early modern hits. At the same time, theater as an urban institution in the kingdoms of the universal Spanish monarchy fostered Baroque charity in ways that both reaffirmed and complicated the boundaries of gender, social rank, and race.

"*The Money That Comes from the Plays*"

COMEDIES AND CHARITABLE URBAN PUBLIC HEALTH INSTITUTIONS IN MADRID AND LONDON

In August of 1586 Diego de Chaves, King Philip II's confessor and a member of the Council of State, wrote to the Count of Barajas who was then serving as the president of the Council of Castile. Chaves reported that he had reprimanded Dr. Antonio González for attending a play when he should have been at a meeting of the council. Several months before, González had been reported for truancy. According to reports, González and several other Spanish officials had failed in their duties because they had succumbed to various entertaining vices.[1] The confessor's reprimands were all part of a reform program, undertaken at the Spanish court of Philip II, designed to prevent courtiers from wasting time on such activities. These reforms dictated a halt to dueling, to indulging in prohibited games of chance, and to "being a friend of seeing [plays]"—especially when officials should be in council meetings tending to affairs of state. Chaves recounted his success with the playgoer turned penitent and noted that González had claimed in his defense that there were extenuating circumstances. He had only been drawn into watching the play because he could see it being performed from the window of the house of the prosecutor Ximenez Ortíz. In the end, González promised, although "he had not seen five more than five hundred," that "from this moment forward he [would] not watch any more plays."[2]

The attempted crackdown on frivolities and distracting pastimes was, of course, indicative of their regular availability in Castile's new and growing capital. Such access to games of chance and performances of plays had been increasing in Madrid over the course of the previous two decades. Even if González's remark that he had not seen more than 505 plays was hyperbole, it nonetheless points to the tremendous growth of the theater business in Madrid in the second half of the sixteenth century. The *corrales de comedias* of the court and capital had developed out of mutually beneficial relationships with religious lay brotherhoods, municipal authorities, and institutions of public health. Since the theaters of Madrid emerged out of connections between the hospitals and charitable confraternities that sponsored theater as a means of charitable funding and evolved into a mechanism for funding the city treasury, they faced routine regulation from urban and court officials, but also attracted regular playgoers from all sectors of early modern Spanish society in the court city. The men and women involved in the commercial theater business utilized the playhouses' function in funding Tridentine piety and public health in order to pursue careers and to justify their occupation. In part, they promoted piety through their regular and contractual performances of *autos sacramentales* during the Catholic feast day celebrations that were so important to lay devotion during the decades following the Council of Trent. Throughout the year, the performances of popular saints' plays, religious morality plays, and the more secular *comedias* fostered lay devotion and charitable activity—even if these activities did not gain universal approval.

Early modern Spanish theater had already begun to develop in other cities—particularly Seville and Valencia. Nonetheless, plays and playgoing became integrated into daily urban life in Madrid to an extent that was unmatched in any other European capital during the early modern era because of the intersecting development of confraternities, institutions of welfare, and playhouses that took place there. This integration, in turn, gave theater the potential to influence public opinion and public health policy. It also helped denizens of the court city make sense of the urban spaces in which they lived. Comparing the development of the centrally located theaters of the Spanish court city and growing urban center to that of the public theaters of London's suburbs, and the private playhouses that emerged in the seventeenth century within the city walls, demonstrates many similarities across confessional and national divides. However, it also solidifies the importance of public theater to public health and expressions of piety in the Spanish case.

In other words, Madrid's relationship with the *comedia* was broadly influential throughout the Spanish Atlantic World, whereas in the Anglo Atlantic, drama was more narrowly associated with London. Indeed, as both Walter Cohen and Jean Howard have argued, London was the only city in England that provided the necessary economic, demographic, and material conditions for a truly thriving commercial theater.[3] Madrid's *corrales* developed a central role both culturally and geographically within the city, and early modern Spaniards preferred to live in cities. All of this helped to promote the spread of these theatrical relationships to provincial cities in Castile and across the Atlantic to cities in Spain's dominions in the New World. By contrast, the public playhouses of London, epicenter of the Anglo Atlantic World, were outside the city walls. Although they were widely attended and took up current social issues and influenced public opinion, they did not have the same central role in the daily life of the citizens of London. This was perhaps especially true during the seventeenth century, when new private theaters drew the wealthier and noble segments of the population away from the older public theaters in the suburbs.

The financing of these theaters and their roles in urban London were also very different, as acting troupes in the English capital relied heavily on courtly and aristocratic patronage for their continued existence. Additionally, while the acting companies of London paid poor rates to the parishes in which their associated theaters were located, they did not help to finance the care of the sick and impoverished to the same degree that their counterparts in Madrid did. Consequently, even though English acting troupes traveled to provincial cities, the development of regular theatrical activity took place at a much slower rate outside of the greater London area, which included the court at Westminster and the London suburbs. In fact, this created something of a feedback loop that served to associate Renaissance English drama almost entirely with London and the court.

Before addressing the construction of Madrid's playhouses, some background information about the growth of the court and capital might be useful for context. In 1561, some twenty-five years before ordering his confessor to chastise Antonio González for attending a theatrical performance instead of a council meeting, the head of the universal Spanish monarchy, King Philip II, had moved his court to Madrid. Madrid's population—approximately 6,000 people in 1561—multiplied quickly in the following decades. Perhaps as many as 85,000 people lived in the court city when Philip II died in 1598.[4]

This rapid growth in population in conjunction with the realities of early modern courtly economies created both a significant drain on the region's resources and an urban landscape that changed dramatically in a period of just a few decades. Such quick expansion fostered architectural innovations such as the infamous *casas a la malicia,* or houses that were built partially below the ground or with windows missing or askew in order to escape the injunction that all houses in Madrid with more than one story reserve their first floor for members of the royal government. The Crown of Castile's dirty capital also inspired the kinds of criticisms that were typical of quickly growing cities in preindustrial eras. For example, Camillo Borghese, the papal nuncio in Madrid and the future Pope Paul V, observed in 1593 that the houses were crude, the privies were lacking, and the stench was unbearable.[5] Others criticized the highly visible presence of women in the city's public spaces and streets and their practice of bathing in the Manzanares River.[6] Problems caused by the lack of infrastructure were among the reasons the court relocated to Valladolid during part of the early years of the reign of Philip III. The court returned to Madrid in 1606. It was then that Madrid truly "began to be seen as the definitive court, and that it began to be talked of without hesitation as the head and even the heart of the monarchy."[7]

Even before the permanent return of the court, a dynamic and successful commercial drama developed there in the crowded chaos created by politicos, lackeys, and their servants in the city's labyrinthine streets. In the first half of the sixteenth century religious celebrations and private patronage of talented playwrights, such as Juan del Encina and Gil Vicente, had fostered the evolution of Spanish drama. During the 1540s and 1550s, before Madrid became the capital and center of Castile and its realms, innovators, such as Lope de Rueda and Alonso de la Vega, became playwrights/directors in important cities, such as Seville. More developments continued during the second half of the sixteenth century. Spanish playwrights, directors, and performers created a theater that was oriented toward audiences comprised of all sectors of early modern urban society: clergymen, nobles, artisans, bakers, students, soldiers, and servants. Jane Albrecht has argued that not all denizens of Madrid could regularly afford to attend the performances.[8] However, I contend that there is no reason to believe that different individual members of lower social ranks did not see plays in the *corrales,* especially on Sundays, which boasted more regular performances than did other days of the week, and on the many feast days that gave laborers a respite.[9] Repeated problems with playgoers entering without paying, the concerns of authorities, polemicists, and playwrights about the unruliness of the audience, ecclesiastical concerns about the way the poor supposedly squandered their money on luxuries and entertainments, and evidence from the archives suggest a wide range of social ranks present at the performances of *comedias.*

Although very little commercial theater existed in Madrid when it became the center of Castile and the universal Spanish monarchy in 1561, this soon changed, as two of the city's new religious lay brotherhoods decided to provide financing for their hospitals by putting on plays in the 1560s. Poverty was not new to the realms of the universal Spanish monarchy or to Madrid, but it was becoming alarmingly visible in the rapidly growing capital. Late medieval and early modern Catholics participated in the cult of poverty that honored the deserving poor, but this worldview did not deem all paupers equal. Some merited alms more than others, and some required different types of aid and assistance. In conjunction "with the reforming spirit of the new post-Tridentine times," reformers and technocrats submitted proposals and ideas designed "to control poverty" and argued for placing cities in charge of the efforts of poor relief.[10] Scholars whose work focuses on the Counter Reformation have demonstrated that the outpouring of lay piety had significant impacts on lived religion and communal daily life in the second half of the sixteenth century and throughout the seventeenth century. During this flush of religious activity many laypeople founded or reinvigorated already existing religious lay brotherhoods in order to participate more fully in charitable works and feast day life and culture.[11] Madrid's rapid growth enabled the rapid development of some of these new *cofradías,* which helped to fund hospitals, orphanages, and dowries to enable the marriages of poor girls.[12]

Some confraternities undertook significant efforts to cure the sick and wounded and to shelter orphans. Philip II granted the Cofradía de la Pasión y Sangre de Jesucristo (hereafter the CdPSJ), founded in 1565, permission to build the Hospital de la Pasión (Hospital of the Passion), an institution designated for the care of sick and poor women, in the calle de Toledo. Several years later, in 1574, deputies of the CdPSJ claimed they had cured more than 2,200 women of their fevers and wounds.[13] Shortly thereafter this confraternity received the exclusive right to put on performances during Corpus Christi to raise funds for their charitable work and hired acting troupes to do so.[14] After initially having plays performed in the courtyard of the hospital, by the late 1560s the CdPSJ began to hire yards for this purpose. Contracted acting companies purchased plays from playwrights and provided their own costumes, though these might be rented or borrowed from others. Initially, the CdPSJ used the Corral de Burguillos, named after its owner, and later it hired the Corral de la Pacheca; both of these *corrales* had their addresses in the Calle del Príncipe. As the process for funding such charitable work in public health continued to develop over the following decades, more women would be admitted to the hospital founded by the CdPSJ, and, although some of them would not leave the institution again alive, most were cured.

The idea of using performances to fund charitable work caught on quickly in the growing city. The Cofradía de la Soledad de Nuestra Señora (hereafter the CdSNS), founded in 1567, began to have plays staged in order to provide funds for the Hospital de Niños Expositos. The *cofradía* had founded this orphanage and home for foundlings in the late 1560s. In 1572 the CdSNS moved the orphanage to a larger space in the calle de Preciados. Sharing the hired yards with the CdPSJ for the proceeds from plays was a source of conflict between the two confraternities until they decided to share the costs and the profits. In 1574 both lay brotherhoods named commissioners of plays and a *mayordomo,* or superintendent, to "henceforth maintain an account book in his keeping where he makes an entry each day of that which comes from each play, and in which *corral* it was made, and which *autor de comedias,* or troupe manager, directed it."[15]

Also in 1574 one of the most famous Italian *comedia dell'arte* players, Alberto Naseli, more commonly known by his stage name Ganassa, came to Madrid for the first time. Having performed all throughout Italy, in Paris, and possibly in England before coming to the center of Phillip II's lands, Ganassa expected to find a court theater in the heart of Castile. Instead he encountered the nascent *corrales de comedias,* which the religious brotherhoods of the court city had rather haphazardly constructed in the courtyards of houses rented from the owners. Early modern theater historians have argued that the actors still probably owned their own stages and erected and dismantled them at every performance. Ganassa's arrival was instrumental in changing this. While the Spanish *comedia* did not take its form from the improvisational Italian *commedia dell'arte,* Ganassa and other traveling Italian performers certainly influenced the development of drama in Spain. Some early Spanish playwrights modeled dramas on Italian dramas of intrigue, and there are numerous similarities between the *zanni,* or clown, of the *commedia dell'arte,* and the *gracioso,* or fool, of the Spanish *comedia.* Additionally, the structure of the improvisational Italian performances may have suggested the division of the *comedia,* as developed by Lope de Vega, into three acts instead of the classical five acts inherited from Roman drama and the humanist tradition.

Ganassa set about establishing a permanent playhouse with a roof, the Corral de la Pacheca. The CdPSJ and CdSNS then leased this *corral* for a period of ten years. On another trip to Madrid in 1582, Ganassa loaned money to the *cofradías* to assist them with the construction of the Corral del Príncipe, the second of the long-standing theaters in Madrid and one that would long outlast Ganassa's Corral de la Pacheca.[16] Ganassa did not do these things solely out of a sense of altruism. He performed in Spanish cities for the next several years, and it was in his best financial interest to have a place to perform in the court and capital as well as substantial connections to those in the theater business there. It is worth noting that those who had benefited from the old system of leasing their *corrales* to the religious confraternities on a regular basis complained about this change. They even took their case as far as Madrid's royal civic council of magistrates, the Sala de Alcaldes de Casa y Corte.[17]

While there were earlier playhouses in Madrid, such as the aforementioned Corral de la Pacheca and the Corral de la Puente, the first truly permanent playhouses in the court city were the Corral de la Cruz and the Corral del Príncipe. Both resulted from the cooperative efforts of the *cofradías*. In October of 1579, the CdPSJ and CdSNS jointly purchased property on the calle de la Cruz and began construction on this new playhouse. They had the benches moved from the Corral de la Puente, which they had been renting, to the new playhouse. Soon the Corral de la Cruz also boasted private boxes and a *cazuela*, or a separate section for the women of the audience, as well as the benches in the pit for the *mosqueteros*, men who watched the plays from the pit.

With the aforementioned help of Ganassa, the *cofradías* purchased two houses and their accompanying yards on the calle del Príncipe in February of 1582. On this property, they laid the foundations for the new theater. When the first performance of a play took place at the Corral del Príncipe on 21 September 1583, the construction project had not yet been completed. The playhouse still lacked stands, windows, and a gallery. Nevertheless, this did not stop the new commercial theater from attracting willing audiences to see performances.[18] The early success of the playhouses caught the attention of both municipal and royal authorities in Madrid. Consequently, the Council of Castile decided to grant the *cofradías* the right to have more frequent performances in exchange for granting one quarter of the admission fees earned to the General Hospital of Madrid, which was an umbrella organization that had come to include the Hospital of the Passion, the Convalescents Hospital, and the Hospital Inclusa, an orphanage for foundlings.

Another important change also took place in 1583. Due to their urban and charitable success, the *corrales de comedias* were placed under the supervision of the protector of the hospitals, an official who also had a seat on the Council of Castile. Shortly thereafter the members of the council decreed that the deputies of the confraternities involved in the theater business "charge each person that wants to see the plays and to sit on the benches of the said theaters 16 *maravedís*, in this manner they must charge four *maravedís* more than the 12 they have until now charged for each seat."[19] The council's decree diverted these additional funds to care for the patients of the General Hospital, in addition to those already going to care for the female patients of the Hospital of the Passion. In doing so, the Council of Castile further solidified the symbiotic relationship that had emerged between the commercial theater and institutions of public health and welfare in the court city.

The importance of theater to various aspects of daily life had ramifications for urban topography. Both of the permanent commercial theaters were close to the heart of Madrid.[20] The theaters were located on streets that intersected near the Plaza de Santa Ana, only a short distance east of the Plaza Mayor and just southeast of the Puerta del Sol, one of the fifteenth-century gates of the city, which during the late sixteenth and seventeenth centuries became an important meeting place in Madrid for the exchange of news, gossip, and letters. Madrid's *corrales* were within the city's boundaries, as determined by Philip II in the 1560s, and within the commercial and social center of the city that his grandson Philip IV ordered enclosed in 1625.[21] The central locations of the playhouses, along with the fact that these locations were in "respectable" neighborhoods, helped to integrate theater into the daily cultural life and social fabric of Madrid. This legitimization by location helped to make the commercial theater a thriving business in the court and capital of Spain.

As the theater business expanded, other entrepreneurial activities that took place in the *corrales* also increased. One way to further commercialize the theater and make it more profitable was the sale of refreshments to playgoers. Soon individuals competed for the contracts to sell fruit, nuts, candies, wine, and *aloja,* a sweet beverage similar to mead, in the playhouses of Madrid. In March of 1587 the deputies of the Hospital of the Passion granted the enterprising denizen of Madrid Francisco Briceño the exclusive right to sell fruit and beverages in both *corrales.*[22] Similarly, in 1602 the *cofradías* subcontracted out the right to oversee the rental of benches and private boxes at the theaters to Alonso and Juan Estébenez.[23] This allowed the theaters to capitalize on the desire for nobles and city fathers to watch performances comfortably and with an ostentatious privacy that projected their rank and importance.

It is clear that by the final decades of the sixteenth century the commercial theaters of Madrid had became popular locations for people who wanted to forget their troubles for a couple of hours for a relatively cheap price of 16 maravedís. By the mid-1580s, when Philip II became concerned that his officials were at the playhouse instead of performing their governmental duties, it already seemed certain that the *corrales de comedias* would be permanent fixtures in the physical space of Madrid, as well as in its social and cultural life. However, the royal government, the municipal authorities, the men and women who wrote for and performed on the stages of the court and capital, and the playgoers themselves were continually negotiating and manipulating the terms under which this integration into the developing urban environment would continue.

For example, a flurry of legislation sought to circumscribe and control the appearance of women on the Spanish stage, including those of the court and capital. In 1580 and again in 1586, the Council of Castile forbade women from performing onstage. However, acting companies, audiences, and authorities alike seem to have ignored the edict. As a result, by the late sixteenth century, women were making use of the developing theater business in Madrid and elsewhere in Castile to pursue careers not only as actresses but also sometimes as troupe directors, playwrights, and food sellers. Actresses provided the Spanish stage with greater verisimilitude than its English counterpart, but they also provoked numerous anxieties on the part of civil and ecclesiastical authorities. These concerns led to attempts to prevent single ladies from joining acting companies and legislation decreeing that women must be married to (or the daughter of) an actor or director in order to be a troupe member. Ultimately, this might not have had quite the impact authorities had envisioned. For as some scholars have argued, some married women actually had more freedom and less watchful supervision than their unmarried counterparts in early modern Spain.[24]

Although legislation attempted to constrain which women could perform, women participated in and sometimes even directed the officially sanctioned acting companies that emerged in Spain. Sometimes this was done jointly with their husbands, demonstrating the paradoxical freedoms from enclosure that marriage and partnership could potentially give at least some early modern women. For example, Jusepa Vaca achieved fame as an actress performing numerous roles as a cross-dressed *mujer varonil,* and married the director Juan de Morales Medrano in 1602. Lope de Vega wrote some of his *comedias* with the popular actress in mind. Archival records indicate that she and her husband frequently received payment for their services jointly. Two of their children also went on to become famous players in their own right.[25] Mariana Vaca de Morales, who married the troupe leader Antonio de Prado, had a similar experience. In addition to directing, she also performed the part of leading ladies in a number of plays. She and Prado had several children who became prominent performers as well.[26]

The Council of Castile also tried to limit and control the movement of licensed acting companies, and troupes could not remain in Madrid or other cities indefinitely. Legally, only Madrid and Seville could play host to more than one acting troupe at a time.[27] Such legislation compelled acting companies to travel. It also meant that, consequently, many provincial cities, such as Burgos and Valladolid, had regular access to commercial theater as directors and their troupes rotated in and out of Madrid and Seville. Thus, while much of the theater business in Castile had its logistical foundations in Madrid, acting companies exported *comedias* and their potentially symbiotic relationships to public health institutions to cities in all of the Crown of Castile's realms. This reinforced the myriad connections between the actors, charitable brotherhoods, and municipal governments throughout the towns of the Spanish Empire.

Spanish acting companies came to be headed by—and associated with—their directors, or *autores de comedias.* These directors had many responsibilities, including petitioning for licenses to hire players and discovering and signing talented actors and actresses who would bring in audiences. The directors of acting troupes also took charge of costuming and the legal documentation involved so that actors onstage could violate normal sumptuary laws and wear the garb of kings and nobles. In October of 1590, the *autor* Francisco Osorio petitioned the Council of Castile for a license "so that he and his fellow workers could wear neck ruffs while they were in the theaters performing."[28] Likewise, they organized the costume rentals and purchases that were key to the theater business, acquiring clothing such as a dress with "sleeves of gold brocade and black camlet, embroidered with silver crests" for the members of their company to don onstage.[29]

For their part, actors and directors organized themselves to defend their own interests in response to persistent government intervention. The careers of those who were successful might span several decades and gain them lucrative contracts with theaters in prime locations. In Madrid the majority of these players lived in the parish of San Sebastián, where the *corrales de comedias* were located. Actors and actresses had access to the benefits of their own lay organization, the Cofradía de Nuestra Señora de la Novena. This *cofradía* was named for an apparition of the Virgin Mary, initially known to locals as the Virgin of the Silence. In the early 1620s an image of the Virgin of the Silence and child was carved and placed in a niche in the calle del León, a street on which many actors and actresses lived. This apparition of the Virgin received a new name—de la Novena—after she miraculously cured the sick actress Catalina de Flores on the ninth day.[30]

This organization protected performers' interests, aided its sick and elderly members, and paid for the Christian burials of deceased members of the profession. It also assisted in caring for the children of deceased actors and actresses. More generally, it gave actors and actresses access to a community and connected them with the charitable giving and religious renewal that was so characteristic of Tridentine Catholicism in Castile. The organization's constitution reminded its members of the importance of humility and charity. It also sought to regulate the profession by decreeing that none of its members could join the acting company of a director who was not a member of the guild.[31] The Cofradía de Nuestra Señora de la Novena received official church approval in 1634 and came under the jurisdiction of the protector of the hospitals at the same time. While there were segments of society that resented the burgeoning theatrical business and the popularity of *comedias* and the professionals who performed them, the *corrales* of Madrid had developed physically and culturally into a key element of urban life in the court city.

The entrenchment of theater in the daily life of Madrid also coincided with efforts at consolidating the hospitals of the court and capital.

In 1566 Madrid had over a dozen hospitals, in spite of its still relatively small size. By 1587, thanks to consolidation efforts spearheaded by the monarchy, there were only four: the Court Hospital, the Hospital de La Latina, the Hospital de Antón Martín, and the General Hospital. The General Hospital moved to the calle Atocha in 1603. Early modern historians of Madrid have suggested the monarchy accomplished the process of combining and streamlining the court's health care and charitable institutions with relative ease because the *cofradías* of the new capital were fewer in number and less powerful than they were in some other Spanish cities.[32] While the hospitals had other sources of income, such as taxes on meat and oil and a portion of money and goods seized by the courts in legal cases, they relied heavily on the theater box offices of Madrid.

In 1590 all the proceeds from such performances at the Corral de la Cruz began to be taken to a counting house, where the accounts of the theater were kept and the proceeds divided. The protector of the hospitals had the job of licensing the plays for performance and introduced the practice of appointing special money collectors who took up their posts at noon and charged admission fees until after the performance of the play began. In 1596 and 1597 the *cofradías* began to make alterations and expansions to the theaters, and this contributed to increased income for the hospitals.

According to Carmen Sanz Ayán and Bernardo García García, by the late 1580s the Cofradía de la Soledad could depend upon several hundred thousands of *maravedís* in alms from the proceeds of the playhouses each year.[33] Between 1586 and the death of Philip II in 1598, for which the theaters closed for a period of mourning, theatrical performances produced 6,298,727 *maravedís* earmarked for good works.[34] The substantial charitable proceeds that the performances of *comedias* brought in for the hospitals of Madrid in the 1580s and 1590s can serve as a baseline for gauging the expectations of the administrators of the hospitals and theaters in the seventeenth century, particularly after the return of the court to Madrid from Valladolid—a period during which the money made by Madrid's theaters, and consequently that funneled into urban social welfare projects, declined substantially.[35]

In 1604, while the court was still in Valladolid, Madrid's *corrales de comedias* came under the official supervision of the protector of the General Hospital. At the same time, all of the box rentals and the selling of food, *aloja,* and other drinks came under the control of the individual who held the lease to running these aspects of the theater business. The lessee took half a real for each performance, a *cuarto* for each bench rental, and the proceeds from the refreshments.[36] This relationship continued to bear financial fruit that enabled the *cofradías* to engage in charitable good works. In 1610 Don Francisco de Heredice Salgado, the treasurer for the Hospital of the Passion, took charge of the 485,996 *maravedís* that came from the plays that had been performed daily from the beginning of January until 23 February of that year.[37] Even though substantial sums continued to come from the plays, as these accounts indicate, the success of the *corrales de comedias* was not always enough to sustain Madrid's hospitals and their work in curing the sick and aiding the poor. Some *comedias* ran to greater success than others, people slipped into the playhouses without paying, and bad weather and rival attractions, such as bullfights or public executions, could always drive down the number of spectators at any given performance. Inflation also compounded these problems.

Because of the continual need for funds, the administration of the *corrales de comedias* underwent a number of changes beginning in the second decade of the seventeenth century. One of these changes helped to spur the further growth of theater both in the capital and beyond. In 1615 the Council of Castile decided to increase the number of approved acting companies from eight to twelve. It also granted a two-year monopoly in the Crown of Castile to troupe directors Alonso Riquelme, Fernán Sánchez, Tomás Fernández, Pedro de Valdés, Diego López de Alcaraz, Pedro Cebriano, Pedro Llorente, Juan de Morales, Juan Acacio, Antonio Granados, Alonso de Heredia, and Andrés de Claramonte.[38]

At the same time that the number of licensed companies increased, government officials significantly altered the mechanisms for funneling proceeds from the playhouses to the hospitals in Madrid. After an extensive audit of the hospital system in 1613 and 1614, it became apparent to administrators that the hospitals lacked sufficient personnel and materials required for the care of patients.[39] On 11 April

1615, the Council of Castile decreed in the name of King Philip III that the General Hospital and its subsidiary institutions should henceforth receive a sum of money from excise taxes equivalent to one-sixth of 54,000 ducats, discounting what came from the charitable proceeds from the playhouses and other alms and donations. The council mandated that payments be made to the hospital in thirds and that "the amount of the final payment should be subtracted from what [the hospitals] have earned from alms and the production of plays."[40] From this point on, until the nineteenth century, the Council of Castile required the municipal government of Madrid to provide an annual subsidy to supplement the income of the hospitals, in case the *corrales de comedias* did not make enough money in a given year to support them. The Council of Castile mandated this alteration in June of 1615. According to city records, the municipal government, "having understood" the terms laid out by Philip III and his council, agreed that the direct funding from "the plays be removed and that in their place that the hospitals receive, in addition to the plays, the subsidy from the excises."[41] The city, with the approval of the royal government, then began to lease the rights to run the playhouses to lessee-managers on the basis of four-year contracts.

The goal of this new system was to make the theater business more efficient and more profitable for the city and its hospitals. In February of 1625, for example, some 1,042,476 *maravedís* were disbursed to the Hospital de Niños Expositos; 1,093,953 *maravedís* went to the Hospital de los Desamparados; and 561,180 *maravedís* went to the women's hospital in Madrid. These funds came from the 519,985 *maravedís* that had come each of the first five months of the previous year from the lease payments on the *corrales de comedias*.[42] The lease of the theaters to Don Juan de la Serna y Haro from 1633 to 1637 produced a sum of 10,700 ducats.[43]

Madrid's municipal government further streamlined the process in 1638, when the leaseholders of the theaters began to make payments directly to the city treasury. The city, in turn, then paid a fixed subsidy to the hospitals.[44] This change also brought the *corrales de comedias* more completely under the control of Madrid's city fathers, although rules and regulations for hours of operation and the selection of plays to be performed still came under the supervision of the protector of the General Hospital. The royal and city governments clearly hoped that the profits from the *corrales de comedias* would be sufficient for the hospitals or that at least the profits would come close to making up the amount of the fixed subsidy that it had to pay the hospitals. In cases when they did not, the brunt of this burden—in theory—fell on the individual leaseholder rather than on the municipality.

For this reason, it was still in the city's best interests that the Corral de la Cruz and the Corral del Príncipe remain open during much of the year and that as many capacity audiences as possible see the performances that took place in them. It was also in the municipal government's best interests to make sure that the members of the audience actually paid their admission fees. This was an aggravatingly persistent problem. In 1632 the protector of the hospitals, José González, complained of the "great disorder that has occurred in the *corrales* due to many people entering them to see the plays without paying, to the great damage of the hospitals and the diminishment of their alms."[45] In an attempt to quash this problem the city fathers demanded that playgoers pay the admission fees or face arrest and imprisonment. The protector of the hospitals ordered that "the guards who are in attendance not consent to this [entry without paying] and that if anyone wants to enter without paying they be put in jail."[46] The city fathers of Madrid ordered that the notice be put up in each of the playhouses so that it could be read and obeyed. However, many audience members in Madrid and other cities continued to illicitly infiltrate the *corrales de comedias*.

They could also be disorderly in other problematic ways. Theater historians have often noted the general unruliness of early modern spectators, who might engage in jeers, whistling, throwing food at actors onstage and at each other, and jangling their keys. Audiences might also riot, as they did at the Corral de la Cruz in May of 1623. In this instance the riot broke out before the play had even begun, when the *autor* Antonio de Prado told the playgoers that the *comedia* they expected to see could not be performed due to an order of the government. Prado begged their forgiveness for not being able to stage *La primera parte del Emperador Carlos Quinto*. He attempted to placate the audience by telling them "he would put on another that they requested or return their money."[47] However, the spectators would have none of this, and the men in the pit expressed their displeasure in no uncertain terms. They "shattered the benches with daggers; tore the taffeta of the costumes to bits; they threw rocks at the actors hitting one of them in the face."[48]

Consequently, those in the theater business frequently sought to take measures to protect themselves and their interests. They hoped to prevent the *corrales* from becoming hot zones of disorder and scenes of more than just dramatic entertainment. They sought to protect the reputations and honor of playgoers by doing such things as installing guards at the doors of the women's section. They also wanted the money collectors, ushers, porters, and other theater employees to be allowed exemptions from the city ordinances that forbade ordinary citizens from going around armed. In October of 1620, Baltasar Ruiz, then the holder of the lease for the *corrales de comedias,* petitioned and received a new amendment to the terms of his lease. He and "his money collectors must be allowed to wear protective armor for the defense of their persons because of the risk to their lives in the said collections without any guard bothering them for it."[49]

The problem of playgoers who did not pay or who engaged in disorderly activities caused the playhouses and the hospitals to take a financial hit. Any closures of the playhouses due to extreme heat, outbreaks of plague (which Madrid was fortunate to largely escape during the first half of the seventeenth century), periods of royal mourning, or periods of governmental antitheatrical policy also caused problems. Naturally, such closures had significant ramifications for directors of troupes and performers, who found themselves out of a job. The most significant of these long-term bans on performance in Castile took place from 1646 to 1651 and came shortly after an earlier closure for royal mourning upon the death of the Queen Consort Isabel of Bourbon in 1644. These bans compelled the troupe director Antonio de Prado to petition the palace treasurer in 1648 for payments he claimed he had never received for private performances staged for the late queen five years earlier. The *autor* begged for compensation from the government since the chamberlain had never paid him and since "he was currently without employment and crippled and so afflicted with gout that he had no way of providing for himself or his children."[50] Although Prado's disability might have prevented him from working even if the theaters had not been closed, it is likely that because of the financial strain on actors and actresses that resulted generally from the closure, the actors' confraternity would have had few means to help an unemployed member of their trade who lived with chronic pain. After all, many actors and actresses were not only currently out of work, but the confraternity had also lost a primary means of asking for alms since it could not post someone outside the playhouse door to request charitable donations.[51] This made seeking payment from royal officials even more necessary for actors like Prado.

Closures of the theaters also had troubling consequences for playhouse lessees and hospital administrators. The General Hospital and all of its subsidiary institutions depended on the tax on the playhouses, which the city government could not always collect from the holders of the leases to the *corrales* if the playhouses were not open for business. This was the case for Antonio de Soria in 1644, upon the death of the queen consort Isabel of Bourbon, Philip IV's first wife. While Soria also drew income from his other business ventures, such as his license to run snuff stalls in Madrid, one of his major entrepreneurial enterprises was the lease of the theaters.[52] His financial success depended on theatrical productivity. In 1644 Pedro Trigoso, the collector of the excise taxes of Madrid, who had not received the full payment from Soria for his lease of the *corrales de comedias,* brought a lawsuit against him. Soria petitioned for relief, reminding the city that the protector of the hospitals, Don Gregorio López de Mendiçabal, "[had] ordered the closure of the said *corrales* and that no other performance of any kind be enacted in them due to the sadness and grief caused by the death of the queen."[53] On 13 February 1645, Antonio de Soria was granted a discounted rent to pay to the municipality because the city fathers and the Council of Castile recognized that "it was the season and the months of winter in which the *comedias* were profitable."[54]

During the second and longer closure of Spain's *corrales de comedias* in the 1640s, hospital administrators throughout Castile petitioned for relief in the form of reopened theaters in the face of diminished resources with which to combat illness and poverty. Disease, poor sanitation, and vagrants caused problems for cities on every basic level, taxing their premodern capacities to deal with such difficulties. In Madrid, the lack of significant preexisting infrastructure to support the tremendous growth that took place during the sixteenth and seventeenth centuries compounded these problems. The contrast between the lavish luxury of the court and its attendant high-ranking courtiers, and the poorest beggars of the city, must have been striking.[55] By 1617, Madrid had almost 150,000 inhabitants and by the early 1640s some estimates put Madrid's population at almost 400,000.[56] Among the growing populace were increasing numbers of the destitute, the sick, and the orphaned. Thus, the hospitals of early modern Madrid waged an unending campaign against poverty and disease.

This is not to say that care was always consistent in Madrid's charitable institutions. At times shortages caused problems. An audit of Madrid's hospitals authorized by King Philip III in 1613 and led by the Marquis of Valle as well as Juan de Hoces revealed that the hospitals lacked sufficient bedding and clothing and deemed six servants necessary for more adequate upkeep and care.[57] At other times particular staff members caused significant problems and financial setbacks. The extensive 1613 audit revealed a number of problems, including some related to the behavior of Brother Antonio Valerio, who had been "accused of not being present at the visits of physicians and surgeons, not attending meals with the sick, of being cruel to the poor, and throwing out anyone who disagreed with him." Similarly, he was under suspicion for showing favor to "people who exploited the resources of the hospital for their own benefit."[58] The auditors also interviewed a number of witnesses who testified that the Hospital of the Passion's matron Sor Juana Ruiz engaged in a number of uncharitable and cruelly despicable acts that harmed patients and would-be patients. On 4 September 1613, Sister Catalina de la Sossa, another employee of the hospital, stated that the matron "refused to give clothing to the sick even though they had repeatedly begged for it" and that she was "bitter" and "cruelly treated the sick and the nurses." Her testimony also revealed that another nurse, Maria Perez, "had mistreated and given lashings with a whip to a poor sick woman, who then died."[59] Depositions of other workers confirmed and elaborated on the misdeeds of Juana Ruiz and Maria Perez.

The election of new deputies may have been part of a housecleaning effort that resulted from the scandal and corruption associated with the General Hospital and clearly revealed by the 1613 audit.[60] That year its subsidiary the Hospital of the Passion chose twenty-four deputies to serve the hospital. One of their primary responsibilities was to collect and use "the money that comes from the plays" to provide for the poor.[61] These funds, along with those that came from charitable donations and endowments, were kept in a treasury chest that required three keys, one of each of which was kept by the hospital rector, one of the city's aldermen, and one of the deputies.[62] This system of using a strongbox was maintained even as the system for funding the hospitals underwent other changes during the seventeenth century, as later documents pertaining to the finances of Madrid's General Hospital reveal.[63]

Although care was not always consistent and funding levels might fluctuate, the hospitals undertook important public welfare efforts that had important practical consequences for Spanish society. Consequently, the overall message of tracts by hospital administrators was clear: Madrid's public health institutions could only care for and cure the patients for whom they could afford to provide care, food, and space. They required sufficient funding, and this funding remained connected to the commercial theater of Madrid. Without the *maravedís* of playgoers, there were far fewer ducats to buy the bread and wine or pay the rents and wages of hospital staff.

In 1666, Gregorio de Aldana y Arellano, the official accountant of the royal hospitals, wrote a report, which he dedicated to the Queen and Regent Mariana de Austria, assessing the state of work undertaken by the hospitals in Madrid. Aldana carefully reminded the Spanish monarchy of the importance of continuing to provide additional financial aid and royal protection to the hospitals they had endowed. This treatise also justified the expenses paid out to the General Hospital and the Hospital of the Passion for the previous year. The accountant and administrator traced the history of each institution, the composition of its employees, its many commitments and responsibilities, and its great value to the capital. Aldana reminded the queen of the roles played by those who served in these hospitals and their obligations. For example, he pointed out that the *hermano mayor*, who was elected for a three-year term by the Council of Castile to serve in the hospitals, and the *enfermero mayor* who served under him, had the duty "of caring for and seeing how the remedies were applied, attending first to the supervision of the doctors, surgeons, and barber-surgeons, later to that of the mid-day and evening-meals."[64]

Aldana and other hospital administrators had to carefully tread a fine rhetorical line between advertising the hospital system's charity and benevolence and assuring his royal patron that the hospital was fiscally responsible with the resources provided by the royal government and the municipal government of Madrid, which subsidized these funds through the performances that took place at the *corrales de comedias*. A significant portion of these resources went to paying the salaries of staff members, providing bed linens for patients, and purchasing food. Aldana assured his readers that this was managed with a balance of care and frugality: "ordinarily for lunches they give them raisins, biscuits or fatback and during the summertime healthy and fresh fruits."[65] A decade later in 1676, the hospitals purchased some 127,398 loaves of bread at different prices totaling 13,629 Spanish ducats to feed their patients. Likewise, the expenses of the General Hospital and the Hospital of the Passion included other dietary staples. Meat, wine, eggs, bread, biscuits, oil, and fruit, along with other ordinary foods, made up a large part of the annual budget.[66]

Leonardo Galdiano y Croy, who had been secretary of the Hospital's Junta and then received an appointment to the position of *contador*, or official accountant, of the Hospitals of Madrid, wrote a similar tract in 1677. In *Breve tratado de los hospitales y casas de recogimiento desta corte*, Galdiano y Croy reported on the budgets, provided lists of employees, and enumerated in precise terms the benefits that the hospitals provided to those for whom they cared. For example, he listed all the offices held by the some 160 employees of the General Hospital in the previous year. Madrid's General Hospital had a staff that included twenty-four brothers, an accountant, a scribe, a lawyer, four physicians, two physician's apprentices, two surgeons, two phlebotomists, a head cook, four kitchen helpers, six laundresses, eighty servants for the rooms, and two priests. Meanwhile, that same year the Hospital of the Passion employed another thirty-three persons, as did the Hospital de Niños Expositos, including twenty-five wet nurses.[67]

According to Galdiano y Croy, in these branches of the court's hospital system, during 1676 some 9,807 inmates sought relief from poverty, hunger, and disease in these institutions and 8,278 people were cured. Only 967 died during their stay in the hospitals, and another 562 were still in the care of the hospital system in December of that year.[68] If these numbers are accurate, we are left with a picture of institutional success. This was a remarkably high cure rate, and these numbers suggest the efficacy of hospital care that had been developed in the court city over the previous 115 years. It is worth noting that 1676 was not a plague year in Madrid, so statistics such as these might have been very different from a tract that dealt with the hospitals in 1602, when the plague created a crisis in many Castilian cities, including Madrid. Even so, this high rate of cure and release suggests that the patients of the hospitals of Madrid had access to medicines, nourishment, and a chance for curing their illnesses and improving their overall health—something difficult for impoverished, vagrant subjects to do.

Madrid and London both fought uphill battles against poverty, disease, and sanitation problems during the early modern period, but they did so differently. This divergence existed partly as a consequence of their different historical infrastructures, partly because of their religious differences from the mid-sixteenth century onward, and partly because of how public theater became incorporated into the daily lives of the two capitals. During the Middle Ages, London grew in population and trade. After the devastating arrival of the "Great Pestilence" of the fourteenth century, which may have killed more than half the medieval metropolis's population, the city recovered over the next two centuries, and commerce increased to such a degree that by the end of the sixteenth century the area between the city of London and the court at Westminster had become fully urbanized.

With the court at Westminster and with the city fathers in control of the city itself, the jurisdiction of London could be complicated and contentious. Jurisdictional problems became compounded by London's continued growth during the early modern period: its population roughly doubled between 1520 and 1620. Along with the growth in population, much of which stemmed from immigration from the countryside, came increased problems with crime, vagrancy, and poverty. During the sixteenth century the suburbs outside the city walls also expanded, and a significant segment of poorer Englishmen and women and a sizeable number of foreigners came to call these neighborhoods home.

It was in these poorer suburban neighborhoods, which many early modern elites associated with crime, vagrancy, and disorder, that the public theaters of early modern London first became established. Unlike in Madrid, in early modern London the first public playhouses, such as The Theatre, The Swan, and The Globe, were outside the walls. In other words, while Madrid's audiences might consist of people segregated by rank and sex into different parts of the playhouse, locality also segregated and splintered London's audiences into multiple theater publics. This trend became even more pronounced during the seventeenth century with the building of a number of private playhouses in the city that catered to a more elite crowd of playgoers.

In spite of these differences in the urban geography of playgoing, English playwrights, like their Spanish counterparts, participated in a substantial buyer's market as a result of this growth in theatrical activity. Their plays, like those written by Spanish dramatists, had to pass through censorship controls. As early as 1574 an Act of the Court of Common Council prohibited performance of plays that had not been "pervsed and Allowed in suche order and fourme and by suche persons as by the Lorde Maior and Courte of Aldermen."[69] As time passed and the repertories of acting companies expanded, there was less demand for new material, since older plays could be kept in constant rotation. By the 1620s and 1630s, acting companies in London commissioned few new plays—this was rather different from the market demand in Madrid, where new plays remained sought-after commodities in the *corrales*.[70]

London's acting troupes usually employed eight to twelve players, who were all typically sharers in the company. They hired assistants for smaller parts and musicians to provide additional entertainment. Three or four boy apprentices studied under the sharers and played the roles of female characters onstage. This was a significant distinction between English and Spanish acting companies, which employed actresses and were even sometimes under the management of women directors. English boys in acting companies, who usually began their apprenticeships around the age of ten, received lower pay than the hired assistants. After a period of several years, they might become hired men and then eventually full members of the company.

The reliance on boy actors on the Renaissance stages of England also led to a brief vogue of acting companies entirely comprised of boys—a tradition that had origins in the academy and older medieval mystery cycles. During the Tudor period, children's troupes performed fairly regularly during royal banqueting or as entertainment for aristocrats.[71] The first of these groups, The Chapel Children, performed beginning in 1576 at the Blackfriars playhouse, which though within the city was not under the city's jurisdiction until 1608. The Children of Paul's were the most active of these groups. They performed from 1557 to 1590, when they became implicated in the Marprelate Controversy. The anonymously printed tracts and short books provoked controversy in early modern England less for their pro-Presbyterian theological stance and more for their irreverent departure from "conventions of decorum that had governed debates about the church since the Elizabethan Settlement."[72] As polemic debate heated up, Paul's Boys and a number of other acting troupes in London performed anti-Martinist pieces. In late 1589 the Elizabethan state banned such performances on the grounds that they treated material not fit for the stage. The Paul's Boys were once again playing by late 1599 or early 1600.[73] The troupe experienced a resurgent popularity from 1600 to 1606. Their demise in 1606 and that of the King's Revels Children in 1609 marks the end of the vogue for child actors in Renaissance English drama.

At the same time that the popularity of boy companies declined, a new trend was emerging that continued the fragmentation of theater publics in England. During the seventeenth century new private theaters emerged in more respectable neighborhoods of London. Significantly more expensive than their public counterparts, these theaters catered to a more fashionable and higher-ranking clientele. Peter Thompson has contended that by the end of the sixteenth century, the Puritan-dominated City of London Corporation in Guildhall was making life in the theatrical business of the suburbs more difficult. He claims that theater survived in London due to royal and aristocratic protection and, during the reign of James I (1603–1625), became increasingly oriented toward private rather than popular audiences.[74]

As early as 1574, civic authorities in London had undertaken efforts to discourage unruly behavior in the emerging theaters and to make them profitable for the city. Some of this money was designated for poor relief. However, the hospitals had difficulty in collecting it, and were instructed to collect the money from the acting companies directly.[75] Acting troupes did ultimately pay poor rates to the parishes in which they were located; they provided jobs in more economically depressed parts of the greater metropolis; and after 1598 those actors who were part of an established acting company with noble patronage became legally categorized as deserving poor rather than as roguish undeserving vagabonds.[76] These changes helped them to integrate into the communities with which they interacted, as the work of scholars such as Mark Bayer and Melissa Aaron has shown. However, the charitable function of the London theaters generally did not take on the same level of importance that it did in Madrid or many other cities in the Spanish Empire—or even as clearly as it did in Bristol.[77] Perhaps this was a consequence of the rapid growth of London as a major center of trade and burgeoning capitalism. Using literary evidence from London city comedies such as William Rowley's *A New Wonder*, Jean Howard contends that English playwrights used plays to ideologically position ideas and spaces in the tremendous commercial flux of the seventeenth-century London metropolis. In Rowley's play, "civic endowments and adherence to a doctrine of Christian charity are offered as a solution to the wild fluctuations that mark the financial careers of the play's chief characters, but the implausibilities and contradictions of the narrative allow one to see the inadequacies of this seductive, backward-looking paradigm for addressing the rapidly expanding culture of credit."[78]

Regardless of the reasons why such charitable endeavors became less important in London than they were in Madrid, they did. This lesser importance also perhaps reflects how the role of charitable good works and the visibility of piety and poor relief was relegated to the margins of the metropolis rather than being made a central feature of urban daily life as it was in Spain. Certainly, while giving alms retained some importance to English Protestantism and while parishes benefited from the payment of the poor rates, these sources could not satisfy the needs of London's hospitals. They relied heavily on royal endowments, private charity, and income from monopolies on salt for their income, which was often not sufficient to deal with the problems of poverty in a rapidly growing city.

In early modern London the main institution for dealing with vagrants and beggars until the middle of the seventeenth century was Bridewell Hospital. Founded in 1552 by Edward VI, Bridewell had been created to house the poor, particularly women and youths, who had been engaged in disorderly conduct. The foundations of this innovative London institution of public health and welfare lay in particular English circumstances. The English Reformation, as well as the inflation of the 1540s and the failure of statutes that founded the country's poor law, led to the creation of Bridewell and the development of London's hospital system.[79] Initially Bridewell had a training and vocational capacity, but by 1600 it had attained a primarily penal function.[80]

Other hospitals, such as St. Bartholomew's, St. Tomas's, and Christ's Hospital, cared for the sick, the elderly, and the orphaned inhabitants of London. Those among the deserving poor also included veterans of military campaigns, who were sometimes disabled as well as being impoverished and, in some cases, foreigners.[81] In the London suburb of Smithfield, Henry VIII refounded St. Bartholomew's, which had been in existence since the Central Middle Ages. It also cared for the sick, vagrants, and criminals, who might, like the "Maideservant in London, who foreswore herself, and now lies rotting" in the hospital, serve as cautionary tales for London's moralists.[82] Its surgeons and physicians also undertook forensic investigations and wrote learned medical tracts.[83] Christ's Hospital was founded in the aftermath of the Dissolution of the Monastery at Grey Friars. It cared for orphans and foundlings until it burned down during the Great Fire of 1666.

The relationships that developed between such institutions and the charitable and communal life that supported them varied in strength, as did their relationships to the playhouses and acting companies that formed part of the fabric of early modern society. In Madrid, even after 1615 and 1638 when the municipal government and the Council of Castile altered the mechanisms by which this relationship worked, the hospitals—and thus the charitable poor relief and the care of the ill—remained closely linked to the success of the commercial theater of the Spanish court and capital. All aspects of this connection in Madrid were more centralized, whereas in London and its suburbs the benefits the playhouses provided to charity remained largely local.

In both cases, city authorities scrutinized the playhouses as sites of disorder and potential disruption. Some scholars have argued that the constant regulation of the theater by city and royal governments made for a public drama that was subservient to the tastes of the crown, but the reality was more complicated than that.[84] The playwrights and acting companies of Madrid negotiated a metaphorical middle ground, just as the *corrales de comedias* themselves took root in the middle of the city and owed their success to the link they provided between two theoretically marginal groups: actors and sick beggars. The plays performed before the audiences of the public theaters of Renaissance Madrid allowed playwrights, directors, and actors to have a livelihood, a theatergoing public to be entertained, and hospital patients to be admitted and cured.

Actors, audiences, and playwrights knew the cities and neighborhoods in which they lived and worked. Both metropolises provided excellent fodder and a great setting for numerous plays as well as boasting large populations of potential audience members. Dramatists who wrote for the public—and later the private—theaters of London spent time resident there. Likewise, many of the most famous playwrights of the Spanish Golden Age, such as Lope de Vega, Tirso de Molina, and Calderón de la Barca, lived at least part of their lives in Madrid, and many of their plays were written with not only the actors, but also the playgoers and even the physical spaces of Madrid in mind.[85]

For example, in *Los balcones de Madrid*, a play dating from the 1620s and often attributed to Tirso de Molina, the pair of young lovers, Elisa and Juan, exploit the easy proximity of the balconies of the houses of the court and capital to surreptitiously visit each other. They contrive to see each other with the help of Coral, Juan's servant, who constructs an extendable bridge between the two balconies. Meanwhile Elisa's father, Don Alonso, becomes suspicious that his daughter has been disguising herself with a veil and is somehow making use of a secret passage. He is right on both counts—though he is still unaware that this passage is actually through the air, from balcony to balcony in the close quarters of the city. Elisa's servant Leonor's knowledge of theater and savvy recognition that her mistress's father is an avid playgoer also saves the lovers from discovery when she realizes that her mistress should not stash her veil up her sleeves in order to hide it from her father. She warns Elisa that this is a "bad idea, for once in a *comedia,* I saw them hide it like that." Alonso must have seen the same play or another that used a similar plot device because he demands that both of the women let him inspect their sleeves.[86]

Numerous other plays set in Madrid, such as Tirso's *Don Gil de las Calzas Verdes* or Lope de Vega's *El acero de Madrid,* make use of city geography and play on stereotypical views of life in the court and capital. The "streets of this court, imitators of the confusing Babel," were important to the development of the confusion of the characters in *Don Gil of the Green Breeches.*[87] Tirso's characters make several direct comparisons between Madrid and Babel, including the lament of Don Martín, who complains, when he gets his just deserts, that the streets of Madrid are ones "always trodden by lies, as flattering to the rich man as they are harsh to the poor." Not only are they "out of control" but they are full of "*casas a la malicia,* at all hours home to spite and vice."[88]

Just as there were many Spanish *comedias* that relied on the audience's intimate knowledge of Madrid's geography, architecture, and social conventions, there were numerous city comedies that were set in London. Unlike the city comedies set in the Spanish court and capital, the London comedies that became popular on the Jacobean stage during the early seventeenth century tended to pit one social group of London against the other, with some playwrights championing middling merchants and others mocking them. After all, Renaissance English actors and playwrights had nobles, not middling merchants, as their patrons and the private theaters were too expensive for poorer citizens of the English metropolis to afford, so it should not be surprising that many of these plays were written about citizens of London rather than for them.[89]

Many of these comedies also depicted London as a site of sinful behavior and vice. In Thomas Middleton's city comedy *A Chaste Maid in Cheapside,* the main plot revolves around a young couple, Moll Yellowhammer and Touchwood Junior. In typical manner, the Yellowhammer family objects to their courtship, and Moll's father intends for her to marry an older knight, Sir Walter Whorehound. While the play abounds with extramarital affairs, sexual humor, and puns, the title of the play was perhaps the biggest joke of all. In the early 1610s, when this city comedy was first performed, contemporaries knew Cheapside for its large number of prostitutes and a seedy reputation.

Nonetheless, some literary critics and theater historians have contended that the characters in *A Chaste Maid in Cheapside* were more varied than in other city comedies in the same vein. They have also suggested that Middleton treated the romance more sympathetically than he did in his other comedies because *A Chaste Maid in Cheapside* was actually written for performance in The Swan rather than in the private theaters, where the gentry preferred to see a mockery of the citizen class.[90] Jean Howard gives a fascinating reading of this play in her book *Theater of a City,* arguing that in it Middleton reveals how the changing economic nature of London had destabilized gender roles to the extent that "the pursuit of gold leads to a whore's conversion into a wife and a wife's conversion into a whore."[91]

Although theater probably has never had the ability to influence its audience to the extent that many of its polemical opponents hysterically claimed it could, or the ideological sway that playwrights might have hoped, there is some evidence to suggest the power of theater events and the theatrical language of plays could influence the vocabulary of politics and political events in early modern society. This was the case in October of 1600 in an incident involving the French ambassador that took place in Madrid and had implications for relations between Spain and France.[92] Several days before the incident there had been a performance "in the public playhouse a certain play about a King of France." This *comedia* contained language that was "contemptuous and insulting to the French nation."[93] Inspired by the anti-French nature of the *comedia* that they had either seen or heard about in the streets of the city, some men shouted insults at the ambassador's coach. One of them yelled, "how go the Lutherans!" prompting one of the French ambassador's footmen to get out of the coach and slap one of the men who had compared his master to a Protestant. The situation was about to escalate to the point of drawn swords, when the ambassador and his companions got out of the coach and somehow managed to diffuse tensions and disperse the crowd. Still, the ambassador complained. Consequently, the city fathers imprisoned the actors who had performed the play and exiled the *autor*. They also found themselves in the somewhat awkward position of having to arrest one of Madrid's constables for not intervening to keep the peace during the potential diplomatic debacle. Even if the constable had wished to apprehend the disturbers of the peace, it would not have been an easy task. After all, as the ambassador discovered, he was to be taunted a second time; he still had to endure laughter at his expense in the city streets until the gossip died down and the public's attention turned to other affairs and the content of other plays.[94]

A similar diplomatic debacle occurred because of a performance in London a quarter of a century later. In 1624 Henry Herbert, then the Master of the Revels, failed to censor a play that by several standards should never have made it to the stage. That August, London playgoers at The Globe saw a new play by Thomas Middleton, *A Game at Chess,* which ran for an unprecedented nine days straight due to its immense popularity. The play capitalized on the recent failure of marriage negotiations between Charles, then the Prince of Wales, and the Spanish infanta, Philip IV's sister María Ana, by hilariously and viciously dramatizing Spanish foes. The play also violated English law by portraying living Christian monarchs and other court personages. Most famously—or perhaps infamously, depending on one's point of view—*A Game at Chess* mercilessly mocked Diego Sarmiento de Acuña, the First Count of Gondomar and the former Spanish ambassador to the court of King James I. Gondomar had served as a diplomat in this capacity from 1613 to 1618 and again from 1619 to 1622. From the point of view of many at the court and in London, he was a "papist" and a plotting politician, known for three things: his seeming ability to bend the ear of King James, his fistula, and the special chair he used because of this painful medical problem.[95]

When James I returned to his capital he was greeted with a letter, dated 17 August, full of complaints about the play from the new Spanish ambassador who had replaced Gondomar, the Valencian Don Carlos de Coloma. The response of the English court was immediate but ultimately rather ambiguous. The Privy Council briefly closed The Globe and put an end to *A Game at Chess*'s unprecedented run, but it remains uncertain whether authorities ever imprisoned or fined Thomas Middleton. Three days after he had written to the king of England, Coloma also wrote a letter to the Count-Duke Olivares, the so-called favorite of Philip IV, to pass on the news of the recent incident, which had been so insulting to the Spanish. In his missive, he described the plotline of this "play so scandalous, so impious, so barbaric, and so offensive to my lord, the King."[96]

In both of these incidents, dramas that began on the stage and in the playhouses of Madrid and London took on lives of their own. These plays influenced public opinion, carried religiously charged xenophobic sentiments into the city streets, and even made waves in the circles of international diplomacy. Certainly, such cases demonstrate that the theater had the ability to sway audiences and public opinion. In Madrid, the reliance on the ticket sales to *comedias* for funding hospitals and other institutions of public health opened up both real and discursive spaces for commercial theater to operate, to judge, and to be judged. Of course, this was not without potential legislative ramifications. Plays could be censored and actors could be imprisoned. This was also so in London. *A Game at Chess* was not the only play with a political edge. When actors played on underlying confessional tensions or patriotic sentiments, this influence could become even greater, potentially creating a feedback loop of sorts in which the play became more popular as a result of public chatter and caused more public chatter as a result of its popularity.

Similarly, the drama of the playhouse and the drama of the streets commingled in certain settings and at certain times, such as religious processions and executions of political prisoners. One such example of political theater was the execution of Don Rodrigo Calderón in October of 1621. Philip IV's court intended to use Calderón's execution to demonstrate that the royal government was distancing itself from corruption and misdeeds, like those allegedly committed by Don Rodrigo. However, his religious awakening and the way he behaved on the scaffold swayed public opinion in his favor and had a negative impact on perceptions of Philip IV's government. Calderón no doubt had ample material from which to draw during his performance as penitent: he had had his own permanent, private box in the theater in Valladolid and the Corral de la Cruz in Madrid.[97]

The Spanish playhouses, where men like Rodrigo Calderón had boxes and where men like those who taunted the French ambassador watched plays, developed in the chaotic atmosphere of early modern Madrid. At the *corrales,* actors and actresses treated the public—comprised of women and men and people of all social ranks and occupations—to a couple of hours of entertainment and relaxation. These comedies provided for the charitable relief of the poor, the sick, and the orphaned of the city's hospitals. The space for the theater to become integrated into daily life and public opinion in Madrid was heightened by the central location of the theaters and by the theatrical nature of the court and capital of Castile and its realms. Of course, Spanish and English theater moved beyond Madrid and London. However, there was no English city that could rival London in its theatrical activity, and, while Valencia in the Kingdom of Aragon was an important center for theater with links to Italy and the Mediterranean and a large and thriving community of actors, *autores,* and playwrights, there was only one city in Castile that could truly rival Madrid in theatrical output and life. This city was early modern Seville.

Playing in the Port

THEATER IN EARLY MODERN SEVILLE AND BRISTOL

After the court and capital of Madrid, Seville was the second most important city for theater in the early modern Spanish world. With its strategic and defensible location as an inland port on the Guadalquivir River and its prominent political and social position within the geography of the universal Spanish monarchy, Seville was a crossroads for people, wealth, and goods traveling between Europe, America, and Africa. The medieval *Primera Crónica General de España* described the city as the most perfectly situated in the world for trade between the Mediterranean and Atlantic, and during the early modern period it continued to attract commerce from all over the known world.[1] Seville also attracted migrants from Andalucía and beyond. It was a large city with many churches, charitable institutions, hospitals, businesses, and people of diverse ranks and occupations. This most noble and loyal city—an appellation won during the reign of Alfonso X (1252–1284)—was a key location for humanism as well as for commerce. In what some dubbed the New Rome, *sevillanos* made major contributions to Spanish Golden Age art, literature, and theater.[2] However, Seville was also a city compelled to cope with significant problems caused by poverty, disease, and—according to many ecclesiastical and secular authorities—crime and social disorder.

The English provincial city of Bristol was similar to Seville in a number of these regards and experienced many of the same issues on a smaller scale. With its natural harbor, Bristol was second only to London in commercial activity in seventeenth-century England. It was a major regional market city and had important connections with other coastal settlements in England and abroad, including to cities in Iberia, such as Lisbon and Seville.[3] Bristol served as a hub for wider Atlantic transport, and many people who went to colonies in the Anglo Atlantic as traders and indentured servants came from or passed through it. By the early seventeenth century Bristol had one permanent privately owned theater, and evidence suggests the possibility of a second in simultaneous operation. No city in England, aside from London, boasted as much regular theatrical activity as part of urban daily life.

Looking first at Seville and then at Bristol, this chapter contextualizes and compares the development of their commercial theaters. In both provincial centers, commercial drama developed quite centrally in their respective urban topographies and landscapes. Both provided important funds that assisted hospitals and poor relief in these port cities that were frequently in a state of flux and demographic change. In spite of the many parallels between theatrical activity and public health in these two cities, such a comparison is inherently asymmetrical because of the differences in these two cities' sizes, levels of documented commercial theatrical activity, and expressions of piously motivated poor relief. Ultimately, these differences demonstrate the heightened role that the integrated Spanish theater played in urban life in Castile and its dominions.

As in Madrid and elsewhere in the Spanish Empire, in Seville popular dramatic entertainment and public health were linked through the charitable function of the *corrales de comedias*. However, since Seville's theaters did not have the direct links provided by *cofradías* between the theaters and the hospitals but rather ones between the municipality and the city's coffers, they had a civic dimension that at times ironically helped to stabilize early modern Seville even as the playhouses were known focal points for disorder in the city. The confusion may have been notable—as a character in Lope de Vega's play *El Arenal de Sevilla* exclaims—but so were the proceeds that benefited charitable good works in this Baroque and theatrical city.

Seville was both a city with numerous commercial theaters in which performers gave countless dramatic entertainments and a city with a tremendously theatrical civic culture. During the sixteenth century, the metropolis became known as the New Rome because of its role as a center of classicizing humanist learning in Renaissance Spain.[4] As the New Rome, Seville's inhabitants included nobles, clerics, scholars, wealthy merchants, and less prosperous urban dwellers, including the so-called deserving poor who had a more "marginal place in respectable society."[5] The city, whose council met on Mondays, Wednesdays, and Fridays and whose royal governor was a direct representative of the Hapsburg monarch, had jurisdiction over many towns and hamlets in its vicinity.[6]

Yet others referred to the city as the Great Babylon of Spain because of its chaotic mix of peoples, goods, and tongues. This is perhaps ironic because the Roman world that sixteenth-century Castilians wanted to emulate also had problems with crime, unemployment, fire, and disease, and its gladiator games and arenas attracted patricians and plebeians, including in provincial cities like Italica. At least according to reactionary reformers and concerned authorities, Seville was successfully copying Rome in this regard. It had a sinful and disorderly underworld, which included, among others, criminals, beggars, the unemployed, persons held in the bondage of slavery, and itinerant and unlicensed actors. In early modern Seville, the boundaries between the New Rome and the Great Babylon blurred on the streets of the city, especially during the festivals of Holy Week. They also merged together in the *corrales de comedias*.

One aspect of public dramatic life in Seville began with the Corpus Christi festivals in the High Middle Ages. Although these processional pageants had been instituted by Pope Urban IV in 1264 and made obligatory by Pope Clement V in 1311, there is no documentary evidence for a Corpus Christi procession in Seville until 1454.[7] Religious one-act plays formed the core of these public and sacramental spectacles, which continued to evolve during the early modern period, as Seville's *cofradías* performed processionals during Holy Week. In the sixteenth and seventeenth centuries these processions featured detailed, life-like sculptures capable of inducing tears, cries of anguish, and other strong emotional responses from the spectators who lined the streets of Seville. The affective nature of the Holy Week spectacle even led some to believe that the spirit of the Virgin Mary inhabited these processional statues. Thus, it is not surprising that the desire to put on the most elaborate and emotionally evocative spectacle generated fierce competition between the confraternities—and occasionally large amounts of debt, as these brotherhoods frequently pawned their silver in order to pay for these sculptures of Jesus and the Virgin Mary.[8]

At some point between 1504 and 1541, the city officials, rather than the guilds, began to control the production of the Corpus festivals.[9] Possibly spurred by the arrival of a troupe of Italian performers led by "Il Mutio" in 1538, during the 1540s and 1550s more routine commercial drama emerged in this city.[10] Lope de Rueda and Alonso de la Vega, both from Seville, created the first organized theatrical companies, possibly as a result of experience with the Italian players but equally likely as a result of participation in processions and religious festivals.[11] They wrote their own material for immediate performances, many of which took place at the market during daylight hours for audiences primarily consisting of groundlings.[12]

Lope de Rueda was successful in Seville, and in 1552 the city council of Valladolid engaged him to come to perform and direct Corpus plays at what was then the court city. He also performed at the prince's pleasure at Toledo in 1551 and at Benevente in 1554 to mark the future king Philip's journey to England for his marriage to his cousin Queen Mary I of England. Rueda returned to Seville in 1559, when he performed two *autos sacramentales* during the Corpus Christi festivals. While some literary critics have considered Rueda a playwright of dubious skill, he clearly possessed a talent for exploiting existing material and a willingness to experiment with it. He became incredibly famous and was the recipient of the kind of royal patronage that could accompany such celebrity, being asked repeatedly to perform at the palace in Madrid for Philip's third wife, Elizabeth of Valois, during the 1560s and earning a large sum of ten ducats a performance for his efforts.[13]

While initially still typically limited to feast and public days, theater became a regular feature of daily life in Seville in the second half of the sixteenth century as theatergoing and play-reading publics expanded and theater became more widely accepted by both secular and ecclesiastical authorities.[14] Additionally, Italian *commedia dell'arte* players, in search of economic opportunity in the form of new audiences, visited Spanish cities, including Seville. One of these itinerant players, the aforementioned Ganassa, also played a part in shaping the early modern theater landscape of Seville.[15] When he arrived there in the 1570s, he received permission from the city's authorities to put on performances two days a week, but this caused a number of problems and conflicts.[16] In 1575, after first petitioning Philip II for the removal of the Italian troupe, the city fathers decreed that Ganassa could only perform on holidays because his performances in the Corral de Don Juan were prompting many of Seville's denizens to "go there for that novelty, resulting in great harm and detriment to the city."[17] This evidence implies that Ganassa's improvisational performance of the *zanni*, or clown, was such a novelty that it provided an even greater draw for entertainment seekers than the performances of plays by their fellow Castilians.[18] The injunction by the city fathers against Ganassa also indicates that the municipal government wanted to impede the foreign competition with its popular innovations from not only distracting urban laborers from their jobs but also negatively impacting the financial development of Spanish theater in Seville.

And Ganassa did have local competition, even if it required some boosterism. This growth in theatrical activity also took place in the physical development of urban spaces for dramatic performances. For, in spite of city taxes and opposition by some secular and ecclesiastical authorities, the commercial theater flourished in Golden Age Seville to such an extent that it was able to sustain theatrical activity in multiple playhouses. Seville came to be the only city aside from the court and capital of Madrid to be legally able to support more than one acting troupe at any given time, as was stipulated by decree in 1615 and again in 1641.[19] And this legislation may have resulted in part from the frequency with which numerous acting troupes visited Seville. By the final decades of the sixteenth century the Corral de Don Juan was only one of the eight or nine houses and inn-yard theaters being used to stage performances in the port city. Although less is known about some of these spaces, they also included the Corral de Don Manrique, "whose houses were encircled by three streets . . . Boceguinería, Soledad, and Aire."[20] Three different acting companies were performing plays written by Juan de la Cueva in at least three of these other theaters.

One of the most important *corrales de comedias* in early modern Seville was the Corral de Doña Elvira.[21] This playhouse was likely constructed in the early 1570s, and documents refer to it in 1578. This *corral* was certainly in existence by March of 1579, when the Doña Elvira's leaseholder and administrator, Diego de Vera, authorized by contract for Juan de Granado and his company of actors to have use of the space "in peace and without any impediment or obstruction" in exchange for 12 *reales de plata* for each day that they performed *comedias*.[22] Juan Ganassa and his Italian troupe performed on the Doña Elvira's stage in 1583. This playhouse was named for the late Doña Elvira de Ayala, the daughter of the Chancellor of Castile Pedro López de Ayala, and built on her descendants' property in the parish of Sagrario. Located near the residence of the Counts of Gelves, the Doña Elvira drew large audiences of entertainment seekers thanks to its superior acoustics, in spite of efforts to prohibit performances there in favor of having them in the newer structures built in the seventeenth century.[23] It was only permanently closed in 1631.

Purpose-built playhouses, like the Doña Elvira, were physically integrated into the topography of the city. They were near the Casa Lonja, built by Philip II as the Casa de Contratación, which was the hub of commercial activity between the Old World and the Americas; the Cathedral of Santa María de la Sede; and the Real Alcazar. In the seventeenth century, the Coliseo and the Corral de la Montería, in the Patio de la Montería, were central and unavoidable features of the urban space of Seville. Their highly respectable locations stemmed from their popularity and from the role the theaters played as moneymakers for not just acting companies and theater leaseholders, but also for the municipal government and thus, by extension, for the hospitals of the city.

The Coliseo, which belonged to the city government of Seville and was sometimes referred to as the Corral de los Alcaldes, was an important commercial theater in early modern Seville. The city council decided to build the Coliseo in the parish of San Pedro in the calle de las Alcázares as part of an effort to better regulate public performances and to exercise greater control of the profits being earned by the city's successful commercial theaters. The leaseholder of the Coliseo, in return for a substantial share of the profits, was responsible for paying taxes to the public prison and to the hospitals of Seville. The first incarnation of this playhouse was finished in 1607. It did not originally have a roof, and this caused certain problems for performances there—particularly the issue of spectators who did not pay their admission fees. Inhabitants of the neighborhood could and did watch the performances from the roofs and windows of their houses, rather than paying the price of entrance, which was half of a *real* for a seat.[24] Certain officials, not unlike the aforementioned Antonio González, might even have empathized with an inability to resist such an easily accessed and unobstructed view of the performances.

Despite the efforts of some to avoid paying for their entertainment, it is still apparent that these playhouses contributed significantly to urban culture in early modern Seville and to the coffers of the municipal authorities and city efforts at charitable relief, as the numerous *comedias* staged brought in sizeable sums.[25] The Coliseo was rebuilt in 1614, and, in its refurbished incarnation, was more lavish, with marble and paintings decorating it. After it burnt down in 1620, it was rebuilt again in 1624. The lessee Diego de Almonacid, whose family sought to control a significant sector of the theater business in Seville, undertook much of the effort and expense of the construction project. The terms of Almonacid's lease also required him to pay an annual subsidy to the Hospital de la Misericordia.[26]

In spite of the efforts of Almonacid and other leaseholders, such as Captain Alonso Vergera Catano, Gaspar Diaz Catano, and Juan de Roxas, and in spite of many performances in this playhouse by acting troupes, including that of Roque de Figueroa, the Coliseo once again began to fall into disrepair.[27] It was refurbished in the 1630s, when "this said city and the parties authorized to act in its name consent and agree that the corral named for the Alcaldes that now they call the Coliseo where they present plays . . . must be remade and refurbished, with a new design, convenient for the public good."[28] The city fathers of Seville authorized yet another renovation in 1641. The Coliseo burnt down in 1659, at which point the city lacked the money to rebuild it, so the municipal authorities granted the *autora* Laura de Herrera and her company the right to use the Coliseo for a period of forty years with no rent, in exchange for rebuilding the theater at their own expense.

Herrera's company rebuilt the playhouse, but it burnt down again in November of 1698 in a deadly fire that killed numerous women, many of whom were trapped in the *cazuela*.[29]

In the 1620s the officials of Seville's royal palace decided to build another even more sumptuous *corral de comedias* in the spacious Patio de La Montería. By official decree the Montería, which was constructed in an unusual oval shape, would be built at the expense of the first lessee, who could then take "all the proceeds that came from or might be taken from the street entrance to the second door" of the theater.[30] Diego de Almonacid, who was working to monopolize the administration of commercial theatrical activity in the city, was the first leaseholder of the new *corral*.[31] The company directed by Roque de Figueroa performed the inaugural *comedias* upon the opening of the playhouse in May of 1626.

The variety of spaces available for theatrical performance meant that, even when a given playhouse was in disrepair, commercial drama could and did take place regularly during much of the year. Although performances lapsed during Lent or during waves of unbearable summer heat, hundreds of performances might be given over the course of a year.[32] Theatrical activity played a central role in the daily public and cultural life of the city. Contracts negotiated between administrators of the *corrales* and the directors of acting companies provide insights into these relationships. The contract made between Diego de Almonacid and Antonio Granados, a troupe director who had come from Madrid to Seville in 1623, required that Granados not only stage forty plays during his stay in Seville, but also that "in each week [of his contract] two new plays be performed by order of the aforementioned Almonacid."[33] This clause indicates the regularity and variety theater administrators demanded of acting companies resident in Seville. It was in the interest of all parties to attract large audiences of paying playgoers to performances, and new plays helped to satiate audience demand and, by extension, meet the economic interests of municipal authorities. Similarly, the contract negotiated between the leaseholders of the Coliseo and the company of Roque de Figueroa in 1632 stipulated that the players should present ninety *comedias* for the period beginning 1 November 1632—"give or take four days"—and ending

Shrove Tuesday of 1633. It also mandated that the *autor* and his troupe should not leave the city and that they present "two new plays every seven days."[34]

The Coliseo's special arrangement as the playhouse owned by the municipality meant that its managers got the first choice of the acting companies touring Seville. Yet the Montería's leaseholders also managed to attract and contract with talented *autores* and actors. As discussed previously, although actors and actresses, especially itinerant players, often lived on the margins of early modern society, they could become famous celebrities. Since two companies could be present in Seville during the seventeenth century, actors and actresses frequently made up part of the urban milieu there and were more visible than marginalized. These were professionals, whose lives consisted of a sometimes burdensome daily schedule of learning their lines for the required performances of new plays, rehearsing in the day, and performing at the *corrales de comedias* and before government officials and elite patrons into the night.

While the lifestyle of professional players carried with it the potential for glamour and celebrity, as evidenced by the fame of María Calderón, often called La Calderona, or by the decision by Alonso de Olmedo, who had been the Count of Orpessa's page, to join an acting company when he became enamored with an actress onstage, it also had drawbacks. Even the more respectable members and directors of acting troupes could run afoul of authorities in theatrical cities like Seville. The imprisonment of Roque de Figueroa in the city's royal jail in 1634 provides a glimpse into just such an incident. After he had left Seville with his contract to deliver ninety performances in the Coliseo unfulfilled, the managers of the playhouse contracted with Figueroa's rival, Bartolomé Romero, whose company began performing in the newly renovated *corral de comedias* in January of 1633.[35] Figueroa was arrested, and in January of 1634 authorities seized and assessed his goods in order to pay his outstanding debts. These items included props and costumes used by his company. Among the director's possessions were numerous tunics, coats, sleeves, hoses, and breeches, "a skirt of black watered camlet with trimming," and "a red taffeta dress with beading."[36] Having experienced so many problems in Seville, once he was released, the *autor* took his company to Salamanca and was directing performances there by September of 1634.[37] By the next year, he was causing a different kind of trouble in Madrid. In May of 1635, Figueroa's company was in the middle "of performing the first act" of a play at the Corral del Príncipe when "Simon González, city constable, and two soldiers of the Spanish Guard" noisily interrupted the performance and took the *autor* and his company to the palace to put on a play at the pleasure of the king.[38]

Troupe directors and actors who met the terms of their contracts might still find themselves subjected to unwanted scrutiny and the negative attention of authorities. One of the reasons for this was the potential for playhouses to be sites of disorder in early modern Spain. When audience members in Seville's playhouses did not get what they wanted, they threw cucumbers, lemon peels, and other missiles and jangled their keys in displeasure.[39] They might get into brawls or break out into riots. Even without riots, the theater could be an unsettled space into which people illicitly forced their ways. Not only did some of the denizens of Seville gather together in noisy groups on rooftops to watch the performances that took place in the initially roofless Coliseo, but they also created problems for public order in their numerous attempts to enter the *corrales* without paying.[40] As a consequence of the city government's direct control over the charitable proceeds of public drama, there was an increasing attempt by royal and city authorities to control theater in Seville as early as the end of the sixteenth century. While this also occurred elsewhere, authorities in Seville, as well as Madrid, seemed especially concerned with trying to regulate and minimize disorder, with quite mixed results.

Numerous disorderly incidents took place at the Corral de la Montería. In November of 1632 a man in black "caused a disturbance at the second entrance [by] shouting that he wanted to enter without paying in order to see the play being performed."[41] Two months later one of the Montería's guards was wounded when five or six young men—likely university students, as witnesses testified that they were wearing typical student garb—tried to force their way into the main entrance of the Montería without paying for admission and wounded one of the theater's guards in the process. There were also problems with men infiltrating the *cazuela* and sexually harassing women by lifting up their skirts and touching their legs. When a man did this in 1654, the city punished him with imprisonment followed by exile.[42]

In 1642 playgoers rioted at the Montería because the Inquisition had banned the *comedia* due to be performed. When the *autor* offered the performance of another play to the audience, the disappointed playgoers refused and quickly made their disappointment quite vocal. They began to loudly chant the name of the play that had been forbidden: "San Cristobal! San Cristobal!" Soon, their anger erupted into violence. They vandalized the theater, destroying seats, tearing up scenery, and ripping up costumes left behind in the actors' dressing rooms. This was also a moment in which the frustrations of the lower ranks of city dwellers with their wealthier, elite neighbors boiled over, as some of the rioters targeted the lattice screens of the private boxes that afforded the privilege of privacy to nobles and authorities when they attended plays in the Montería.[43] Disorderly incidents such as these suggest that, despite city and royal officials' attempts to control the theaters and maximize their profitability, they remained raucous places rife with the potential for scandal.

As in Madrid, the *corrales* in Seville were semi-compartmentalized. Working-class men paid their half *real* for a seat, and crowded into the central patio. Playgoing allowed the men of Seville to see and be seen, to be entertained and to take part in a public activity. Although members of the theatergoing public came from all classes of so-called respectable society—including nobles, merchants, artisans, and members of the cathedral chapter, who certainly believed that they deserved a clean and decent place to view the *comedias*—the structured spaces of the *corrales* sought to maintain class boundaries and gender divisions.[44] With an attendant to escort them to their seats and guard the door to their area of the theater, the women of the lower and middle classes watched *comedias* from the separate space of the *cazuela*. However, these divisions were not always properly enforced, as a 1627 proposal by the municipal authorities indicates. To prevent women from sitting with the men in the *corrales*, one of the city fathers suggested that men and women be required to enter the theater and their respective seating sections through separate doors.[45] It is easy to imagine that such efforts met with at least some continued resistance, just as those attempts to compel people to pay entrance fees did. Meanwhile, noblewomen might accompany their husbands, fathers, or brothers to watch a play in the more private space of a rented or owned box.

Seville's political and social discourses were heavily steeped in theatricality. This is what some scholars have described as a theater state in which religion and secular authority merged in the public spectacle of the exercise of power and authority.[46] The trappings of Seville as a theater state and a theatrical society became apparent during executions of convicted criminals, when dialogues between the convicted and Jesuit priests took on aspects of pedagogical and penitential performativity, even as a number of Jesuit priests condemned the formative nature of theater and its promotion of social vices. The power of the theater state was also on display during the city's celebration of religious festivals.[47] Such festivals required the efforts of acting companies and carpenters as well as clergymen, guilds, artists, and dramatists such as Ana Caro Mallén de Soto. Although only a handful of her works have survived to the present, Caro, who spent most of her life in the port city, received payment from the city fathers for penning two of the *autos sacramentales* for Seville's Corpus Christi festivals in the 1630s and 1640s.[48]

The performances of one-act religious plays involved the same directors and acting troupes that drew crowds to the commercial theaters. For instance, in 1624 Seville's Corpus Christi Commission authorized a payment to the *autor* Tomás Fernández "for his arrival in this city and for his decorations and costumes for the floats for the performance." For his generosity in providing "such good religious plays" the municipal authorities drew 50 ducats from their coffers to pay him.[49] These festivals also generated competition between troupe directors to secure lucrative contracts and remuneration for the best performances. In June of 1644 Antonio de Prado petitioned the commissioners for compensation, claiming that he and his company were "the most brilliant and had put on the best *autos* and interludes in the festival and for which he had been forced to add four more men to his troupe which had added 500 *reales* to his expenses."[50]

Actors and other performers also sought payment for their individual efforts from Seville's corpus commission. In 1638 Iñigo de Albaisa, an actor in the troupe that had staged a one-act play about Ferdinand III, the saintly king who had led the reconquest of Seville in 1248, petitioned the festival commissioners. Albaisa asked them for financial assistance because "he and his wife had performed the roles that had taken the most work and care. In order to serve your lordships with splendor we have made the dresses and costumes that were necessary in concordance with the intent of the said performance [and] from which much cost and debt have followed us." He also noted that these costumes were especially financially burdensome since "they would not be used for any other occasion." In response to Albaisa's need, the commission paid him 6,800 *maravedís*.[51] Documents such as these not only give historians a sense of which companies and actors were in Seville and when, but they also point to the complicated and symbiotic relationships between acting companies, municipal authorities, and festive culture in early modern Seville.

Unlike those of many other cities in Castile, the commercial theaters of Seville had developed for the most part without many substantial connections to the religious lay brotherhoods of the New Rome. Nevertheless, there were some occasional exceptions to this more general tendency. For example, the confraternity of La Limpieza de Nuestra Señora y Conversión de la Magdalena petitioned Seville's city fathers in 1586 to allow more frequent performances during the week in order to help fund its charitable activities. Sometimes confraternities produced dramatic performances in conjunction with feast days, as the monastery of the brotherhood of Nuestra Señora del Rosario y la Oración en el Huerto did in 1608.[52] However, such connections were less common in Seville than they were in Madrid during the sixteenth and early seventeenth centuries. In all likelihood, some of the reluctance of the *cofradías* to associate themselves with the *corrales* stemmed from the repeated ecclesiastical injunctions on acting troupes and public theatrical productions.

However, in addition to the well-known negative perceptions about actors, which could be compounded when they performed religious drama, the timing of both the development of the commercial theaters and the network of religious brotherhoods was different in Seville, and this probably also mitigated such entrenched connections. Unlike the *cofradías* of Madrid, which largely emerged at the same time as the city expanded as capital and used theater to fund their charitable good works, many of those that operated in Seville had existed prior to the development of commercial theatrical activity there. Considering the large number of residents of the city who were members of confraternities and the numbers who attended the performance of *comedias,* it seems that the charitable brotherhoods missed out on an opportunity for alms-giving on a much greater scale. Instead, the municipal government took on this role at an early stage, helping to entrench theater into the daily life of the city.

The *cofradías* played substantial roles in religious processional drama and in public welfare programs for the city of Seville.[53] While they varied significantly in size and in membership demography, many performed good works and acts of mercy in a display of Baroque piety. In the port city confraternities organized spectacular processions for religious festivals that could potentially augment their abilities to perform pious works by motivating members and witnesses to make donations and bequests. Sometimes Seville's confraternities organized spectacles of pain even outside of their normal Holy Week activities, as in 1599, when one confraternity, La Oración en el Huerto, organized a procession of self-flagellants who cried out for all to pray against the plague as they whipped themselves.[54]

Many of Seville's hospitals provided assistance to small numbers of sick and poor men, women, and children. The Hospital Real, founded during the reign of the thirteenth-century monarch Alfonso X, could only house twelve men. The Amor de Dios was larger, with 45 beds for patients, and the Casa Cuna housed 150 orphans and foundlings.[55] Many of the smaller hospitals had been established by "individual effort or, more frequently, by the work of charitable associations," and over time their liens and rents had become devalued.[56] During the 1580s when Seville's population had grown to as much as possibly 150,000 inhabitants, the Spanish crown undertook efforts to cut the confraternities out of the hospital business and to consolidate the small hospitals into just a few general hospitals. More than one hundred hospitals—seventy-six different ones in the parish of San Pedro alone—merged into two institutions of charitable care and hospitality, the Espiritu

Santo and the Amor de Dios.[57] By the next decade, these efforts at centralization faltered because the newly consolidated hospitals were still unable to meet the needs of the city's sick and poor. Outbreaks of plague, which hit Seville repeatedly and much harder than it did Madrid during the seventeenth century, increased the demand for care and heightened the public health crisis. The number of hospitals once again increased; by 1673 there were at least twenty-four hospitals in Seville in spite of a significant decline in population.[58]

Historians have debated the efficiency and quality of these institutions. Evidence suggests that some of the smaller foundations were not even functioning as hospitals and could be called such in name only. In spite of patrons' recommendations, such as the requirement that the bedclothes of hospital patients be changed as regularly as once a week and more often if necessary, some of these institutions became characterized by poverty and neglect. Even when hospitals offered significant aid, they were often unable to do much to aid the sick, poor, and injured who entered their doors. Some patients were likely too far gone. This was the case in November of 1639 when a certain Don Pedro, who was not originally from Seville, received a serious chest wound during a brawl at one of the theaters. The fight escalated out of a heated argument about which of the actresses, Antonia Infanta or Jacinta de Herbias, was the best. While his attacker fled the scene with his sword still unsheathed, Don Pedro was carried first to the changing rooms and then to one of the city's hospitals, where he died two days later.[59]

Although the confraternities only rarely connected themselves with public theater in Seville and the income of the *corrales de comedias*, early efforts were undertaken to use proceeds from playhouse admissions to fund public health and charitable works in the port city. As happened in some other cities in the Spanish Atlantic World, it is probable that some sixteenth-century performances took place in hospital patios. A synod of churchmen held in Seville in 1575 decreed that no performances should take place in churches, convents, "or hospitals or other pious places without our express permission."[60] This may have been a miscalculation from a fiscal point of view for hospital administrators and others involved in poor relief efforts. In 1593 Gaspar Benítez, who was the administrator of the poor of Seville's city jails, petitioned the Spanish monarchy for a special license to "create a theater and restrict performances to it" in order to aid the poor of the city. This petition suggests that the private leaseholding of the theaters that was already taking place in Seville undercut the amount of aid to the hospitals and poor relief that the *corrales de comedias* had the potential to provide.[61] Even though theatrical activity was not restricted to one theater in the manner Benítez had hoped, as the continued existence of multiple playhouses and issuing of leasing contracts demonstrates, by the seventeenth century proceeds from performances had become charitably linked to the hospitals of the city in significant ways.

Municipal connections and authorizations were important in the development of this symbiotic relationship. In April of 1614 a decree required that everyone who entered the playhouses of Seville "be charged eight [*maravedís*] more and that these serve to help discharge the pledge" owed to the city. The money, like that earmarked for the hospitals and orphanages in Madrid, was stored in a special strongbox with three keys. Such an increase in entry fees had a potentially significant impact, as "from the eighth day of April 1611 until the first day of February of 1614, 526 *comedias* had been performed, 258 in the Coliseo and 268 in the Corral de Dona Elvira bringing in a total sum of 53,346 *reales*."[62] An increase in entry fees helped to ensure that the leaseholders could pay the acting companies the amount stipulated by their contracts, meet the other obligations of their leases, and bring in thousands of *maravedís* over the duration of an acting troupe's stay in Seville to provide charitable aid to their less fortunate neighbors.

Sometimes individual, contractual, financial obligations written into the leases of the playhouses supplemented the money that came from admission fees paid by playgoers. When Diego de Almonacid took over the administration of the newly refurbished Coliseo in the middle of the 1620s, he agreed to make an annual payment of 100 *reales* to the Hospital of the Misericordia for as long as his lease of the Coliseo should last.[63] The contract also required that these disbursements of charitable funds be made in silver and not in more depreciated coinage made of silver alloy or *vellón*.

The importance of the financial connections between the theaters and hospitals of the city can also be seen in a petition to King Philip IV.

Although it was not dated, Melchor de Alcazar likely composed this appeal at some point after 1646, when the Spanish monarchy had issued a long-term theater ban in Castile, and prior to the severe outbreak of plague in 1649. Alcazar noted the deplorable state of the patients of the Royal Hospital of Seville and their "very great necessity and poverty" and implored the monarchy to allow that the performance of *comedias* be resumed in order to alleviate the burden on the city.[64] In deferential yet urgent language, he reminded the monarch that there were, after all, "three places where plays were performed" in the city and claimed that such action taken "in order to succor the poor [would be] without aggravation or harm to the persons [nearby]."[65] His claims may have helped reopen the *corrales* with certain conditions, as a document from November of 1648 indicates. However, he might have been overly optimistic in his promise of no aggravation, as the deputy mayor of Seville Don Antonio Mendoza issued a decree in a fit of exasperation over the noisy and disorderly behavior that was taking place at the Corral de la Montería. He threatened people "of all stations and qualities to stop disturbing the peace" at the Montería with their shouted requests for "speeches, dances, and other things," and cautioned them "that they should let the director and his company perform what they wanted." Mendoza promised to punish disturbers of the peace with "public shame and two years in the Moorish dungeon" or "10,000 *maravedís* and two years in the city's jails."[66]

Even with the charitable financial assistance brought in by the *corrales de comedias*, which attracted so many jocular and rowdy entertainment seekers of "all stations and quality," neither Seville's hospitals nor its cemeteries could keep up with the problems of the living and dying populace of the city. The physical circumstances of urban living did little to alleviate many of the early modern health problems. Vermin infected people with typhus and other diseases. Medical doctrine was preoccupied—largely unsuccessfully—with how to get rid of these pests, balance humors, and purge the air of putrid miasmas. As Seville grew in the sixteenth century, problems with urban cleanliness and waste only worsened. Dirty, sewage-infested water ran through the streets and public plazas of the city. People urinated and defecated in public and even sacred spaces.[67] In spite of the efforts of physicians and civic authorities who issued regulations—such as the 1586 city ordinance that decreed that nothing should be emptied onto the streets before midnight and that, if waste was thrown into the street during the day, the person tossing out the contents of the chamber pot should give vocal warning three times before doing so—there was little alleviation of public health problems.[68]

Such run-of-the-mill sewage disposal and issues of sanitation became compounded during times of plague and natural disaster. For example, a plague outbreak that lasted from 1599 to 1601 brought deadly interruptions to all aspects of Seville's society. Bad weather disrupted daily life in 1635–1636 when a terrible drought created a grain shortage and general famine. Torrential rains and the flooding of the Guadalquivir took place in 1629 and from 1642 to 1649. The fact that the later years of this crisis coincided with a time during which the theaters had been closed by the Spanish monarchy only worsened the financial aspects of the public health crisis. A devastating plague outbreak that swept Seville in 1649 further compounded the catastrophe when the river flooded so high that as many as one-third of the city's inhabitants were unable to get to their homes except by boat, and the putrid waters carried disease and death.[69] Some scholars have estimated that this outbreak killed as much as half of the city's population. Others who could afford to do so fled, at least temporarily furthering this demographic collapse.

Although civil authorities implemented measures to try to restrict the flow of goods and movement of people around the port city and undertook quarantine efforts during outbreaks of epidemic disease, individual people could petition for exemption from quarantine.[70] These exemptions likely spread contagion. Disasters such as floods and droughts led to shortages of even the most basic staples of life, which were already difficult for the urban poor to obtain. As an observer noted in a 1655 publication, Seville's poorest went to the river to collect dead fish for their sustenance.[71] Such desperation put added pressure on city hospitals, apothecaries, medical practitioners, public officials, and poor relief efforts. As theaters tended to be closed during outbreaks of disease, which eliminated a substantial site of potential contagion for the city's populace, this also meant that the additional charitable funds the performance of plays provided ran dry. This was further complicated in the late 1640s by the Spanish monarch's ban on performances.

When not hindered by plague outbreaks and natural disasters, the theater of Seville came close to rivaling that of Madrid—if not eclipsing it at times. By contrast, the commercial theater that developed in London did not get exported to provincial and colonial cities to the same extent. The theaters and theatergoing publics of Seville were more active than those of early modern Bristol. However, that does not mean that there was not substantial ceremonial, festive, and dramatic activity taking place in this English provincial port. Indeed, there were numerous theatrical performances in the sixteenth-century city, and by the first decade of the seventeenth century, commercial drama was taking place routinely in a permanent, privately owned playhouse in Bristol.

Prior to the Reformation there were numerous public ceremonies related to Catholic feast days and political activity. Inaugurations of new mayors and officeholders in Bristol were opportunities to bind the urban community together and came with displays of splendor and the taking of sophisticated oaths.[72] These formal rituals also denoted the symbolic change of authority and potential for new beginnings for Bristolians. Civic ceremonies and public processions related to the celebration of St. Clement, the patron saint of Mariners, and to St. Katherine, whose feast day took place only two days later, featured prominently in Bristol's cultural life. Such festivals also involved feasting, drinking, and public performances of plays. Like in Seville, Corpus Christi productions involved pageantry, if of a somewhat different style, as authorities in Bristol banned wheeled carts and wagons due to the extensive system of sewers and underground warehouses in the city. While the records do not demonstrate any guild-produced drama in connection with the Corpus Christi celebrations, the parishes put on processions and hired lute players, harp players, minstrels, and torchbearers.[73]

Such feast day celebrations came to an end with the reigns of Protestant monarchs Edward VI and Elizabeth I. However, civic celebrations remained important to urban life. Mayoral inaugurations continued to be celebrated with festive rituals, music, and bonfires. While evidence for strolling players performing at fairs in Bristol is notably absent, there is significantly more evidence for touring professional entertainers, including acting companies, tumblers, and bears and their keepers, coming to Bristol during the early modern period.[74] Schoolboys' dramatic performances, royal entries, and other special occasions also provided some opportunities for entrepreneurs in the theater business and for citizens of Bristol to see spectacles, participate in revelry, and enjoy entertainment. For example, the early modern adventurer Richard Ferris, who rowed a green boat from London to Bristol, arrived to a welcome extended by the mayor and aldermen whose rejoicing was "wonderful to see and heare." According to Ferris's account of his adventure, "the people came in great multitude to see us, in so much as by the consent of the Magistrates thye took . . . and carried our saide Boate to the high Crosse, in the Citie."[75] The next morning the populace of Bristol, accompanied by musicians and standard-bearers, gathered to carry the boat once more. Although they numbered fewer than in Seville, the inhabitants of Bristol enjoyed the novelty of such events and the more routine performances of plays.

During the early decades of the seventeenth century, John Daniel received a license to create a boys' company, The Youths of Her Majesty's Royal Chamber of Bristol, "to use ane exercise the arte and quality of playing Comedies histories Enterludes morralles Pastoralles Stage-playes and such other like as they have alreadie studied . . . in and about our said Citie of Bristoll in such usuall houses as themselves shall provide."[76] However, the records do not suggest that this company, which has become more commonly known as the Children of Bristol, ever actually performed in Bristol—at least not under its own name.[77] In spite of the lack of direct evidence, it is likely that this company did perform and was likely the troupe that gave a performance in 1622.[78] Certainly, playgoers did have opportunities to see professional companies, as the mayor's audits reflect relatively routine payments to acting companies, such as the "kinges players" and "the Ladie Elizabeths players" as well as to other unspecified companies during the first half of the seventeenth century.

During the sixteenth century dramatic performances had taken place in a variety of places and spaces in Bristol. These included the mayor's door, the free school of St. Bartholomew, the Marsh, and the

Guildhall. Evidence suggests that a playhouse in Wine Street may have become the focal point for dramatic activity in the first decades of the seventeenth century. This playhouse, which was located close to several churches and not far from Guildhall, was owned by Nicholas Woolfe, a cutler, and closed around 1625. By 1626 the property had passed into the hands of a tailor named Anthony Bassett.[79] Nicholas Woolfe's property was also a residential playhouse rather than an inn-yard one in spite of the fact that Woolfe's extensive property ownership would have enabled such an inn-yard theater to exist. Some theater historians have observed that this demonstrates the continued Bristolian preference for dramatic performances to take place inside.[80]

While it remains uncertain when Richard Barker built Bristol's second privately owned theater, the Redcliffe Hill playhouse across the Avon River, and when this playhouse began to operate, it is certain that the property was included in Sara Barker's will in 1637–1638. Both of the Bristol playhouses were private ones, and they may have operated concurrently, which was an unusual phenomenon for a provincial urban setting in England during the early seventeenth century.[81] This speaks to the vitality of dramatic activity and playgoing in the city, even if it was not as developed as that of the more populous and theatrical city of Seville.

Although evidence does not suggest as deep and consistent a connection as those that evolved between the theaters and hospitals in Spanish cities, the playhouses of Bristol did provide some financial assistance to local institutions of public health. From 1614 to 1619 Nicholas Woolfe's playhouse in Wine Street provided an annual income of 30 shillings to Queen Elizabeth's Hospital, which had been founded in 1586. This amount is equivalent to approximately half of what Diego de Almonacid's 1625 leasing contract stipulated that he should pay annually to the city hospitals.[82] Considering the smaller size of Bristol, this indicates a substantial relief effort on the part of Woolfe. Such individual bequests were likely especially welcome, as this hospital and Bristol's charitable relief may have been significantly in debt to the city's corporation in the amount of almost £3,000 during the early seventeenth century.[83]

Woolfe's theater also regularly paid annuities to the churchwardens of St. John Baptist and to the poor of that parish. The churchwarden's accounts indicate that these funds were then distributed to the poor in the almshouse.[84] Upon his death, Woolfe made a provision in his will for a bequest to Queen Elizabeth's Hospital of an annual annuity in perpetuity in the amount of 30 shillings to be paid out of the proceeds made from his playhouse.[85] Theater scholar Mark Pilkington contends that the Wine Street Playhouse aided six different charitable institutions and made an important impact on the cultural life of this urban location in the first half of the seventeenth century.[86]

As in other early modern cities, Bristol had to contend with difficulties caused by the pressures of population, poor sanitation, and outbreaks of epidemic disease. In 1613 its city fathers banned performances because the plague was then ravaging the countryside and had created a fear of strangers, including the traveling playing companies.[87] Such fears of plague outbreaks were not unreasonable, considering the devastating toll they could take on cities and towns. It is also worth noting that Bristol's medical practitioners, even though relatively numerous, would have been unlikely to keep up with the demands of an epidemic.

The occupations of Bristol's citizens can provide some insights into community structures and the still comparatively limited role of theater there. According to the research of David Harris Sacks, between 1607 and 1651, the city of Bristol employed sixty-two barbers and barber surgeons and eight physicians. However, Sacks only documents five people who held the occupation of musician during the same period, and he makes no mention of any actors or playwrights resident in the thriving commercial town, which served as home for 293 merchants and 537 dealers and retailers during the same period.[88] While acting companies visited the city, they did not spend the same amounts of time there that they did in Seville, where the larger population demanded numerous and new performances of plays in the *corrales de comedias.*

Considering Bristol's link to the Atlantic and the New World, it is perhaps surprising that there is no extant corpus of city plays set in this port city prior to the eighteenth century. Aside from *The Bristol Tragedy,* which was performed in 1602 by the Admiral's Servants, and *The Fair Maide of Bristol,* performed for James I and Anne of Denmark in 1605, there do not seem to be others.[89] Added to this, little is known about the performances of specific plays in Bristol's playhouses. However, theater historians can catch glimpses of specific theater events in the dramatic record. Philip Powell's Commonplace book describes what he saw on a trip to the theater in Bristol when he was visiting the city in 1620. In this instance a fool—or character of Vice—named Kendall appeared on the stage and "spake extempore as foloweth, in dispraise of the noble Brittains, if thou art a Brittaine borne, it fitts thee to were ye horne." To this speech John Brittan, an apprentice of Thomas Dean of Bristoll, who was a member of the theater's audience that day, patriotically replied, "A Brittans name I truly beare, I leaue the horne for thee to were:/ the horne becomes the saxons best/I kisd thy wife supose the rest."[90] Such unplanned improvisation by both the actor and the audience suggests that verbal disorder may have been common in the provincial playhouses of Bristol even if audience members there did not riot or disturb the peace as they more commonly did in the *corrales de comedias* of Seville.

Seville, like its theaters, was a place of both order and disorder. It was both the "very noble and very loyal" city of arches, towers, and statues open to the public view and described in great detail by humanists of the New Rome like Juan de Mal Lara, and it was the criminal underworld of secrecy and shady dealings, brought to life by Miguel de Cervantes in his satirical novella, *Rinconete y Cortadillo*.[91] As a port city, Seville served as a doorway between the Mediterranean and Atlantic Worlds. In part, it was the emigration to and the trade from the Americas that transformed Seville from a peaceful provincial city into a bustling and crime-ridden center of unpredictable and flurrying activity, which unleashed consternation on the part of authorities about disorder and a general lack of patriarchal control.[92] Many of Seville's inhabitants were on their way to or from the Americas; others publicly conformed to Catholic Christianity while privately holding on to Islamic or Jewish beliefs, with their doorways serving as physical thresholds over which they passed back and forth; and women, left behind by their ocean-bound husbands and fathers, crossed over, sometimes many times a day, between traditional and subversive gender roles, between enclosure and freedom. Reformers hoped that at least separate doors for men and women to enter the playhouse would prevent them from mingling even as it did not prevent them from entering.

Such a theatrical city provided excellent material for playwrights, and numerous Golden Age *comedias* were set in Seville. Seville served as the setting for many plays such as *El Arenal de Sevilla* by Lope de Vega, *El Burlador de Sevilla* by Tirso de Molina, *La Estrella de Sevilla* now attributed to Andrés de Claramonte, and *El médico de su honra* by Pedro Calderón de la Barca. Such dramas also allowed readers and playgoers in other locations to imagine the port city. They tapped into the imaginations of spectators and capitalized on the familiarity that many would have had with Seville through personal experience, family connections, gossip, news, and reading.

Lope de Vega's 1603 play, *El Arenal de Sevilla,* provides an example of theatrical art imitating life in the port city. In many ways, it is a typical romantic comedy, involving lovers, a love triangle, and comic scenes in which disguises lead to comic and chaos as a prelude to a happy ending that culminates in marriage. Although the broad plotline is standard for an early modern Spanish play, it also captures much of the essence of this early modern metropolis. "Notable is the confusion" in Lope's rendition of the port city, which bustles with characters of all social ranks and genders: gentlemen, soldiers, *moriscos,* galley slaves, thieves, gentlewomen, women of color, and gypsies, both real and feigned.[93] These men and women (and the actors and actresses who portrayed them) visited the "colossuses, amphitheaters,/ beacons, pyres, mausoleums/ one of a kind and alone,/ the statues, temples, and theaters" of grand Seville.[94] In the port of Lope's play, as in historical reality, many things shift and change—as did the Guadalquivir and the eroding sands of the *arenal.* Most of the action of the *comedia* takes place along this sandy shore where sailors, persons held in slavery, and foreigners interact and where confusing movement and deceptions mimic the chaos of Golden Age Seville. Clothing proves to really be rags of threads and paper—but only after a gullible visitor to the city finalizes his purchases of them.[95] Don Lope's love for Doña Lucinda quickly changes into love for Doña Laura. Doña Lucinda transforms herself from noblewoman to gypsy.[96] Even her broken heart and injured pride transmogrify from wounded to healed, as she becomes accustomed to the relationship between Lope and Laura, but not before she manipulates Don Lope's identity, by convincing him to disguise himself as a gypsy, as well. The effects of the unusually large number of thirty-two characters' manipulations, machinations, and metamorphoses in the play are dizzying. Their constant movement and their ever-changing relationships with each other produced in the reader or spectator a simulacrum of the same confusion that characterized the streets of early modern Seville.

In the case of *El Arenal de Sevilla* the theater could and did hold up a mirror for society, and the image it reflected was one of movement, confusion, and disorder. Such activity was part and parcel of early modern city life, especially in a place where social lines could become blurred, crossed, and subverted. Men could and did sneak into the women's section of the playhouse, priests mixed with laypersons, actresses turned themselves into gypsies and men, and common-born players became royalty if only for the space of three acts and so long as their director's goods did not get seized by authorities due to breach of contract.

Seville and Bristol were port cities in which theater became integrated into the daily life of their inhabitants. However, this took place at much different paces and under rather different circumstances. Both the private owners of Bristol's playhouses and the administrators of Seville's *corrales* paid annuities designed to assist their poor and sick neighbors. When people of a variety of social ranks and occupations visited the theaters of Seville and Bristol, they sought entertainment. In the case of Seville, when they paid their entry fees, they provided financial assistance to the charitable relief of the city's hospitals. And this system, along with many of the men of Seville, sailed down the Guadalquivir and across the Atlantic Ocean to the overseas kingdoms of the Spanish monarchy—to seek fortune and entertainment in the Americas.

Comedies in Colonial Contexts

THEATER IN EARLY MODERN MEXICO CITY AND DUBLIN

In 1626 the members of the *cabildo,* or city council, of Mexico City indulged in a self-aggrandizing conversation about how the playhouses of the viceregal capital of New Spain did not provide some of their highest-ranking audience members with the comfort and luxury they desired. The city councilmen keenly felt this supposed lack of propriety. After all, such a dearth of private boxes in the *corrales de comedias* prevented them from having one of the key symbols of status that they thought correct and necessary in the colonial world they inhabited. The council's scribe chronicled the complaints of the city fathers, who claimed that they did not go to the theater as often as they might "because they did not have a designated private box in which to attend, as [was] customary in Madrid, Seville, and the other cities of Spain." The scribe recorded the officials' earnest pronouncement that "as [Mexico City] is the head of this realm, it is right that it should have a box with complete ornamentation and decency, where the magistrates can [sit] comfortably."[1]

The city fathers soon had a better box, at least in one of the two public playhouses then in use in Mexico City. Cristobal de Molina, one of the members of the *cabildo* who was an opponent of the infamous *encomienda* system, was also apparently an expert on the public theater back in Spain. On 25 January 1627, he reported to the council that "in all the cities of the kingdom of Castile, in all the playhouses, the city councils have clearly designated boxes in the best places" in the *corrales.*[2] Within six months, the city council and the superintendent of the Royal Indian Hospital had reached an agreement to make improvements to their private box "that is in the said hospital" and to provide a steward to ensure that the box was kept locked so that no one who was not a member of the *cabildo* could enter it to watch the plays when the members of the municipal government opted not to attend the performance.[3] The relatively speedy action of the council in this instance and the officials' desire for a more ornate and "decent" box exemplifies both the concern for physically demonstrating class and rank in Baroque Mexico City and the centrality of theater in the life of the capital of the Viceroyalty of New Spain by the early decades of the seventeenth century. Additionally, the presence of the playhouse in the hospital patio and the city councilmen's concern about their box in it clearly demonstrates that the symbiotic financial relationships between theaters and hospitals had rapidly spread from the heart of Castile to the Spanish colonies.

Theater played a prominent role in urban life in Mexico during the colonial period. The Spanish colonists of the New World transported the mutually beneficial arrangement between the institutions of the *corrales de comedias* and the hospitals to their new environments, and this helped shape theatrical and daily life in the colonial context. In fact, in Mexico City, these two institutions became even more tightly linked together than they were in some Spanish cities, such as the previously discussed case of Seville. In Mexico's court city the inn-yard theaters were physically connected to the hospitals. Although some historians of Mexican theater in the early twentieth century worked under the erroneous belief that this connection did not actually manifest until the second half of the seventeenth century, evidence from a variety of archival and print sources complicates this view and suggests the link between theaters and hospitals in Mexico City had begun to form during the sixteenth century and became solidified during the first years of the seventeenth century.[4]

Drama in the cities of New Spain, while similar to that in Castile, initially had new uses in the violent colonial setting of Mexico. Here performances and festivals became tools for religious conversion and efforts at Europeanizing indigenous populations during the sixteenth century. Public theater and the performances of *comedias* also became mechanisms for reasserting the Spanish identity of both peninsular Spaniards and creoles in early modern Mexico City. Divided by the Atlantic, the Spanish *comedia* helped to shrink the physical distance of the far-flung empire for peninsular and creole playgoers and readers in the cities of Spain and of its realms during the sixteenth and seventeenth centuries. Public drama developed much more quickly in the cities of the Spanish Atlantic than it did in the Anglo Atlantic, so that by the middle of the seventeenth century Mexico City's public theater outpaced that of Dublin.

Dublin was in many ways a colonial city; it was the seat of viceregal power as the Tudors and Stuarts respectively considered the kingdom of Ireland as part of their dominions. The so-called Irish Plantation was rife with political and confessional tensions. In part this stemmed from the contestation over monarchical power in Ireland. During the period of Tudor rule, there were plots to recognize a variety of alternative claimants to the throne of Ireland. These included James V of Scotland, Philip II of Spain, and Hugh O'Neill, the Earl of Tyrone. After 1603, theater largely became a tool for the expression of Stuart power in Dublin.[5] Dublin's nascent and court-based theater had a limited existence of only a few years before military rebellion and civil war shut the doors of its playhouse in Werburgh Street in 1640. Even after the English Restoration, commercial theater remained dependent on the patronage of the court and was more apt to draw audiences of gentry. While more centrally located in Dublin than many of the theaters were in London, commercial drama in Dublin remained a less crucial factor in the public life of the city than was the case in Mexico Metropolitano.

Pre-Columbian Mexico was a fertile ground for theatrical activity in which indigenous performances and festivals had thrived. The Aztecs and the Maya already had raised earthen platforms on which ritual and religious performances took place when the Spanish conquistadors arrived. In the case of the Aztec Empire many of these dramatic rituals had ties to religious sacrifice and the celebration of religious festivals. Although many of the Iberian victors undertook efforts to physically and spiritually eradicate indigenous cultures, some Spanish administrators and clergymen preserved some forms of pre-Columbian art, knowledge, and culture. In addition to tracing the dynastic, political, and military histories of the Aztecs, the Dominican friar Diego Durán also described pre-Columbian social and religious practices, including performances and spectacles.[6] In his codex, which was compiled in the 1560s, he wrote about a number of indigenous festivals, including those that he condemned for "cruel and horrific sacrifices" such as the feast associated with the month of Tlacaxipehuatliztli, which celebrated warfare and agricultural renewal and involved the donning of sumptuous dress and ornate labial rings and other jewelry, and the consumption of a vast array of poultry, meats, breads, and "drinks of chocolate and wine in the old style."[7]

Durán penned lengthy passages about other festivals that involved brilliant costumes and dances in his *Libro de ritos y ceremonias en las fiestas de los dioses y celebración de ellas*. He provided lengthy descriptions of the feast days, spectacles, and devotional practices of the indigenous inhabitants of the recently conquered lands of New Spain. His work has an overarching theme of Catholic victory over "superstitious ceremonies and false cults of the false gods that [the Indians] worshipped."[8] However, in the process of preserving knowledge about pre-Hispanic cultural practices, the Dominican also opened himself up to criticisms from other mendicants and colonial administrators who feared that he was an enabler of continued idolatry and religious backsliding among Mexican indigenes.

In addition to being an ethnohistory, Duran's codex also serves as something of a theater history. It provides numerous details about feast-day customs, the training of indigenous youth to participate in dances, and the types of performances that took place. The preparations for—as well as the celebrations of—the festivals, such as the ones for deities like Tlaloc, Totec Xipe, and Nauholin, were intense, required labor and training, and involved the rehearsal of numerous songs and dances. The props and costuming used to celebrate feast days were elaborate, and performers disguised themselves "some times like eagles, others like tigers and lions, others like soldiers, others like jesters, others like hunters, other times like wild animals and like monkeys and dogs and a thousand other guises."[9] During the celebration of religious festivals associated with the goddess Xochiquetzalli in Mexico City, the celebrants used extensive props, including a house made of roses.

Farcical elements and the performance of a fool elicited humorous reactions from spectators. Dancers dressed like birds and monkeys flew through the air. Feigned drunkenness along with "dances and farces and interludes and songs" resulted in "much contentment."[10] Although the Dominican friar considered certain elements of these celebrations and spectacles unsavory, dishonest, and diabolical, indigenous religious activities and performances found resonances in the evangelical theater that developed as part of the experience of lived religion in the wake of Castile's victory.

In 1524, just a few short years after conquering the heart of the Aztec Empire with the assistance of thousands of Mesoamerican allies, Hernán Cortés carefully staged a scene with twelve Franciscan missionaries who had come to Mexico as Christian evangelists. Adam Versényi persuasively argues that through the act of kneeling and kissing the hems of the friars' robes, the wily conquistador combined religion, politics, and theatricality in New Spain in much the same way that clerics orchestrated evocative combinations of these elements in public festivals and executions back in Castile. Although historian Matthew Restall has argued that the incident was a later construct created by Franciscans, one of the myths of conquest is that Cortés had allegedly already used performance to take full advantage of Montezuma II. According to the Franciscan fiction, Cortés did this not only by wearing the Quetzalcoatl costume of feathers and gold that the Aztec emperor had sent to him, but also by at least partially performing the role of deity for whom he had possibly been mistaken. Even if Restall is correct and the leader of the Mexican conquest had not actually donned the garb of a god, Cortés nonetheless utilized the performance of ritual exchanges to his benefit. He also took advantage of the ritual of homage to gain the alliance of the Franciscan missionaries and simultaneously reinforced the power of the Franciscans in the eyes of the conquered Aztecs.[11]

By the 1530s Catholic missionaries had begun to write and to direct religious dramas in Nahuatl, as evidenced by a performance of *The Conversion of Saint Paul* staged by Indian actors in the parish church where the Cathedral of Mexico City now stands.[12] Similarly, in 1533 Andrés de Olmos had a Spanish *auto sacramental* translated into Nahuatl and then performed as a method of proselytizing to the indigenous population, which was now allowed and encouraged to perform, sing, and dance for Christ.[13] On 20 June 1538, the first documented *autos sacramentales* for festivals to celebrate Corpus Christi were staged in the Viceroyalty of New Spain. These religious plays, *The Annunciation of the Nativity of Saint John the Baptist, The Annunciation of Our Lady, The Visitation of Our Lady to Saint Elizabeth,* and *The Nativity of Saint John,* took place in Tlaxcala, and served the purposes of both religious pedagogy and celebration. After the performance, the festivals concluded with numerous baptisms of Indians—a pattern that became the norm for several decades. This practice of mass baptisms, which the Franciscans frequently used, was not without vocal critics, who feared new converts had not truly embraced Christianity and would thus be more prone to what Christian ecclesiastics viewed as spiritual backsliding into paganism and idolatry.[14]

Although initially adapted and improvised by the mendicant orders as a tool of conversion, at least one variant of the religious theater brought to Mexico by its new conquerors was soon following a markedly similar pattern to that of Spain, where guilds and then city fathers took charge of Corpus Christi performances. The pageantry of the Corpus Christi festival was meant to be an outlet for civic pride and religious fervor, as well as a mechanism for repentance and potential conversion. As early as 1526, the tailors of Mexico City requested a site on which to build a hospital and a hermitage for the poor, who might come forward in need on Corpus Christi.[15] The poor referred to by the tailors may have included indigenes as well as impoverished Spaniards, and such a hospital would have attempted to provide both corporal and spiritual care. These ideas had crossed the Atlantic with colonists and clerics, but with the added element of evangelism directed toward indigenous peoples of the Americas.

To convert Indians and keep them within the fold of the Church, mendicant friars, particularly the competing Franciscan and Dominican Orders, drew on both the evolving Spanish model of religious theater, the *auto sacramental,* and on the blurred division between performers and spectators in various dramatic traditions, including those they encountered in pre-Columbian dramas. The conquistador,

Bernal Díaz del Castillo, and the famous opponent of the cruelty of Spanish colonization, Bartolomé de Las Casas, witnessed and described a set of two such hybrid theatrical events that took place in 1539. The rivalry between the Aztecs and their old enemies, the Tlaxcalans, found a new performative outlet through the evangelical drama of the Spanish mendicants. There were no more Flower Wars, but there was still a competition with different theatrical stakes. The Mexicans performed *The Conquest of Rhodes* and the Tlaxcalans tried to outdo them by performing *The Conquest of Jerusalem* during the Corpus Christi festivals. Franciscans seeking to evangelize their audiences had written both plays, which used desired—if not actual—Christian military victories, which would be led by the Emperor Charles V, over Islam to solidify Christian victories in the Americas, where Rhodes and Jerusalem represented Tenochtitlan and Tlaxcala.[16] The proselytizing playwrights manipulated an old, established theatrical and political rivalry to assist in this process. This set of performances constituted a "public, visible assertion of public legitimacy, community pride, and devotion to the sacred powers—however people actually conceived of those."[17]

Franciscan friars choreographed and produced *The Conquest of Rhodes,* which was performed in the Plaza Mayor of Mexico City. Apparently, the city council of Mexico spared little expense in financing the sumptuous performance that celebrated the inclusion of thousands of Aztecs as soldiers of Christ. According to Las Casas, the spectacle included "large structures like false [military] theaters as tall as towers" and even "castles and a city made of wood." Although Las Casas was perhaps prone to exaggeration and high counting, it is safe to assume that, even if there were not actually 80,000 Aztec actors, large numbers participated as performers or spectators. The grand scale of the production also celebrated the peace treaty between Charles V and Francis I made the previous year.[18] The performance of these two elaborate spectacles points to the existence of a thriving evangelical theater, operating in the language of Nahuatl and beginning to do so in the Spanish language as well. It is also indicative of the readiness of the municipal government and the Spanish populace of Mexico City for more performances, festivals, and the presence of regular performances of commercial theater by the mid-sixteenth century.

However, in spite of the willingness on the part of potential playgoers, the commercial theater of New Spain took comparatively longer to develop than its counterpart in Castile did. At the same time that the commercial theater of Lope de Rueda was revolutionizing drama in Seville, theatrical activity in Mexico faced a serious obstacle to its development. The first archbishop of New Spain, Juan de Zumárraga, barred dramatic performances and dances from church premises in Mexico City in 1549. Fearing their potential ability to undermine Christian belief, Zumárraga denounced theatrical spectacles for allowing idolatry to survive in spite of the diligent evangelical efforts of the regular and secular clergy in New Spain. This prohibition and others limited theatrical performances to only approved religious topics. At the same time, other outlets for religious fervor and other colonial construction projects, such as the building and opening of the university in Mexico City, slowed but did not stop the pace of further theatrical development during the middle of the sixteenth century.

Concurrently, epidemic disease and transatlantic migrations—both forced and voluntary—led to continued significant demographic, social, and cultural changes. They not only devastated indigenous communities, increased the numbers of Africans who had been sold into slavery in Mexico, and solidified the presence of white European colonists, but also impacted daily urban life and the pace and course of theatrical development in New Spain. In many parts of Mexico, including the court and capital of the viceroyalty, the Indian population decreased significantly due to continued virulent outbreaks of epidemic disease, such as the plague of 1545–1548, which may have killed as much as three-quarters of the indigenous population. Meanwhile, increasing numbers of Spaniards began to try their luck in the wider world of Spain's extra-Iberian dominions, and the secular clergy and the laity began to outnumber the members of the mendicant orders in New Spain.[19]

Among the waves of new arrivals to Mexico City in the second half of the sixteenth century were members of the Society of Jesus. As they did elsewhere, the Jesuits focused on education and evangelization, and they used theater as a didactic tool. In 1578, upon the receipt of holy relics sent to the Jesuits by Pope Gregory XIII, the Jesuits put on an elaborate festival in Mexico City, which included a procession and performances. One of these was the staging of a five-act tragedy, *El triunfo de los santos.*[20] Performed by students as part of the six days of celebration, the play exemplified the Jesuits' use of both classical and innovative forms of drama as a means of religious and intellectual instruction. Such educational theater helped to promote translation of works from Latin into the vernacular and to advance the general standing of performances in colonial society.

It is plausible that the growing population of Spaniards and creoles wanted to see the types of performances they had attended in the cities of Castile or had heard about from family members, friends, and associates in letters and conversations. Certainly, theatrical activity of not only evangelical and educational natures, but also of more commercial ones continued to develop in Mexico during the 1570s and 1580s. In addition to continuing to import dramatic texts from Spain, some colonists began to compose dramas in Spanish for readers and playgoers in the viceregal capital and other cities of New Spain, and some of these reflected current social and political issues and triggered very immediate responses in the public sphere.

An example of such a moment when the commercial, evangelical, and public natures of theater collided in Mexico City took place in December of 1574. Juan Pérez Ramírez, who was born in Mexico in 1545 and whose father was a conquistador, wrote the play *El desposorio espiritual entre el Pastor Pedro y la Iglesia Mexicana,* which was performed as part of the festivals to consecrate the new archbishop of Mexico Pedro Moya de Contreras. The festival also included less allegorical and more potentially scandalous pieces, including a performance of a "very funny" interlude possibly written by a cleric named Fernán González de Eslava "that provoked much laughter and merriment in the audience."[21] It also just happened to satirize the tax collectors of Mexico City. The issue was a particularly volatile one because a sales tax had recently been introduced. According to the Viceroy Martín Enríquez de Almanza who denounced it to Juan de Ovando, president of the Council of the Indies, "it turned his stomach." He implied that the performance of the interlude had not only caused an uproar, but it had also turned the consecration into a farce.[22] Although Eslava swore he did not write the offending interlude, the playwright, the director Juan de Victoria, and a mixed-race actor who performed in it all met with the ire of the authorities and all spent time in jail. The actor received the harshest punishment of the three.[23] The *cabildo* as well as the high court and the viceroy censured the archbishop for allowing the performance—indeed, these officials had already made their displeasure clear when they had walked out during the middle of the interlude's performance in protest.[24] This incident also indicates the failure of Zumárraga's ban on performances on hallowed ground to stick. After all, the new archbishop was a fan of plays and interludes.

In the immediate aftermath of the "very funny" interlude and the ensuing protest at the consecration, Almanza used his alliances with members of the Audiencia of New Spain to gain the upper hand over the new archbishop. The high court's officials decreed that "in concordance with the Archbishop, the dean of the Cathedral, and the church council," no *comedias* should be performed in the church without prior approval from and licensing by the high court. The Audiencia insisted that this would prevent the plays from having anything "superfluous or indecent" in their content.[25] It also noted that since "sometimes plays [had] been presented [to the Audiencia] with very few days [prior to performance] there [had] been some oversights and mistakes." Given the immediate context, this snidely implied that previous orders to follow this procedure had been disregarded by the archbishop. We can speculate that it also indicates that confraternities and companies of actors and the judges themselves may have been lax in their duties to prevent the performance of plays that contained more profane and potentially scandalous material. Sancho Lopez de Agurto, the Audiencia's scribe, recorded that accordingly, "performances to be put on should observe and satisfy the said order [that had fallen out of use and has been mentioned]." The court also "decree[d] that no place should be given to works before the High Court has seen and examined them [especially] not in the aforementioned church because it is here that the service of God and his Majesty are undertaken."[26] Thus, the officials were able to smugly imply that Archbishop Moya was not fully competent in undertaking such service. As Moya described it, this was done "to have me understand that they could order me about and treat me like a sacristan."[27]

In the years following the conflict between the viceroy and the archbishop, theater became integrated into urban daily life in spaces outside of the cathedral. Over the next several years, attending the performances of plays and reading plays became such central features of life in Mexico City that a Society for Plays emerged there in 1597.[28] The Society was located near the Hospital de Jesus, which also further suggests the developing link between public entertainment and health in the Viceroyalty of New Spain. Likewise, a far-reaching book trade flourished in Mexico, bringing *comedias,* romances, and religious tracts from Spain, and the development of the printing industry in Mexico allowed for the circulation of printed texts authored there.[29]

Alonso de Buenrostro brought a professional acting company from Spain to Mexico in 1586, and there is evidence to suggest a permanent structure was being used in Mexicó Metropolitano to stage *comedias* by the following year. Archival evidence proves that by 1597 another permanent playhouse, owned by Francisco de León, had been constructed and was attracting audiences, as it was "very good for performances." When petitioning the viceroy for a license, Francisco de León was sure to mention that his theater had a *cazuela* "so that the women would be seated separately from the men, thus completely maintaining respectability." He also noted that he was in the process of having a separate entrance constructed for the women's section of the playhouse. This would enable the respectable women of Mexico City to avoid coming through the same door as the men and avoid potential harassment.[30] As we have seen and will see again, such concern about gender segregation at the playhouse was a repeated issue for Spanish authorities. For both reasons of Baroque piety and order, they hoped to prevent the mingling of men and women in audiences and to maintain women's physical safety as playgoers.

In November of 1597 Francisco de León and Gonzalo de Riancho requested a license to perform plays on Sundays, feast days, and two days a week for the next six years. They offered to pay 800 pesos a year for the right to do so.[31] Gonzalo de Riancho testified that he "was the first founder of a playhouse in Mexico City and that his acting troupe had been presenting plays for ten years and continued to present plays with great enthusiasm and with great appreciation."[32] The petition also included a request that for two years no other acting company could perform in León's playhouse.

As the municipal authorities considered the request, they put several questions to the theater entrepreneurs. Riancho and León claimed that one of the reasons they wanted what essentially amounted to a monopoly was that there were "other people putting on poor quality plays, without having a real playhouse for them nor a dressing room and set of costumes." Once again, they assured the city fathers that their plays would not only be "very good" but also done with "complete decency and integrity with good costumes."[33] Their request and their respectability politics met with approval. On 22 November 1597, the magistrates recommended to the viceroy that he grant them the license, as the playhouse had "great utility for the republic because many people joined together and congregated to see the [plays].[34] Francisco de León also purchased a license to put on the Corpus Christi festivals in 1599.[35] These incidents demonstrate shifts that would continue to characterize colonial theater in the viceregal capital. As the seventeenth century dawned, theater events in New Spain came to be dominated by the emerging form of the *comedia nueva* performed by Spaniards, creoles, and persons of color in licensed troupes in established commercial theaters, and these same professional actors performed the religious *autos sacramentales* that had become an integral part of the annual Corpus Christi festivals.

The poetry of Arias de Villalobos, who was a peninsular colonist, a sometime *autor de comedias,* a distinguished literary figure, and eventually a priest, offers further insight into the development of the commercial playhouses and their integration into routine daily life in Mexico City.[36] He described the colonial court city at the turn of the century in his epic poem *Canto intitulado mercurio.* Composed for the arrival of the Viceroy the Marquis de Guadalcázar in 1612, the poem glorifies the conquest of Mexico and the subsequent century of Mexican history under Spanish rule. It also provides anecdotal evidence about a number of colonial institutions. Regarding Mexico City's commercial theater, Villalobos wrote there were "For seekers of pleasure/Two houses of public merriment/Actors of imported plays/recently delivered there."[37] In the notes to the 1623 edition of the poem, Villalobos claimed that there were three acting companies sharing the two public theaters of Mexico City. Since a similar system of sharing the *corrales de comedias* between companies of actors had developed in Madrid and Seville during this period, Villalobos's claim seems both plausible and probable. It also indicates the potential opportunity for acting companies in the colonies to avoid the same degrees of legal restrictions they faced back in Castile, where in most cities multiple troupes could not be resident at a given time. The growth of the industry is also reflected by the competition for and naming of two *autores* to direct the performances at Corpus Christi festivals and by compensation paid to playwrights and directors for new dramatic works. In *Canto intitulado mercurio,* Villalobos also boasted about the *cofradías* and the hospitals of the capital of New Spain. Writing in a genre that glorified his urban setting and established his patriotism on both a local and imperial level, the former *autor* painted a picture of a thriving city that featured public playhouses and was part of an expansive and glorious universal Spanish monarchy.

Like Villalobos, the poet Bernardo de Balbuena also positively portrayed the city in his lyric poem, *La grandeza Mexicana,* first published in 1604. Balbuena was a peninsular Spaniard, but he spent most of his life in New Spain. He celebrated a Mexico Metropolitano that, along with gold and other riches, was home to grand public buildings, elaborate façades, and urban dwellers "of diverse color and occupation,/ of various ranks and various appearances." The thriving urban society he described included "muleteers, officials, contractors/peninsular Spaniards, soldiers, merchants, well-heeled young men, gentlemen, litigants/ clergymen, friars, men and women."[38] Such people from different trades, backgrounds, and classes made up audiences of playgoers in the capital of New Spain as the seventeenth century began. Balbuena observed the actors' propensity for provoking laughter and also suggested that there were new plays and interludes on a daily basis for the audiences of the *corrales* of Mexico City to enjoy.[39] Although it is important to take Balbuena's rosy picture of a pristine, gleaming, and colorfully harmonious imperial capital with the proverbial grain of salt, archival and other evidence suggests that his depiction of a thriving theater business was not particularly exaggerated. Playgoers in this imperial capital could see the same *comedias* that their counterparts in Madrid and Seville had enjoyed with increasing regularity.

Colonists could also engage in an ever-increasing print culture that allowed them to read the plays being performed in the playhouses of Mexico City, Seville, and Madrid. Furthermore, the *cabildo* of Mexico City ensured that the Corpus Christi festivals each year were extravagant affairs that included dramatic performances. During the final years of the sixteenth century, troupe directors promised municipal authorities "good plays of great appearance and display" and asked for the funds and opportunity to put them on with "costumes comprised of Castilian velvets and gold adorned cloths."[40] Several years later, in 1606 the city fathers mandated that *comedias* be performed and that fireworks and other spectacular things, such as dancers, accompany the performances. The painstaking preparations and financial outlay for these festivities demonstrate a remarkable commitment to the theater as a necessary institution of the ideal Spanish imperial city because the magistrates were also dealing with the difficulties of "little health and much business" that the recent problems with flooding in the viceregal capital had likely compounded.[41] This is perhaps not surprising since Mexico City was in many ways, like the Castilian court city of Madrid, emerging as a center of consumption and administration for the wider region.[42]

Spanish secular authorities increasingly viewed both commercial and religious theatrical activity as falling under their domain and sought to control the types of spectacle more rigidly. In April of 1612, when the *cabildo* of Mexico approved "all the concerts of dances by Spaniards" for the Corpus feast day festivities, it added "that they should not be performed by blacks or mulattos and that everything else should be done as is correct and customary and that the festival be very brilliant and of great ornament."[43] Of course, the very fact that the council had to make this decree implies that the religious theater of the Corpus Christi festival was becoming a site for contending expressions of cultural and social values in Mexico City. This also is indicative of the possibility that some performers, as well as numerous spectators, were Afro-Mexicans and persons of mixed race. In other words, festive engagement and theater might be intended to Europeanize but they were not simply Eurocentric—especially not in a city that was home to many persons of color.

These contending cultural expressions and conflicting perspectives were not limited to feast day celebrations. The commercial theater played an increasingly integral part in the urban environment and the social fabric of Mexico City, and its growing connection to the charitable functions of the hospitals fostered this development. Such a relationship required a certain amount of regulation, which is reflected in a decree of 1602 that no *comedias* be performed outside of the designated playhouses without an express license from the viceroy to do so. The penalty for violating this decree was a hefty 100 gold pesos and ten days in the city jail for each infraction.[44] In his efforts to streamline poor relief in the city, Viceroy Juan de Mendoza, the Marquis of Montesclaros, earmarked half of the takings from Indian tribute for two years for hospital construction projects for the Hospital Real and had continued to utilize the theater that had at some point been founded by Gaspar de Zúñiga, the Count of Monterrey, who had served as viceroy from 1595 to 1603, to provide charity for sick Indians. A decree from Philip III approved the decision to "among other things take advantage of the *corrales de comedias* of the said city." The king's decree noted that, as he understood it, the playhouses were "good for providing mercy and alms for the hospital for the present."[45] By the time the Marquis of Montesclaros left New Spain in July of 1607 for his new appointment as Viceroy of Peru, he wrote the Council of the Indies informing its members that the construction of the Royal Indian Hospital was complete and funds from food and beverage being sold at performances were also augmenting the funds for poor relief in Mexico City.[46]

As the viceroy's plans for using theater to fund public health were making their way to the king's chambers, not all were content with the way the situation operated. In January of 1605 Archbishop Jeronimo García de Santa María Mendoza y Zúñiga urged the royal government to take action in regards to the increasing needs of the Hospital del Amor de Dios, the plague hospital of Mexico City, which Juan de Zumárraga had founded in 1534. However, this was a complex issue because of the privileges of other charitable institutions and the complicated finances and accounting practices of the hospital itself. On

25 October 1604 the Marquis of Montesclaros had reported that "the Archbishop has supplicated his majesty on behalf of the need of the Hospital of the Amor de Dios of this city and that in order to repair it and its buildings begs Your Majesty that the plays be performed in a yard in the hospital and not in any other place." The Council of the Indies' minute of Montesclaros's letter indicates that this had been an ongoing matter; the viceroy had observed that "this has been an issue brought up by the Archbishop many times with my predecessor [the Count of Monterrey] and with me" and that some of the problems stemmed from competing jurisdictions since the Royal Indian Hospital was under royal patronage and "the lien on the Amor de Dios [was] more than 12,000 pesos."[47]

Philip III agreed with the viceroy that it was not convenient to move the location of theatrical performances even if it was at the archbishop's request. His twice-rubricated response in the minute's margins states that regarding the Hospital of the Amor de Dios, the following procedure should be followed: "with care and accuracy they should undertake accounts in the form they had been undertaken other times without any value being lost from the Royal Patronage, safe-guarding that which has been ordered by the said patronage."[48] In the end, the high court of New Spain decided to place a limit on the overhead expenses paid by the Amor de Dios and to maintain the *corral de comedias* in its current location.

Even without losing the proceeds from the theater to the Amor de Dios, the Royal Indian Hospital still faced serious problems due to a lack of sufficient funds. The newly arrived Viceroy Luis de Velasco observed in a report from December of 1608 that the hospital had "great need" because many Indians from the city and from all over the kingdom of New Spain came to seek assistance there. At times the hospital cared for "more than 170" people at a time. It appealed for a share of tributes the colonial government levied on indigenous communities in 1607.[49] Velasco's account suggested that while charitable donations and activities of the religious orders provided some relief, there was not enough to alleviate routine problems of poverty and disease. Nonetheless, Velasco praised his predecessors for changing the method of distributing tribute and founding stores and offices of administration on hospital property.[50] However, some were already in need of expansion or repairs, and these repairs extended to the theater. This was an ongoing process, as every few years the need for refurbishment, repairs, or better boxes resurfaced—as was the case when the city fathers of Mexico Metropolitano later wanted a better box in this *corral.* Yet these administrative issues demonstrate the ways in which the theater connected to this hospital both financially and in terms of physical space. For officials, it became apparent that the answer to this financial problem was to continue to strengthen the link between the public theater and this hospital that cared for the impoverished indigenous population of Mexico City, including its immediate physical needs, its spiritual care, and to some degree its educational needs.

The symbiosis between the commercial theater and the hospitals helped to enable the economic and cultural activity of acting companies. During the first two decades of the seventeenth century, much of this development took place under the direction of directors/actors such as Gonzalo de Riancho, Alonso Velázquez, and Juan Ortíz. As in Castile, these companies included women and were sometimes even directed by them. The acting company of Alonso Velázquez included his wife, Maria Manuel, his daughter Ana, as well as a number of other actors.

At times there was competition between the acting companies in New Spain over the contracts to put on the plays for festivals or to perform in the playhouses of the capital or Puebla. Obligations to the hospitals as well as the realities of everyday life could complicate these rivalries. For example, in 1632, the Marquis of Cerralvo, who was serving as viceroy, demanded that the company of Fernando Ramos leave the provincial city of Puebla de los Angeles, where the *autora* Anamaría de los Angeles would be left to monopolize the theatrical business with her troupe of children, and come to perform in Mexico City for the relief of the Royal Hospital. Cerralvo decreed that any delay due to stopping to perform elsewhere would result in a fine of 50 pesos. However, Ramos begged the viceroy to excuse him from complying with the order because his wife was pregnant and traveling would be a risk to her health. Ramos was prepared to include the testimony of physicians and midwives to that effect and also suggested that his competitor Anamaría de los Angeles should come to Mexico City instead.[51]

With the increasing number of plays arriving from Spain and a growing number of skilled troupe directors, actors, and actresses in the colony during the first half of the seventeenth century, the commercial theaters of Mexico City, like those of Madrid and Seville, became places where playgoers could simultaneously enjoy entertainment and participate in Baroque piety. However, even with the connection forged between the playhouses and efforts of poor relief and hospital welfare, there were deeply entrenched problems of poverty and public health. On 4 November 1621, the Viceroy of New Spain the Marquis of Gelves wrote to King Philip IV, bemoaning the impoverished state of his subjects and requesting 2,000 pesos in alms to be distributed to the poor.[52]

Even if the playhouses could not solve all the problems of illness and poverty, they were locations where a multitude of people converged and were entertained in a way that connected them to a theatrical spectacle and occasionally a kind of discourse that put them in touch with their counterparts in Castile. Theaters also became sites to gain both celebrity and publicity in Mexico. Occasionally, the city fathers offered a prize for new *comedias*, as they did in 1619, when they ordered that Juan Ortíz be paid 100 pesos for putting on a new play.[53] Famous and celebrated *autores* in New Spain, such as members of the Riancho family and Juan Ortíz, thus had potentially lucrative opportunities to pursue. These men—and occasionally women—were to direct the *comedias* imported from Spain or written in New Spain, and to ensure that lavish and appropriate Corpus Christi performances would be put on each year. At times their skills were in high demand among the elite officials of colonial New Spain. Similarly, the playhouse also enabled more privileged members of this hierarchical society to demonstrate their rank and privilege off-stage. It was exactly this kind of representational publicity that the city councilors of Mexico City sought with their ostentatiously ornamented box in 1626. From their box, comfortably appointed with "rugs and chairs," they could be entertained "all the days that there were plays."[54]

However, their newly achieved level of publicity was short-lived after a flood devastated Mexico City in 1629. Parts of the city remained submerged under floodwaters for the next five years, and numerous homes and shops and the *corrales de comedias* met with destruction or serious damage. The stagnant floodwaters carried pestilential diseases that killed many of those who had survived the flood event itself. Mexico City had experienced bad floods previously in 1555, 1580, 1604, and 1607, in part as a result of soil erosion in the growing center of empire.[55] Royal officials had ordered the construction of a *desagüe,* or overspill channel, after the flood of 1607 brought increasing public pressure on the government to find an effective way of dealing with such destructive inundations. The final creation, built through the use of *repartimiento* labor, "was an eight mile long drainage canal, half tunnel and half open trench, which was to conduct the floodwaters of the Valley of Mexico . . . into the Tula River, from which they would flow to the Gulf of Mexico."[56]

An initially impressive structure designed by engineer Enrico Martínez, the desagüe fell into poor maintenance and was never enlarged. Work on it largely halted in 1623 due to bureaucratic obstacles. Vera Candiani suggests that these obstacles were not so much the result of a lack of funds but rather the consequence of what she calls "the limited motivations" of urban elites who envisioned the desagüe as protecting the imperial city instead of as enabling agriculture in the area.[57] When the summer rains came early, frequently, and in large quantities, culminating in a terrible storm in September of 1629 that purportedly lasted forty hours, the incredibly expensive structure could not channel the massive amounts of water, and Mexico City was inundated. Biblical allusions to forty days of rain aside, in the aftermath of this destructive deluge, one-story houses fell, buildings collapsed, and people found themselves stranded in the upper floors of their homes. The theater was severely damaged by the flood and the resulting lack of care on the part of its stewards, who were dealing with seemingly more pressing issues.[58]

After the flood most theatrical activity, along with many residents of the city, moved to nearby Puebla for the next couple of decades. As discussed in the next chapter, Puebla had a theatrical tradition and playgoing public that made such a transition relatively easy. It was, however, not without consequences for both cities. Since the patio of the Royal Indian Hospital had flooded and no longer had public entertainment to regularly contribute to its finances, the public health situation of the city suffered even beyond the immediate effects of the flood.

The lack of commercial drama also damaged civic pride and lowered the quality of life for many inhabitants of the capital of New Spain at a variety of levels. In April of 1630 the municipal government decided that it was necessary for the city "to bring an acting company back to the city from wherever it is. For it is not right that the city be without entertainment."[59] In all likelihood, the city fathers of the viceregal capital turned to nearby Puebla to send for a troupe of actors to fill this entertainment vacuum. Though the proceedings of the city council suggested that the religious theater of the Corpus Christi festivals continued during the 1630s, it seems that the commercial theater of the viceregal court city did not regain its pre-flood prominence until the 1640s.

In 1640 and 1641 the city council of Mexico Metropolitano proposed to renovate its boxes in the Corral del Coliseo, which was the name increasingly used for the theater in the patio of the Royal Indian Hospital. The *cabildo* noted that petitions had been received since the boxes were "wretched and abject."[60] Just two years later, in April of 1642, the newly arrived Viceroy of New Spain, the Count of Salvatierra, García Sarmiento de Sotomayor, in a more theater-friendly act than his short-term predecessor the antitheatrical Bishop Juan de Palafox (who will be discussed at greater length in the next chapter) took measures to give financial support to the aforementioned hospital, which continued to struggle to make ends meet. He ordered that the wood left over from repairs to the Hospital Real be used to build additions to the theater as "before it was impossible to take care of the sick that were [in the hospital]."[61] The desired solution was to use wood from the hospital to enlarge the theater, bringing in more playgoers and therefore more money for the care of patients. Additionally, 12,000 pesos were earmarked for the playhouse's construction. One of the officials involved was Luis de Berrio, who had been named as a magistrate to the Audiencia of Mexico and given permission to embark from Spain in 1636. Berrio had lived in Seville and participated in one of the renovations of the Coliseo there, and he recommended that the repairs be based on those of that playhouse. Even so, complications arose, as hospital officials noted that this plan would impede the primary function of the hospital patio, which was to provide light and air to the infirmaries.[62]

The city government had continued to mount Corpus Christi festivals in the period after the flood, though evidence of such things as complaints about the poor quality of costumes suggests they might have had to make do with what was available.[63] During the same period of expanding and refurbishing the Coliseo, the municipal government of Mexico City also passed a motion that during the Corpus Christi festivals "there not be three-act plays but rather religious one-act plays that are dispatched outside of Mexico"—in other words, the city fathers wanted Spanish *autos sacramentales* for these important festivals.[64] The city council approved the necessary arrangements for the performance of a religious one-act play, *Los cisnes* by Lope de Vega, during the Corpus Christi festivals in 1642.

Gaps in the council records during the 1640s make it difficult to clearly ascertain whether the theater ban that shut the doors of the *corrales de comedias* in Castile and Aragon also affected New Spain in 1644–1645 and 1646–1651. However, it would seem that commercial theater had either never been banned outright in New Spain or that the injunction had been lifted by 1649, as it had essentially been in Madrid and Seville due to the pressure that the hospitals placed on the royal and municipal governments. In July of 1649, the city council of Puebla received an order that the famous Jerónimo Ortíz and his company of actors should depart for Mexico City at the request of the superintendent of the Royal Indian Hospital. In order to fund the coffers of the court's hospital, the authorities greased the wheels by threatening Ortíz with a fine if he did not arrive with his company swiftly.[65]

Some of the celebrity that these men and women attained in New Spain can be glimpsed in an incident that occurred during the following year. In July of 1650, Don Gregorio Martín de Guijo, a prominent citizen of Mexico City, recorded the arrival of the new viceroy in his diary. According to Guijo, his Excellency Luis Enríquez y Guzmán, Count of Alba de Liste and Marquis of Villaflor, processed through the capital of New Spain in the typical fashion of new viceroys with a large crowd—an audience, really—that included city officials, gentlemen, and other citizens. At least one person in the crowds that thronged the ceremonial procession was an actor. Upon the viceroy's return to the cathedral, this actor explained the painting of Hercules in the portal and the verse that accompanied it.[66] Though Guijo did not mention the comic by name, the fact that one had been selected to explain this bit of the urban landscape to the new viceroy suggests that actors were capable of acquiring stature, and not just notoriety, in the society of seventeenth-century Mexico City.

Thus, in spite of setbacks caused by flooding and other destruction, the commercial theater continued to develop and draw audiences in Mexico City during the middle and second half of the seventeenth century, and the relationship between the public theaters and the hospitals continued in the viceregal capital into the eighteenth century. The *corral de comedias* of the Royal Indian Hospital underwent additions and renovations in the 1640s and then again in 1665. When a fire burned down the structure in 1722, a new theater, the Coliseo, was built. These structures, like those in Madrid and Seville, were located centrally within the city—not far from the main square. And they formed an integral part of the urban landscape and the daily life of colonists of different ranks, genders, and castes throughout the early modern period.

As the sixteenth century drew to a close, Dublin, unlike Mexico City and also unlike London and Bristol, was not yet home to any permanent public playhouses. Thus, it may not be surprising that for a long time the historiography of Irish theater was bound to a resulting narrative that there was no native tradition of public drama. However, this is not to say that there was no history of performance in Ireland. For example, fools amused noble audiences and *braigetóirí* entertained their audiences through the olfactory and auditory arts of the fart in addition to jesting and singing—at times depicted derisively by Elizabethan English colonizers as evidence of the uncouthness of the colonized. There was also a developing tradition of liturgical drama and civic professions during Corpus Christi. Although the evidence is cursory, troupes of itinerant performers may have been entertaining in Ireland as the early modern period began.[67] Some might have performed a mixture of indigenous Gaelic and imported English entertainments at both private and public celebrations. Decrees and other evidence also suggest that buildings like the town hall and corporate and civic buildings provided a space for visiting performers to entertain audiences in the absence of purpose-built playhouses.

Historian of Irish theater Christopher Morash begins Dublin's theater history, if not its history of performance, with the production of *Gorboduc,* an English play by Thomas Norton and Thomas Sackville, performed at Dublin Castle in September of 1601 for the Lord Deputy Baron Mountjoy. He notes that, although the "archaic" play was forty years old, its focus on fratricidal conflict and civil war set in a mythologized English past resonated with the political climate of the times. Ireland was then embroiled in the Nine Years' War, a politically and religiously motivated war between the English colonizers and the Gaelic Irish, led by Hugh O'Neill.[68] Thus, a play that established abdication of the throne as the catalyst for bloody conflict provided an impetus for political elites to consider and explore these fraught issues just as they had much earlier in Elizabeth's reign when the play had first been staged at the Inns of Court.[69]

However, as fitting as this performance of *Gorboduc* may have been for the political climate in Ireland in 1601, the work of Alan Fletcher places the beginning of theater history in Dublin much earlier through his examination of the evidence for both religious drama, such as Christmastide plays, and civic dramas. Similar to cities in Castile and in New Spain, Dublin featured Corpus Christi celebrations that involved significant pageantry and may at times have featured the performance of plays. This continued to be the case into the 1560s, and Dublin's Corpus Christi guild survived the Reformation. It may have even continued to persist after the Lord Justice Sir Nicholas Arnold reminded the city fathers in 1565 that Dubliners "schuld nat kepe corpus christi day a hally day but that ewry man and womane schuld worke as they dyde ewry other worken day . . . A pone A great penallytie."[70] Nonetheless, as the pageantry of Corpus took off in Mexico Metropolitano, it was being suppressed in Dublin. Just a few years before Arnold's rejoinder to enforce the ban on Corpus, the Irish parliament had decreed that any person who "in any enterludes, playes, songs, rimes or by other open words, declare[d] or sp[o]ke any thing in derogation depraving or despising of the [Book of Common Prayer]" would be subjected to fines, confiscation of property, and imprisonment.[71]

While expanding the definition of dramatic performance incorporates many activities that took place in Dublin during the sixteenth century, it remains the case that private performances for nobles became the main form of Irish theater until Thomas Wentworth, the Earl of Strafford, arrived as lord lieutenant in July of 1633. Once there, he set out to make Dublin into a symbol of English royal power and would become known for his harsh methods and autocratic mindset—for ruling like an absolutist.[72] In the process of promoting royal power, Wentworth—like viceroys and royal officials elsewhere—drew on rituals to do so. In Wentworth's case he focused particularly on using the rites associated with the conferring of knighthood; he also took advantage of ceremonial occasions and patronized artists in an effort to utilize political imagery.[73]

Since theater was an important part of court life under Charles I, Wentworth required that a permanent playhouse be built in Dublin for the court there. Dependent on the court and castle, it was in a respectable location not far from the castle. Although a lack of evidence has prevented theater historians from precisely dating the opening of this theater, it was clearly open by July of 1637, as a letter of Wentworth's to Archbishop William Laud makes reference to a playhouse. In all likelihood, plays were being performed there prior to mid-1636, as the Archbishop Lancelot Bulkeley had the playhouse closed during Wentworth's absence.[74] John Ogilby took charge of the arrangements and later served as the first Master of the Revels in Ireland. Since the London theaters were closed due to a plague outbreak in the late spring of 1636, Ogilby was able to recruit a professional troupe of English players with experience performing at the Red Bull and the Cockpit to come to Dublin.[75] In November of that same year Ogilby convinced James Shirley to come to Dublin as the resident playwright. Shirley had possibly become a Catholic in the 1620s, leaving his living as a minister near Saint Albans. He then began to teach and later to write plays for the acting troupe Queen Henrietta's Men. Relatively prolific by English standards, he wrote some thirty plays—at least four of them while in Dublin as the resident playwright from 1636 to 1640.[76]

In January of 1638 Shirley's *The Royal Master* premiered in the Werburgh Street Theater. This romantic comedy, set in Naples, about a king's favorite who plots to increase his power by marrying the king's sister and thwarting the duke who is his rival, was probably the first of the new resident playwright's works to be performed in the Werburgh Street Theater. A special performance of it was also held at Dublin Castle, and *The Royal Master* was published both in Dublin and London. Despite the reputed success of this play, the prologues of other plays known to have been performed at the playhouse in Dublin lamented the "forsaken stage" and indicate that the size of the theatrical public fostered by the Anglo-Irish there remained quite small during the seventeenth century even as royal officials attempted to foster its development.[77] This is in contrast to the many people who congregated to see plays in Mexico City, which was also a much larger urban center than Dublin, three decades earlier. Although Dublin's audiences may have been small, the plays performed provide an insight into the ways that theater could be used, though not necessarily entirely successfully, to shape and foster identities and connections. London city comedies and the typical fare performed for the private theaters in London made up Werburgh's repertoire. Undoubtedly, this type of drama attracted a certain clientele, including those who were familiar with or sought to imagine themselves in London. Yet others in the audience were harder to please, and Alan Fletcher has traced Shirley's growing resignation with the different standards of Dublin's audiences. In the last plays likely performed there, he included more Irish topics and sensational effects.[78]

Unfortunately, as tensions in the three kingdoms escalated into violent military conflicts, Dublin's emerging theater became caught in the maelstrom. In early 1640 the professional players began to leave, and on 16 April of that year Shirley also left for London. On 17 March 1640, even as political tensions mounted and as some of the actors departed, there was a hopeful moment in which theater might have swayed public opinion and assuaged religious conflicts. Henry Burnell's tragicomedy *Landgartha,* which theater scholars consider to be the first extant Irish play by an Irish author, was staged in Werburgh Street. Burnell, an elite landowner, became a prominent Catholic royalist. However, in the spring of 1640, his play offered the audience a glimpse of the potential for harmonious relationships between English Protestants and Irish Catholics who, in the wake of the Bishop's War in Scotland, also seemed to be increasingly headed toward war.

Burnell based *Landgartha* on a Danish tale about a Norwegian king (an allegorical representation of the English) who is aided by an Amazon-type maiden of a Norwegian lady, Landgartha (an allegorical representation of Ireland). The title character is steadfast, ethical, chaste, and courageous. Through her, Burnell urged for a politics infused with morality. The comic subplot centers on two lower ranking characters, Marsisa and Hubba (also representative of the Irish and the English), who by the fourth act end up kissing and decide to "build upon [each other's] constancie."[79] The ending of Burnell's play suggests the potential for a happy marriage between English and Irish—so long as the Catholic religion is upheld.[80] However, the dramatist's proposition of a happy marriage of kingdoms faced an increasingly hostile political climate. Even as his play was being printed with a title page proclaiming that it had been performed "in the new Theater in Dublin, with good applause," the political situation reached a crisis that would close the playhouse and bring war and bloodshed to Ireland.[81]

The situation worsened for Wentworth, too, and he was indicted for bad government in the Petition of the Twelve Peers.[82] Numerous members of Parliament realized that an army raised to put down rebellion in Ireland could also be used by the king against them. Anti-Stafford polemicists accused the former lord lieutenant of usurping royal prerogatives—a decidedly negative final outcome of his performances of princely power. His treasonous crimes included his lax attitude to Catholicism, evinced by acts such as his bringing an alleged Catholic to Dublin as resident playwright. His securing of Irish Catholic parliamentary votes for subsidies to be used against the Presbyterian Scots had been a divisive issue among members of the English Parliament, and the petition claimed that the malefactors who had caused fear and discontent included both Thomas Wentworth and the Arminian Archbishop Laud. Parliament condemned him to death, and on 12 May 1641 Wentworth was executed.

In the meantime, the lords justices Sir William Parsons and Sir John Borlase closed the Werburgh Street Theater, turning it into a military stable. Later Dublin's first permanent theater fell into utter ruin. The

Irish dramatist Henry Burnell, who had replaced Shirley as the resident playwright, fled from Dublin to Kilkenny. Burnell later became a member of the Confederate Assembly—a body that was formed in October of 1642 by the Irish and the Old English as an alternative government and lasted until 1649. Kilkenny, which had long maintained a performative culture and had continued to mount Corpus Christi festivals after they had been repressed in Dublin, became the center of any substantive Irish theatrical activity that might have taken place during the 1640s.

With the monarchy's restoration in 1660, a new flush of theatrical activity took place in Dublin, as it did in London. James Ogilby saw another opportunity for profit and publicity, and he petitioned to be remade Master of the Revels of Ireland. The king had already given the potentially lucrative position to William Davenant, but he rescinded this commission and granted it to Ogilby on 8 May 1661. Returning to his post as the Master of the Revels, Ogilby began work on a new theater in Dublin in Smock Alley, near the quays on the River Liffey. The playhouse, which opened in October 1662, was the first of the Restoration theaters to "have been built and designed as a performance space from the ground up."[83] Like The Cockpit in London, Smock Alley had a proscenium arch and a music loft.

Although Smock Alley was a public theater, it relied heavily on the support of royal officials such as James Butler, the First Duke of Ormond. It was his patronage and social standing that drew audiences from the inner court circle to performances during the 1600s. Smock Alley also had other problems, in that it was tied to Dublin Castle for its continued existence. Since it remained so dependent on political appointments, during the 1670s the theater was frequently closed. The fact that the upper galley came crashing down during a performance of *Bartholomew Fair* in 1670 also further stunted growth of the commercial theater in Dublin, even as the city itself was growing at an incredible rate, from an estimated population of under 9,000 people in 1659 to almost 70,000 people less than thirty years later in 1687.[84]

As was the case with Werburgh Street, Ogilby recruited actors from across the sea, and they performed a mixture of plays written in England and in Ireland. This was similar to what developed on an even larger scale in the late sixteenth and early seventeenth centuries in New Spain. Archival records demonstrate that the dramatic works of Juan de la Cueva, Lope de Vega, Francisco Tárrega, Tirso de Molina, Juan Pérez de Montalbán, and Pedro Calderón de la Barca were all shipped to Veracruz, and from there they passed on to the bookshops and into the libraries of colonists in New Spain's cities.[85] In the hands of their readers, these plays provided entertainment in a far less bulky form than the chivalric novels that had been so popular in the colonies during the sixteenth century. In the hands of troupe directors they provided material for dramatic performance.

The staging of these plays in the commercial theaters of New Spain allowed colonists to feel a bond with the court and capital back in Castile. This connection is reflected by government officials' knowledge of what took place in the *corrales* of "Madrid, Seville, and the other cities of Spain."[86] Although the records do not frequently indicate which plays were performed in Mexico City during the sixteenth and seventeenth centuries, the role of the Inquisition as censor and the legislation passed regarding the performance of *comedias* provides evidence of a commercial theater that thrived primarily on imported plays from Spain but that also supplemented its repertoire with ones written in Mexico. Without a doubt, the *comedias* of Spanish playwrights with their typical love triangles provided entertainment, but they also provided colonists living in Mexico with a link to Iberia. Scattered with bits of news and gossip, the *comedias* of Spain served to promote a sense of Spanish identity. Spanish plays were luxury goods sent from the metropole and consumed in the colonial periphery. The plays written in Mexico for performance there made reference to current events, such as the arrival of new viceroys and the greed of tax collectors, and could seek to influence public opinion on particular matters.

Sor Juana Inés de la Cruz, the Mexican playwright of the second half of the seventeenth century, whose fame and talents earned her the title of the tenth muse, did not write for the audiences of the commercial theaters. Instead, her dramas were staged in convents and the private homes of peninsular and creole elites in New Spain. Sor Juana's target audience for her plays as performance texts included high-ranking administrators among the circles of the viceroy and vicereine, who served as her major patrons. This not only brought her significant prestige but also enabled her to influence the opinion of elite members of colonial society—many of whom were transatlantic agents who returned to Castile after serving terms in the Americas. Indeed, as Amy Fuller has recently argued, although Sor Juana was a creole and composed some of her works in Nahuatl, she was also a subject of the Spanish Crown who was seeking a primarily Spanish audience through publication of her works. Fuller reads the corpus of Sor Juana's *autos sacramentales* as "an apologia for the conquest."[87]

Likewise, playwrights occasionally more explicitly sought to influence public opinion about and perceptions of the colonies held by Castilians by writing more directly for the stages of the metropole. This was certainly the case with some of the works of Juan Ruiz de Alarcón y Mendoza, a creole born in New Spain in the early 1580s. Alarcón, the son of a superintendent of the mines in Real Taxco, a silver mining town one hundred miles southwest of Mexico City, was small of stature, redheaded, and hunchbacked—all characteristics that brought him the scorn and ridicule of others in an early modern society that believed external features represented internal qualities.[88] In 1600 he traveled to Spain, attended the University of Salamanca, and went on to practice law in Seville for a few years before returning to New Spain and receiving his M.A. from the University of Mexico in 1609. In 1611 he went back to Castile and began seeking a court appointment. Frustrated in his early efforts, Alarcón wrote *comedias* for the theaters of Madrid until he finally received a permanent appointment to the Council of the Indies in 1626. At this point, he stopped writing plays.

Although he had a much shorter and less prolific career than his more popular and famous rival Lope de Vega, Alarcón was an influential playwright of the Golden Age. His drama *La verdad sospechosa* was the model for Molière's *Le menteur,* which many consider the first great play in modern French. The main character of *La verdad sospechosa,* the mendacious Don García, fabricates an identity as an *indiano* recently returned to Madrid from the New World. As a creole Alarcón was able to supply his character with tales of the New World that were just as convincing to audiences and readers as the many other duplicitous tales that Don Garcia weaves throughout the course of this play.[89]

Thought to be one of Alarcón's first plays, *El semejante a si mismo,* probably written between 1611 and 1616 and first published in 1628, is for the most part typical of the genre.[90] However, it is the only one of Alarcón's plays that specifically mentions an event in New Spain. One moment in this first act of this play demonstrates Alarcón's wider understanding of the Spanish empire, as a highly educated, competent, and well traveled yet frustrated creole. The developing action of the *comedia* is suddenly interrupted as one of the characters describes the flood of Mexico City in 1607 and its major public works project, the desagüe. As the first act opens, Don Juan and Don Leonardo and the servant/comic relief, Sancho, are in Seville. They are people-watching and cattily gossiping, when out of the blue Don Leonardo mentions the drainage works in Mexico. Sancho, playing the part of the ignorant *gracioso,* responds, "speak plainly, sir." Leonardo responds by launching into a lengthy description of "Mexico the celebrated head of the world of the Indies that they call New Spain."[91] Don Leonardo knows of Mexico's valley and lake. Interestingly, he claims that the flood occurred, not in 1607, but in 1605, when the water entered the houses. Leonardo and, by extension, his playwright creator praise the Viceroy Velasco for beginning the project of the *desagüe,* "after a thousand consultations with learned people and ancient authorities."[92] Of course, Leonardo's claims that the *desagüe* would bring eternal peace to the colony and eternal fame to its engineer were not exactly true. And the playwright must have known that the immense public works project—once impressive—had not been enlarged after the flood of 1607 and was falling increasingly into disrepair at the time he wrote *El semejante a si mismo.* Certainly, he hoped that Leonardo's glorious description of the drainage ditch, which had cost 100,000 ducats each year, and Sancho's incredulity would demonstrate this irony to well-informed audience members and remind more ignorant audience members of Spain's imperial realms and perhaps even its obligations to them.[93]

Alarcón was not the only playwright to write about Mexico or the Indies. It is plausible that many who were not born in the colonies and did not carry the social stigma of not being peninsular-born Spaniards themselves even felt a greater freedom to write about the so-called New World. Although a relatively small number of the surviving plays from the period focus entirely on Spain's overseas colonies, a number of *comedias* contain references to America, set some of their scenes there, or include characters with experiences of travel or living in the Indies. Alarcón's most famous contemporary and rival in the quest for fame and patronage, Lope de Vega, wrote at least a handful of plays that fall into this former category. The best-known of Lope's works about the Americas was—and still is—*El mundo nuevo descubierto por Cristóbal Colón.* Likely written between 1598 and 1603, this *comedia* features a certain Columbus who predicts the existence of the Americas and convinces the magnanimous Catholic monarchs to support his exploratory endeavor.[94] His efforts result in the New World and its inhabitants being physically incorporated into the realms of the Spanish monarchy, spiritually into the folds of Christianity, and ideologically into subjects of a transatlantic empire in the eyes of his seventeenth-century audiences.

Lope's *Arauco domado,* written during the same decade, dramatized the earlier poem by Alonso de Ercilla about the initial stages of Spain's war with the Mapuche Indians of what is now Chile. Victor Dixon has compellingly argued that Lope received a commission to write it as part of "a protracted publicity campaign" to advance the reputation of Don García Hurtado de Mendoza, who had served first as governor of Chile and then as Viceroy of Peru.[95] As such, it comes as no surprise that the character of Don García is steadfast and praiseworthy not only in contrast to the fearsome and cannibalistic characters of the fictionalized indigenes in the play but also in contrast to his greedy, lustful, and inept Spanish compatriots.

The prolific dramatist also wrote plays about Mexico. His *La conquista de México* or *La conquista de Cortés* was lost during the early modern period. However, Lope portrayed the Spanish invader of Mexico in yet another work, *La mayor desgracia de Carlos V y hechicerías de Argel.* In this *comedia,* Lope's Cortés is a defender of the valor of the Aztecs—admittedly, one with a vested interest in promoting his own honor through acknowledging the difficulty of the conquest that he had undertaken.[96] Such a portrayal simultaneously depicted the Aztecs as alien others and as a new group that would be symbolically if not politically incorporated into the developing idea of Spanish imperial identity. This conceptualization paralleled colonial administrative policies, including those related to poor relief in a society with intersecting hierarchies of race, class, and gender in colonial Mexico.

Thus, certain ideas about the New World and its inhabitants—indigenes, Spanish subjects, and their descendants—and even about Mexico City entered into the public lexicon of Castile through the performance of *comedias* as well as through the arrival of letters and news. In Mexico City, the institutions of entertainment, public health, and charity reinforced understandings of what it meant to be a Spaniard. As elsewhere in the dominions of the universal Spanish monarchy, the urban space of the viceregal capital of New Spain fostered these centrally located institutions where colonists could feel both their imperial identity and a sense of local pride as they participated in activities deemed "useful for the public good."[97]

In early modern Dublin and Mexico City, authorities sought to constrain and utilize theater to promote the agendas of colonial projects as well as to enjoy the entertainment performances provided. In the sixteenth century, friars in Mexico used theater, including plays drawing on indigenous performative customs, to proselytize and to educate—yet they had to walk a fine line lest they be suspected of encouraging idolatry or enabling spiritual backsliding. Authorities in Dublin sought to curtail Catholic festivities in the 1560s and to prevent theatrical mocking and jest of Protestant practices and the Book of Common Prayer. Preferences for plays from London or Madrid reflect the desire of elites in these colonial societies to imitate and to connect with their counterparts across the sea. Representatives of the king in both cities drew upon pageantry and performance to enhance their political power. The theaters of both cities faced crises of destruction in the seventeenth century. However, it was the privileged place of the *comedia,* its integration into urban daily life, and its connection with Baroque piety that helped theatrical development in Mexico City rebound more quickly after its crisis and to outpace that of Dublin during the early modern period.

"Aware That It Is a Public Work"

COMMERCIAL DRAMA IN PUEBLA AND WILLIAMSBURG

In 1639 Antonia Sanchez de Prado petitioned the municipal government of Puebla de los Angeles for an extension of her family's lease and license to operate a theater. She reminded the city fathers of her late husband Juan Gómez Melgarejo's significant contributions to theatrical life in Puebla. Her claim noted that if they turned over the lease to her competitor Juan Otríss del Espinal, who owned the land on which her husband had built the *corral,* the magistrates would be leaving her in very dire straits, as now she was "a poor woman and widow." Sanchez de Prado also reminded the council that together, she and her husband had made numerous renovations and repairs to the playhouse's boxes (in which many of them sat) at their own expense over the years.[1] Carefully deploying civic rhetoric, she petitioned the *cabildo* to recognize her family's contributions to urban life, reminding them that the inn-yard theater was "a public work."[2] Seemingly the council was aware of the truth of her words, and her petition was successful. The playhouse remained with the family. As this incident indicates, Mexico City was not the only place where colonists could seek opportunity and entertainment in the *corrales de comedias* of Spain's overseas kingdoms. Puebla de los Angeles, often called Puebla or Angelópolis, about eighty miles east of Mexico Metropolitano, became another important site for early modern theatrical activity in New Spain.

In this provincial city colonists used urban institutions, including the *corrales* and hospitals, to bolster their identity as subjects of the universal Spanish monarchy. At the same time, these very institutions could paradoxically heighten local identities and concerns. Puebla's theater history provides an instructive case study for examining some of the aspects of urbanism in colonial Latin America. It also illuminates the spread of the charitable system of using theater to fund institutions of public health and social welfare beyond the Iberian Peninsula and into the wider Spanish Atlantic World. Additionally, while the evidence is somewhat cursory, the historical development of commercial drama in Angelópolis highlights the tensions between local interests and viceregal authority and how those invested in the theater business maneuvered around and through these tensions to advance their own agendas.

Contrasting the early stages of theatrical development in the colonial cities of Puebla de los Angeles in Mexico and Williamsburg in Virginia, it becomes clear that theater had become a sought-after commodity in the early modern Spanish Atlantic World much earlier and to a greater degree than it did in the Anglo Atlantic. In the city of angels, the commercial theater of the *comedia* developed to accommodate Mexican audiences during the late sixteenth and seventeenth centuries. However, nothing comparable can be seen in the colonies of British North America until much later. In part this was because English colonists arrived later in the Americas and, for some time, in smaller numbers than their Spanish counterparts. They also claimed lands that had less dense populations of indigenous people. The Spanish engaged in city building and by 1678 some 90,000–100,000 people lived in Puebla; in 1755 the capital of Peru boasted a population of 54,000; and Mexico City had a population of more than 100,000 toward the end of the early modern period. Compare this to the colonial populations of British North American settlements. New York's was only about 5,000 in 1700 and 33,000 in 1790, and Williamsburg's population only numbered around 1,400 in 1782.[3] Another factor contributing to the slowness of theater's development in the mainland American colonies of the Anglo Atlantic was the focus of English theatrical activity in the metropolis of London. As has already been discussed, compared to London and compared to provincial cities in Spain, public drama remained less available in provincial cities in England during the sixteenth and much of the seventeenth centuries.

Because of the different trajectories of European imperial designs and the smaller number of residents in these two colonial cities, the comparison is inherently asymmetrical. Looking first at Puebla and then at Williamsburg, this chapter demonstrates that the center of early modern colonial theater was in the Spanish Atlantic. During the seventeenth century, the cavaliers and fortune seekers of Virginia, although generally more likely to be receptive to dramatic entertainments than their Puritan counterparts who settled in New England, did not have the necessary tools or the necessary troupes to establish playhouses until long after they had settled tobacco plantations and fought destructive wars with indigenous tribes. This is indicative of the different priorities of the English colonists, of the lack of substantial urbanization in the colonies of the Anglo Atlantic in the first decades of European settlement, and of the lack of the same vital role that Spanish theater played in daily life, both in the Iberian Peninsula and increasingly in the American holdings of the Spanish Empire.

Spanish colonists founded Puebla during the middle of the sixteenth century. The second Audiencia of Mexico approved its creation as a new town in the hopes of reducing vagabondage. An additional aim was the prevention of Spanish colonizers from further exploiting the indigenous populace of New Spain. This was a lofty and utopian goal, especially in the aftermath of the violence of the conquest of the Aztec Empire and the continued campaigns against the Maya. The site of this city even had mystical and evangelical resonances, as it was dictated in prophetic dreams experienced by the Dominican bishop of Tlaxcala Julián Garcés and later recorded by the Jesuit Francisco de Florencia.[4] Founded near three rivers, Puebla promised a sort of utopian ideal for yeoman farmers and artisans. The rivers were real and the evangelical activity and Christian spirituality of many early modern denizens of the city has been well documented. However, the reality of colonial economies of labor meant there were soon not only European settlers in Puebla but also Indian laborers who assisted with the city's building, Africans held in slavery, transported laborers from the East Indies such as the famous "China Poblana" Catarina de San Juan, and many free persons of color.[5]

While the settlement initially grew slowly, by the early seventeenth century Puebla had become one of the three most populous cities in the Viceroyalty of New Spain. Thanks to the contributions of Indian workers and the settlement of many people of a variety of ranks, backgrounds, and occupations, it became a thriving and cosmopolitan city. It became a key transit point for goods and people traveling between Veracruz and the viceregal capital. Many peninsular Spaniards and creoles preferred to reside in Puebla over Mexico City. Puebla had been set up on the grid pattern in vogue during the Renaissance and on the model of the Spanish towns to which they were accustomed; it was also a more hospitable urban environment in some regards, especially in the years immediately following the massive flood that devastated Mexico City in 1629.

By the second half of the seventeenth century, Puebla's population approached 70,000.[6] Its inhabitants had a great deal of civic pride, and many of its denizens undoubtedly saw their city as one that competed with and maybe even superseded the viceregal capital in a number of ways. Puebla's highest-ranking citizens viewed themselves as loyal subjects of the Spanish crown if not always of the allegedly corrupt officials sent from Iberia to serve in the colonial bureaucracy. Magistrates and artisans went to great expense to stage important festivals, such as the annual feast of Corpus Christi or the more irregular entries of viceroys on their way to Mexico City.[7] Puebla was also home to some of New Spain's oldest guilds. Shortly after its founding, mills, baths, and tanneries had been established in the new town, and residents included clerics and priests, artisans such as silk weavers, butchers, carpenters, tile makers, and water carriers.[8] As early as 1604, Angelópolis had become an integral center of Mexico's growing textile industry.[9]

Called his "Rachel"—an allusion to the favorite wife of the biblical patriarch Jacob—by its reforming and antitheatrical Bishop Palafox, who first arrived in the city in 1640, Puebla had much to offer its elite inhabitants. Its more cosmopolitan institutions included some things about which Palafox was much less enthused—such as theatrical options for entertainment and the consolidation of civic pride.[10] Although the surviving archival evidence does not prove its existence at such an early date, some scholars have argued that there was a *corral de comedias* operating in Puebla by the middle of the sixteenth century.[11] If this was the case, the theater was probably not yet in regular use because the absence of archival evidence also implies an absence of a resident acting company—nor does it seem many actors yet lived in Puebla. Later records confirm this. For instance, the minutes of the city council indicate that a "farce" was part of the Corpus Christi celebrations put on at the city's expense in 1598, but the city had to make special arrangements for it. Puebla's city fathers contracted Juan Corral and his company to come from Mexico Metropolitano to put on the performance.[12]

Nonetheless, the rapid expansion of theatrical activity in the city during the first decade of the seventeenth century makes it plausible that Puebla was already a routine destination for actors living in Mexico City and that they may have had a regular location to perform there. By 1600 there was frequent commercial theatrical activity in Puebla. Additionally, the records indicate that the Corpus Christi festivals of some, if not all, years in the last quarter of the sixteenth century included the performances of *comedias,* along with interludes, music, and dancing, in the city's cathedral, which was still under construction for much of the period.[13] In 1588 the city council had paid Diego Lozano 150 pesos for the performance of a play at Corpus, and in 1590 a troupe manager named Diego Diaz received payment from the city council for a Corpus performance in Puebla. In 1600 the *cabildo* took pains to ensure that there would be not only a "*comedia* of the angelic republic" but also "three interludes, music, and dances" for the feast-day celebrations.[14] The parallel development of religious one-act plays and the evolving *comedia nueva* that took place in Spain also occurred in the growing provincial city in New Spain. It is likely that directors and the troupes they employed also offered other performances there at least intermittently, as they were doing in Mexico City.

By 1599 the records of the city council demonstrate that Juan Gómez Melgarejo, a carpenter and ambitious theater entrepreneur, had leased property in order to develop a *corral de comedias.* The city magistrates deliberated over the matter of extending Melgarejo's lease of "the said theater" in the calle de los Herreros on 12 April 1600. Melgarejo assured them that he had invested substantial sums of money into the project, intimating that his solvency depended on their decision. He also made sure to remind them that he had undertaken the construction of "particular boxes so that the city officials who wanted to come and see the said plays from a very comfortable vantage point" would be able to do so.[15] In 1602 the city of Puebla granted a six-year monopoly to Melgarejo, decreeing that in no other part of the city should a theater be erected and that "no other person should construct in this city any *corral* or particular house where they recite and perform plays."[16] In 1603 the Viceroy of New Spain Don Gaspar de Zúñiga Acevedo y Fonseca, Fifth Count of Monterrey, granted a monopoly on performances in Puebla to the troupe directors Antonio Rodríguez and Juan Corral for a period of two months. The viceroy's intervention suggests that Melgarejo's theater was popular enough to elicit competition from bidding managers of acting companies and the regular presence of professional performers in the city.

Melgarejo's playhouse became an institutional fixture of public and cultural life in seventeenth-century Puebla. Yet maintaining a theater in the provincial city was not always an entirely smooth process. After being granted the rights to provide the venue for and to profit from the performance of plays for much of the first decade of the seventeenth century, Melgarejo and his business faced something of a setback. In June of 1613 the carpenter and entrepreneur suddenly found his privileged position revoked and his playhouse in danger. The "Regidor Nicolás de Villanueva Guzmán, Deputy Mayor [of Puebla] ordered that, for the just causes that had been agreed upon" notice had been sent to Melgarejo that no "plays nor performances of any kind should take place under pain of a fine of 200 pesos of *oro común.*" His theater was also threatened with physical destruction.[17] The motivations behind this order and the sudden attacks on the Puebla playhouse are somewhat unclear. It is possible that they were due to competition or to antitheatrical sentiment, and it is possible that plays ceased for some time. What is clear is that Puebla's playhouse ultimately weathered the storm.[18]

By the later 1610s Melgarejo had triumphed again in spite of continued issues that now certainly included competition from others looking to capitalize on *comedias.* In 1618 one of the city's aldermen, Don Felipe Ramírez de Arrelano, petitioned Puebla's municipal authorities because he claimed that he had been given a license from the viceroy to the rights of a twenty-year monopoly on theatrical activity there. According to the alderman, he had already "spent a vast sum of money to construct a patio and a theater for the entertainment and delight of this city."[19] Although Arrelano was ultimately unable to edge Melgarejo out of the theater business, this conflict sheds light on a recurring issue that was not exclusive to the theater business: contestation and negotiation between viceregal and local authorities for control. Ramírez de Arrelano (and others involved in the theatrical business, as we will see again later) drew on the authority of the viceroy to pursue his interests with the municipal authorities. This jockeying for position paralleled other struggles going on in colonial New Spain as fiscal pressures from Madrid increased and as peninsular viceroys and their officials not only snubbed creoles for being born in Mexico but also sometimes ran roughshod over local interests, institutions, and structures of governance.[20]

The previous year, in accordance with the municipal government's demands, Melgarejo had overseen renovations to the private box in his playhouse. These improvements included a new wooden staircase, and the *cabildo* records also demonstrate concerns among Puebla's elite with privacy, decency, and upkeep similar to those expressed by officials in other locations. They stipulated that a caretaker be appointed to make sure that their private box was kept locked and that the porter should take pains to "not allow entry to any person who was not one of the city magistrates or clerks of the said *cabildo*."[21] Of course such stipulations were relatively routine, but they also reflect the presence of lower-ranking city dwellers in the playhouses. They may have also reflected real issues of disorder. Historian Ida Altman has observed that Spaniards carried arms more regularly in the Indies than they did in Castile during the sixteenth and early seventeenth century—an issue that was bound to have fatal consequences when fights or brawls broke out. Indeed, Juan Melgarejo had to intervene in a violent confrontation that involved his stepson in which many swords were drawn.[22] Given the notoriety of playhouses as sites of disorder, it is possible that Melgarejo had honed such peacemaking skills during his experience running the *corral de comedias* on his leased property.

Puebla's theatrical life also had become connected to the charitable work of the city's welfare institutions. During the Marquis of Montesclaros's tenure as Viceroy of New Spain (1603–1607), he had decreed that a portion of all funds from performances be directed to the Hospital of San Roque.[23] San Roque had been founded in the early 1590s as part of the charitable work of the Orden de la Caridad de San Hipólito. Its founder, the friar Bernardino Álvarez, who had come to Mexico from Seville at a young age, spent much of his life creating such institutions in New Spain. From an early date, this hospital was one of convalescence and tended primarily to patients with mental illnesses.

Some thirty years later Don Diego Roque López Pacheco Cabrera y Bobadilla the Seventh Duke of Escalona drew on this precedent, recalling the policy of his predecessor, who had ordered that "from all the plays that they perform in the [city] of angels outside of the Hospital of San Roque should be given four [pesos] of *oro común,*" which would have been about the equivalent of 1200 *maravedís* in the middle of the sixteenth century but by the seventeenth century would have been somewhat more due to problems with inflation. Any performances given within the hospital itself should result in the troupe directors being charged six pesos of *oro común* "from the said plays." The viceroy mandated that these funds be "handed over to the *hermano mayor* who takes charge of them for the assistance and aid of the said hospital."[24] Although it is difficult to ascertain how many performances might have been put on in a given month, these rates for charitable relief seem relatively comparable to those in other Spanish cities, such as Madrid.

This fiscally beneficial relationship between theater and the social work of the hospital of San Roque continued into the nineteenth century. As theater historian Herbert Schilling observed, some 40 percent of the proceeds from the lease of the theater went to the care of patients in this institution.[25] Later documents also point to the fact that in Puebla, acting companies received hospitality from either the lessee or owner of the *corral de comedias* or from the hospital itself. This was described in the 1660s "as the very current fashion in the city of Puebla," which indicates it was not likely practiced during the first half of the seventeenth century.[26] However, it does suggest another way in which the theater and hospitals in parts of colonial Mexico became symbiotically connected as they developed.

At the same time, as the commercial theater in Puebla evolved and expanded, it became linked to charity and public health. Urban public health initiatives became legally connected to the funds from plays. In the summer of 1626 the city magistrates of Puebla sought a license from the Viceroy Rodrigo Pacheco the Marquis of Cerralvo to establish a municipally controlled theater that would help to fund the charitable activities of the city's hospitals. The city's municipal authorities sent a petition to Cerralvo as well as a memo to Juan Antonio de la Reguera, solicitor of the Audiencia of Mexico. The magistrates proclaimed that since Puebla's "neighborhoods and population have greatly increased and each day it is expected that they will be augmented even more greatly . . . it would be of great use to build a playhouse that the city can lease and the rent can revert back to the civic corporation."[27]

Despite the problems that the viceroy immediately faced upon his arrival, including attacks by Dutch pirates, war with France, and the threat of incursions and raids led by Indians in the northern parts of New Spain, he was determined to oversee numerous public works projects designed to enhance urbanism and his own private coffers. In October of the same year, the city of Puebla received a license from the viceroy, who granted it permission to found another theater in addition to the one already in existence and operated by Melgarejo, where the city fathers had been attending performances for at least twenty-five years.[28] The growing city now could "found a theater [and] from the same take six pesos of alms from each play that is performed there to go to the Hospital [Real] de los Indios of this city."[29] This idea, modeled on the efforts of playhouses in the hospital patios of some provincial cities in Castile and those in Mexico City, would extend charitable relief and promote evangelical efforts among Puebla's indigenes. The fact that the plan was considered also points to an elite, and admittedly Eurocentric, perspective about the ways plays could be used to at least shape the identities of members of both the republic of Spaniards and the republic of Indians even if it was implicitly recognized that the lines between the two republics became blurred in colonial realities.

The large numbers of Indians and Africans and increasing numbers of *casta* subjects in the seventeenth century provided an impetus for European subjects to define themselves against peoples of mixed race, indigenes, and Africans. Playgoing was a potential way to do this, as many plays were imported from Spain and provided colonists with an opportunity to perform spectatorship as they would across the Atlantic. This viewpoint, as well as his own love of playgoing, fed into Cerralvo's stipulation that Mexico City should always have at least one acting troupe present.[30] His view of the *comedia* as a mark of urbanism and culture was one shared by many Spanish nobles who held administrative positions in the Americas. For them, a playhouse could serve as a site of European culture, of Renaissance civilization.

Cerralvo's commitment to the theater business fueled his interest in providing the legal possibility for an additional playhouse in Puebla. It is also possible that the large population of creoles and peninsular Spaniards who sought diversion meant that the city could have theoretically supported two playhouses. With one makeshift playhouse long established, the second, it was hoped by city councilors, could provide audiences with more entertainment, actors and *autores* with more opportunities, and the hospitals with even more funds that would not have to come directly out of the city's coffers. This prospect must have had appeal for many members of the municipal government of Puebla because their civic and festive projects, including Corpus Christi celebrations, created a drain on their finances.[31]

Yet identity was complicated in a colonial setting, where there were many people of mixed race and free persons of color who had a variety of lived experiences and held a range of occupations. Although there existed many obstacles to justice in a caste society, Spanish subjects of color also had delineated legal rights. The city boasted a separate *cabildo* for its indigenous population. There were many free blacks in the viceroyalty and a significant number of them served in the colonial military establishment; Puebla had its "own free-colored captains by the 1630s."[32] All this could be further complicated through performance and the act of spectatorship. Some Golden Age playwrights spent time in or came from the Indies, such as Tirso de Molina, Juan Ruiz de Alarcón, and Sor Juana Inés de la Cruz, and even those peninsular dramatists who had not crossed the Atlantic had family, friends, or associates who had. Some *comedias,* while set back in Spain, contained characters, including persons of color, who had lived in the Atlantic colonies. Others were set in the Americas and featured not only Spanish but also indigene characters and persons of mixed race.

While many were stock characters and even more must be viewed with awareness of the Eurocentrism and colonial viewpoints of those who wrote them, some alternative and more nuanced readings of these figures created for the stage should be considered in some cases.[33] Take, for instance, Sor Juana's *Los empeños de una casa*—a play that has been variously translated into English as *Pawns of a Noble House, Trials of a Noble House,* and *House of Desires*—in which a mixed-race *gracioso* named Castaño, whose name means both "Brown" and "Chestnut," cross-dresses and becomes read not only as a woman but also as white. As Morena, the comic seduces a pompous Spanish don into proposing marriage. The spoof undoubtedly elicited laughter among the elite in attendance, but some of this amusement may have been tinged with discomfort. After all, the Castaño/Morena storyline tapped into real anxieties about the potential malleability of gender and the ability of women in the Spanish Atlantic World to transform their rank and caste through clothes, cosmetics, and accessories such as gloves and veils like those worn by the much-maligned *tapadas* about whom Laura Bass and Amanda Wunder have written.[34]

Sor Juana wrote this play for a performance in Mexico City in the private home of the tax collector Don Fernando Deza in 1683. Unlike the theatrical event that caused a showdown between the viceroy and a newly arrived archbishop the century before, the performance of this *comedia* and accompanying elegies welcomed the new archbishop Francisco de Aguiar y Seijas and honored Sor Juana's viceregal patrons the Counts of Paredes.[35] Set in Madrid and focused on what some might call a love triangle or "a chain of amorous pursuit and power dynamics," the play also avoided the pitfalls of commenting on Mexican tax policies.[36]

Although its intended audience was largely comprised of peninsular and creole elites, it is also plausible that some of those who witnessed the performance were persons of color, and that these were not entirely mutually exclusive categories. Even though the standard narrative of colonial Mexican history suggests that the second half of the seventeenth and eighteenth centuries saw a hardening of racial hierarchies and a proliferation of *casta* groups, Joanne Rappaport's recent work cautions us against replicating eighteenth-century *casta* paintings onto sixteenth- and seventeenth-century social hierarchies. Although her arguments apply more specifically to the Audiencia of New Granada than to New Spain, which was not only more densely populated but also had many more mestizos, her warning to avoid monolithic understandings of caste categories is worth remembering here.[37] In the play, Castaño's punny name codes his particular body, but skin color and lineage were not the only considerations that defined these categories for colonial Mexicans. Associations, guild memberships, occupation, and general reputation also played a role in shaping identities. Additionally, some persons of mixed race, particularly those who were of mixed Spanish and indigene descent, still numbered among the colonial elite in both Mexico Metropolitano and Angelópolis.

An earlier example of similar trends comes from Tirso de Molina's trilogy of plays about the Inca conquest: *Todo es dar en una cosa, Amazonas en las Indias, and La lealtad contra la envidia.* Tirso wrote these plays in the late 1620s when he was serving as the commander of the Mercedarian convent in Trujillo. It's likely that Juan Fernando Pizarro had commissioned the plays as part of his bid for the title of marques and the privileges that his ancestor Gonzalo Pizarro had lost the family when he was accused of being a traitor to the crown.[38] Gladys Robalino has contended that the second of these works, *Amazons in the Indies,* was not as effusive in its praise of Gonzalo Pizarro as the other plays in the trilogy are of his brothers. She suggests that this play is one that should be read as an argument about missed opportunities "to ally through marriage with the local nobility" and create an Andean utopia.[39]

The play also features a group of Incan women, who provide a connection to a mythological and Europeanized past in that they are the eponymous Amazons. Martesia, after noting that she could kill Carvajal, claims in "the elegant Spanish language" kinship with the queen of Spain and offers to marry the conquistador.[40] Although this Hispanicization of the Amazons is problematic from a modern perspective and certainly cannot be conceived as an authentic representation of indigenes, it enabled Tirso and his audiences to imagine an alternative to the violence of conquest and to consider a shared humanity among subjects of the crown. Louise Fothergill Payne argues that the marriage proposal in this play is actually somewhat subversive as it provides the prospect (ultimately unrealized in the play) of consolidation of power instead of the loss of it for the Amazonian women and the Inca Empire.[41] Such a message of consolidation and women's roles in this process makes sense when one considers that Francisca Pizarro had founded the Mercedarian convent where Tirso wrote. Pizarro was the mestiza offspring of Francisco Pizarro and the Incan princess Inés Huaylas Yupanqui, also known as Quispe Sisa.[42] Because the evidence does not indicate that Tirso's trilogy was ever performed in Puebla, we cannot know how an audience there would have reacted to it. However, since archival documents and letters sometimes specified the race of actors and actresses and since other plays portrayed indigenes, mestizos, peninsular Spaniards, and *indianos,* or those of Spanish descent who spent time in the Indies, it is possible that denizens of Puebla from an array of caste groups saw themselves represented, with varying degrees of nuance and agency—if not absolute authenticity—onstage.[43]

Around the same time that Tirso penned his Pizarro trilogy, Viceroy Cerralvo became occupied with the disaster caused by the 1629 floods in Mexico City. Yet he remained committed to the new theater project in Angelópolis. The city's second playhouse received a license for construction in August of 1633. The viceroy had decreed that "its rents should be for the city's own use." The plan for the new *corral* was for it to be constructed in the same street as the butcher shop, because "there was capacity enough there for it and at present it serve[d] no [other] use."[44] The city council stipulated that the town crier should publicly read out the decrees about the playhouse and the contracts that would be needed for its construction at about 9:00 in the morning for a period of thirty days.[45] However, it seems these documents projected hopes rather than reality for theatrical development in Puebla. It is somewhat unclear why the construction project stalled, but historians of colonial Mexico have pointed to a general demographic and economic downturn during this period, which may have contributed to this failure. It is possible that Melgarejo continued to have *comedias* staged in his older venue during the interim and that this may have also contributed to the project's ultimate lack of success.

Even if there was a break in regular theatrical activity, the situation gave Melgarejo an opportunity to restake his claims over most of the theatrical activity in Puebla. In October of 1637 the city council registered the receipt of an order from the viceroy, dated 9 September, regarding Melgarejo's prior rights to running Puebla's theater business. The carpenter and shrewd entrepreneur had sought the new viceroy's intervention in the affair. Don Lope Diaz de Aux de Armendáriz, Marquis of Cadereyta, noted that Melgarejo had requested that "the *corral de comedias* be moved from where it presently was to some properties he owned."[46] Melgarejo also used the viceroy's authority to trump the local authority of the *cabildo* as he expanded his business activities into the sale of comestibles and beverages during performances of plays. In the same year he got into a dispute with Antonio de Toledo over who had held the rights to monopolize the sale of the sweetened beverage *aloja* to playgoers.[47] After Melgarejo's death, the *corral de comedias* was still in the hands of his family thanks to his wife's savvy appeal. This remained the case at least through the 1660s, when José Gómez Melgarejo took over the operations of the playhouse.[48]

While commercial theater in Puebla developed in the early seventeenth century through the efforts of Juan Melgarejo, the religious theater that aided the celebration of the end of Lent and the celebration of the physical body of Christ in the Eucharist in Puebla became increasingly ornate. As in Mexico City and in cities back in Castile, both the cathedral chapter, which aided the bishop, and the city magistrates regulated this process. The civil and ecclesiastical authorities of Puebla established commissions to choose the dramatic works that would be performed during these celebrations in the 1620s. This process continued over the subsequent decades, creating a vibrant feast day tradition. Puebla's Corpus Christi commissions made sure to reference the long-standing custom of the performance of plays during the festival and sought to contract with two troupe directors for at least two plays during the annual celebrations.[49]

The provisions that the civil and ecclesiastical councils made for the Corpus Christi festivities demonstrate that there was a significant amount of movement of acting companies between the capital in Mexico City and the city of Puebla during the seventeenth century. The more temperate climate of Mexico allowed the *corrales de comedias* to function at all times of the year apart from the forty days of Lent and times of flooding so long as there was a licensed company to perform in them. Consequently, the acting company managers such as Gonzalo de Riancho, Juan de Sigüenza, and Jerónimo Ortíz moved back and forth many times with their acting companies between the two important cities during the course of their careers.

Gonzalo de Riancho had come from Seville to New Spain with his family around 1595 and spent some three decades as an actor, director, and theatrical entrepreneur in the colonies. Riancho attempted to essentially monopolize theatrical activity in Mexico City in the last few years of the sixteenth century. However, it seems that a system similar to that developing in Castile began to evolve in New Spain, which compelled acting troupes to travel between cities—if for economic reasons as much as for strictly legal ones. Riancho won the contract to put on the Corpus performances in Puebla in 1605. He was in Puebla once again in 1617, when the *cabildo* of Mexico City ordered him to leave the city and return to the capital to perform there.[50]

As mentioned previously, the center of commercial theater in New Spain shifted to Puebla during the early 1630s, when Mexico City was still recovering from the devastation and dislocation brought on by the flood of 1629. This disaster had an impact on the careers and lives of colonial acting troupes and directors as well. Take, for example, the aforementioned case of conflict between the troupe directors Anamaría de los Angeles and Fernando Ramos. Los Angeles had apparently been involved in the theater business in Puebla for some time, but in 1632 she and Ramos got into a feud over who would stay in Puebla and who would go to flood-damaged Mexico City to perform for the royal and municipal authorities there. In the end, she was compelled to leave Puebla and take charge of the celebration of the fiesta of Corpus Christi in Mexico City in the spring of 1632. In 1633 she petitioned the city council of Puebla for the right for her company to perform the corpus plays there again. Perhaps the feud with Ramos is the reason that Anamaría de los Angeles teamed up with another troupe director, Juan Antonio de Sigüenza.[51] It is clear that her career continued because in 1639 she was officially warned that she was not allowed to leave the capital without express permission from the Viceroy of New Spain.[52] These episodes indicate that, although women had opportunities in the theaters of the New World, they faced challenges to their authority and often had to make alliances with men in order to maintain the spaces that they had carved out in the theatrical world. Of course, this kind of competition was not a problem faced exclusively by women in the commercial theater business.

The growth of the number of women involved in the theater business, occurring as the number of actresses, dancers, and directors increased in New Spain, scandalized some elements of colonial society.[53] This parallels the same issue in Castile, and civil and ecclesiastical authorities on both sides of the Atlantic tried to circumscribe and control women's presence on the stage and in the theaters with varying degrees of success. In 1595 authorities in Mexico City had attempted to prevent women from entering parts of the theater as spectators on pain of fines. The third woman to attempt to enter the patio of the playhouse was to be fined 90 pesos, and the performance was to be halted.[54] Such legislation makes it clear that Francisco de León was not simply worried about maintaining respectability in his Mexico City playhouse with a *cazuela*. He wanted to make sure he did not lose out on the admission fees of women.[55]

Yet in spite of attempts to legislate women out of the business or at least prevent them from mingling with men in the audience, it is clear that they continued to go to plays as spectators and to participate in the theater business on a variety of levels, as the cases of Los Angeles and Antonia Sanchez de Prado indicate. Similarly, actresses might gain celebrity in colonial settings. Some commanded comparatively high salaries for their work. In the 1680s, the actress Bernarda de Villegas, who was a member of the troupe directed by Bartolomé de la Cuava, received the annual salary of 450 pesos and was the highest paid member of her company, while the actress Felipa Jaramillo earned 300 pesos a year. In 1683 performers in this troupe on average earned a salary of 302 pesos.[56]

Although acting companies in New Spain might not have achieved the same celebrity status that they did across the Atlantic, they could be in high demand. Some troupes of actors received summons to the viceregal court, which could create something of a vacuum in provincial towns and cities. This was the case in July of 1649, when the city council of Puebla received an order that Jerónimo Ortíz and his company of actors should leave per the request of the superintendent of the Royal Indian Hospital. The viceregal summons also stipulated that the owner of the playhouse in Puebla should not allow Ortíz's company to continue playing.[57] A month later the order was reissued to the *alcalde mayor* of Puebla. Ortíz was apparently dragging his feet and performances in Angelópolis had not ceased. This time, the high court demanded his presence in Mexico City, and appealed to Ortíz's sense of charity and public good, reminding him that he was to serve the poor patients of Mexico City's Royal Indian Hospital and to fill the hospital's coffers. Just in case Ortíz had other ideas, the magistrates of the highest court in New Spain commanded Puebla's magistrates to order the acting company to leave without any further delay "nor any excuse on pain of a 500 peso fine."[58]

As it did in other cities in the Spanish Empire, theater in Puebla provided economic opportunities for enterprising directors, performers, and business-minded men and women. The *corrales de comedias* provided a venue for vendors and a meeting place for the public, where it is likely that deals were negotiated and brokered. Occasionally, as we have seen with the disputes between Melgarejo and his competitors in the business and with the disputes between directors of acting troupes, the theater became a site for conflict and contention, as well. Those in the theater business used conflicts between competing authorities to promote their own interests when they could.

There were times, however, when the continued existence of the theater itself was in jeopardy due to conflict and antitheatrical sentiment. This was particularly acute during the tenure of Bishop Palafox, who became caught up in the turbulence between the creole party and the Viceroy the Duke of Escalona, who was a Spanish grandee and, as would become more problematic, the cousin of the Duke of Braganza—or the new Portuguese king João IV from December of 1640 onward.

For most historians of Mexico and scholars of Baroque Catholicism, the bishop's role in this conflict was his most significant contribution to the history of the Spanish Empire. Palafox, along with the city's councils, cathedral chapter, and a large number of female religious and indigenous communities, fell into one camp, while the viceroy, the Society of Jesus, and a number of magistrates and inquisition officials fell into another. As a precursor to this conflict, both the new bishop of Puebla and the newly arrived Duke of Escalona made spectacular and highly ritualized entrances into the city of angels in the summer of 1640. The festivities included the typical processions, feasting, and performances of *comedias*.[59]

Palafox might have put up with such performances as part of the elaborate staging of civil and ecclesiastical power in 1640, but he certainly came to oppose theater's presence in religious feast days and the fact that, at least according to him, many performances were taking place not only in the theater but also in sacred spaces, including convents.[60] And his antitheatricality had real repercussions in Puebla. In 1644 he responded sternly to the city council's request that the Corpus Christi celebrations include the customary performances of plays. Palafox reminded the magistrates "that it was his decree that no *comedias* be heard nor should the ecclesiastical *cabildo* or any clergymen hear them."[61] The records do, however, make clear that although Palafox may have been able to forbid clerics from attending *comedias*, he was unable to put an end to all theatrical activity in Puebla. It seems that the *cabildo* of Puebla's support for plays was not universal but neither was it completely lacking. And proponents of plays knew from previous experience that they could appeal to the vested interests of competing authorities. Once again, Palafox tangled with a viceroy—though for somewhat different reasons. The city fathers had already contracted with two acting troupes, as was customary. In the wake of Palafox's stern response, they appealed to the new representative of the king, the Count of Salvatierra, who had replaced Escalona and who now ordered that the festival—and the plays—be put on in the customary manner.[62]

While Palafox backed down in this instance, he penned his 1645 *Epístola exortatoria a los curas y beneficiados de la Puebla de los Ángeles* as a chastising response to the worldly desires of his flock. In this tract, Palafox drew on many standard objections to the performance of profane drama and questioned the legitimacy of the public playhouses of New Spain. Calling *comedias* "the plague of the republic," he urged the clergymen under his jurisdiction not to attend performances at the *corrales*.[63] It is possible that in the following couple of years, Palafox won a temporary victory in his battle against spectacles through a combination of rhetoric and threats, and this may have been at least partially enabled by the crisis of the theaters back in Iberia brought on by the monarchy's long-term ban on performance. Palafox warned that any clergyman and especially holders of benefices would be fined 20 pesos for attending vulgar spectacles. However, such bans were short-lived if they were successful at all, as by 1649 acting companies were clearly present in the city of angels once again. Among those in the audience may have been some of the clerics and members of Puebla's ecclesiastical council who had switched sides and realigned themselves with the archbishop of Mexico and the viceroy.

While early modern Angelópolis had developed a rich—if not universally approved—tradition of public drama, things were not the same in Virginia. Puebla had long been founded and even had a makeshift playhouse operating out of property leased by Melgarejo before the English had a viable colonial settlement in the Americas. Indeed, as the performances of plays were being integrated into Puebla's corpus celebrations, Englishmen who were interested in overseas colonization beyond the Irish plantations were still looking for convincing arguments to advance their cause and gain investment and support. Anti-Spanish and anti-Catholic sentiments and Protestant patriotism were not enough. Colonization required financial backing, and schemes for planting in the New World had to appeal to merchants and the mercantile community. Although Richard Hakluyt proposed schemes and manifold reasons for colonization, including that it would "staye the Spanishe Kinge from flowing over all the face of that waste firme of America" in the 1580s, and Walter Raleigh subsequently led an attempt to found a colony off the shores of what is now North Carolina in that same decade, these early attempts failed.[64] It was not until the first decade of the seventeenth century with the foundation of the Virginia

Company that the English truly began their overseas colonial enterprise in the Americas.

Since the Virginia colony quickly came to rely on exploitative plantation agriculture, the settlement preferences for large landholdings compounded this lag in urbanization. Although the English continued to reside close to the Atlantic seaboard well into the eighteenth century, their numbers remained smaller and their communities more diffuse.[65] This was quite different from the Spanish who, following the Roman tradition, saw urban life as a symbol of empire and cities as communities of citizens.[66] In other words, the English in Virginia essentially abandoned living in communities, and the colonists in New England lived in small towns or villages that differed greatly from the large, rectilinear cities of Spanish America with their plazas, monumental and religious buildings, and theaters.[67] One consequence was the later emergence and development of significant urban infrastructure—including playhouses in what would eventually become the United States.

Williamsburg, Virginia was founded in 1632. Initially called Middle Plantation, it had been conceived as a defensive palisade in the aftermath of a coordinated attack on English settlements that resulted in the deaths of 347 colonists in Virginia and led to renewed conflict in the deadly Anglo-Powhattan Wars.[68] This foundation coincided with a twelve-year peace that enabled a significant increase in English control of the Tidewater.[69] When the colonial statehouse in Jamestown burnt for a second time in 1698, the headquarters of Virginia's colonial government moved to Middle Plantation. This move was meant to be temporary, but the presence of the college and the more favorable climate led to the House of Burgesses' decision to permanently relocate the capital there the following year. It was then renamed for the reigning monarch William III. Despite its more grandiose name and status, the population remained relatively small. It has been estimated that the entire population of the Virginia colony was less than 60,000 in 1700 and approximately 538,000 in 1780. Williamsburg's urban population was estimated at just over 1,400 persons in 1782.[70]

Much has been made of the potential performative aspects of early encounters between English settlers and soldiers of fortune like John

Smith and indigenous persons like Amonute—more commonly called Pocahontas—and of the ways they were recorded in chronicles and accounts.[71] However, there was little professionally staged theater in the colonized lands that would later become the United States. The first documented occurrence of a performance of a play in the British North American colonies took place not in Williamsburg, but in Accomack County, Virginia. The reason that this 1665 performance was recorded is that an audience member, Edward Martin, objected to the content of the play, *The Bare and the Cubb,* and the court ordered the actors, William Darby, Cornelius Watkinson, and Philip Howard, to appear before it in costume and recite some of their lines.[72] Although the court decided against Martin, no one sought to build a permanent theater in the British North American colonies until 1716. Then William Levingston, a merchant in Williamsburg, contracted with Charles and Mary Stagg to build a playhouse, provide it with actors, and act and direct in exchange for half the profits. They also had to personally take on half the expense. The profits, it seems, were minimal, as Levingston sought other sources of income—such as renting a bowling green and practicing surgery.[73]

After the death of Charles Stagg in 1735, the playhouse in Williamsburg seems to have largely fallen into disuse, and civic authorities then converted it into a courthouse for the town. Of course, neither the lack of evidence nor the financial problems of the Levingston-Stagg venture mean that there were no performances during the intervening years. As Odai Johnson has argued, the accepted narrative about colonial theater in British North America is skewed and rather dysfunctional because there are few surviving playbills and no surviving playhouses from the period, while the records of legislation or opposition to the performances that took place have often survived. He observes that "compounding the absence of performance evidence is the equally vexing problem of the authority such an aggregate body of legal evidence has exerted over the historical narrative of colonial theatre, rehearsed in a host of studies large and small until the position of theatre as an unlawful and unauthorized entity struggling to gain legitimacy in the social landscape of colonial America has become a cliché of the field."[74] However, the limited evidence of attempts to thwart the theater can also be read in such a way as to suggest that theatrical activity was likely intermittent if not actually illicit and undesired during this period.

In 1751 a new playhouse was constructed, and a visiting troupe of actors led by Walter Murray and Thomas Kean, which had been presenting plays in other cities in British North America, was the first to perform there. This theater became home to William Hallam's company of actors, which included twelve adults and three children.[75] As was common in the this period, the entertainment business became a family affair. One of the troupe's children was Lewis Hallam, who was about twelve years old. Purportedly, during one performance in Williamsburg in 1752, he was overcome by stage fright, forgot his line, and fled in tears.[76]

The acting company faced more significant difficulties, as well. By the 1750s, Williamsburg still had a population of only about a thousand people, and this was really too small for a company to attract audiences to repeat performances of old material. Unlike the Spanish acting companies of a century before, Hallam's company was not large enough to continually produce new plays on a near-daily basis. It is therefore likely that Hallam's members supplemented their incomes by offering dancing lessons. Although they did not leave Virginia for several more months, these circumstances compelled the company to tour the region and then attempt their luck with playgoers in New York, South Carolina, and ultimately Jamaica.[77]

The composition and reactions of particular early modern audiences, whether in seventeenth-century Puebla or colonial Virginia, are difficult to ascertain because the evidence for such issues is especially scarce in the surviving records. However, some glimpses into early modern audiences can be found in the records of the city councils of provincial towns like Puebla and in the antitheatrical complaints of people like Palafox and Edward Martin. The need for Palafox to vehemently write against the theater after being trumped by the appeal to the viceroy reveals that at least some if not many clerics in Puebla regularly attended the performance of plays at festivals and in the *corral,* possibly assuaging their consciences with the knowledge that money from their admission fees helped to fund charitable care in hospitals. The need for someone to lock and guard the box of city magistrates indicates that *cabildo* members went to see plays with some frequency, but so did lower-ranking Pueblans who might seek to elevate their status for an evening by infiltrating the city council's box. Antitheatrical worries about the way poor people wasted their money on frivolous and sinful entertainments make it seem likely that less affluent people in Puebla, including Indian laborers, less affluent whites and mestizos, and free blacks attended plays. The continued efforts of Melgarejo and his family suggest that they were at least breaking even if not profiting from their investment in the playhouse, which leads me to believe that some city dwellers regularly sought the same types of entertainments that Spanish subjects did back in Castile.

In Virginia Edward Martin's legal action resulted ironically in an abbreviated second performance of the play at court, which found no fault with the players and demanded that Martin pay the court costs.[78] More regular theater might have developed had there been the populace to support it during the seventeenth century. Although the evidence is cursory for these earlier periods, later evidence suggests at least some variation in rank and occupation among playgoers in colonial Virginia. During the second half of the eighteenth century, southern colonists had more opportunities to enjoy entertainment, as more companies made appearances in locations like Williamsburg and Norfolk. Here and elsewhere, colonial subjects attended plays and saw the occasional tumbler or automaton. Merchants and artisans in towns and members of the southern gentry, like Thomas Jefferson and George Washington, often comprised a large portion of the audience during these decades. Some scholars have suggested that free persons of color and persons held in slavery were also in these eighteenth-century Virginian audiences.[79]

The charitable function of the theaters in funding the hospitals of the colonial cities of New Spain had no real counterpart in the settlements of Anglo America. Both hospitals and theaters came late to the British colonies and had no regular part in quotidian life in cities until the second half of the eighteenth century. As the eminent historian J. H. Elliott has observed, the societies created by colonists in their new American environments were littered with the "cultural baggage" that these emigrants brought with them. The societies that they created "unmistakably replicated many of the most characteristic features of the metropolitan societies as they knew—or imagined—them at the time of their departure."[80] In the Spanish colonies this tendency meant cities with urban institutions like commercial theater and charitable hospitals. In the English colonies this was not the case during the seventeenth—or even much of the eighteenth—century. This difference was partly due to the century-long period of lag time between the efforts of the Spanish and the English to make new lives for themselves in the Americas, and partly due to the less urban and institutional stances of many of the English settlers. In Virginia colonists did support some theatrical and tavern performances with their attendance and admission fees. They just were not in a position to do so until much later than their Spanish counterparts to the south.

Ideas about what it meant to be a Spaniard were reinforced by the institutions of entertainment, public health, and charity in the far-flung cities of the empire: Mexico City and Puebla, as well as Lima and Cuzco. The urban spaces of the kingdoms of the universal Spanish monarchy fostered these centrally located institutions, like the playhouse constructed by Melgarejo, where colonists could feel both their imperial identity and a sense of local pride. However, the theater, as we have seen, was not popular with everyone, including some church, city, and royal authorities. As I will discuss in the next chapter, opposition to the theater occasionally could close the doors of the playhouses. Such closures complicated the lives of playwrights, directors, actors, actresses, would-be playgoers, and—at least in the case of the universal Spanish monarchy—hospital patients throughout the Atlantic World.

"The Plague of the Republic"

ANTITHEATRICAL SENTIMENT AND ITS LIMITS IN THE ATLANTIC WORLD

As the previous chapters have recounted, urban officials and city dwellers accommodated and enabled to various degrees the integration of commercial theater into the physical, social, and cultural landscapes of cities in Spain and England and their Atlantic realms during the early modern period. However, while many attended performances at the playhouses, some, like the Bishop Palafox, vehemently attacked the theaters, criticizing their pernicious, disturbing, corrupting, and effeminizing effects. Opponents of the stage might have felt the satisfaction of antitheatrical triumph in the 1640s, when both the Spanish monarchy and the English Long Parliament closed playhouses for long periods, during which civil war and revolts catalyzed an already existing sense of decline and made reforming legislation seem more necessary than usual. During the sixteenth and seventeenth centuries, antitheatrical polemicists in the Spanish and Anglo Atlantic Worlds made many similar arguments despite their confessional differences. They drew on many of the same humanistic traditions and ancient authorities. In both cases, they had greater—if still ultimately limited—influence in the wake of serious political crises.[1]

In spite of the nearly synchronous timing of these long-term closures of the playhouses, there were some significant differences between the trajectories of English and Spanish antitheatricality. In particular, even though English antitheatrical writers, such as Stephen Gosson and

William Prynne, are perhaps better known to American and Anglophone academics, the opponents of the stage in Spain were more numerous and wrote and published tracts and sermons opposing the playhouse with greater frequency than their counterparts in England. This was especially true during the first half of the seventeenth century, when printed English antitheatrical sentiment declined. Due to the limited extent of commercial drama and then the playhouse's close connections to the court, little printed opposition to the stage emerged from colonial cities in the Anglo Atlantic, such as Dublin. Because there was not much professional drama in the North American colonies established by the English, there was little immediate reason for opposition to it until the late seventeenth and eighteenth centuries when dramatic performances became somewhat more regular. Conversely, because the theater played such visible and important social, cultural, and economic roles in cities throughout the Spanish Atlantic, opposition to the *corrales* of cities in the domains of the universal Spanish monarch continued to appear at frequent intervals. These polemics contributed to perceptions that the state had once been a healthy organism but had developed a wasting and womanish disease. As a result, some opponents of the stages joined with other reformers in the Spanish Empire in expressing concerns over the health of an increasingly problematically gendered body politic.

The theater made a convenient target for anxieties felt during such periods of perceived degeneration and decline because public drama was such a regular and highly visible feature of urban life in cities throughout the Spanish Atlantic World. What is more, this visibility and prominence stemmed from the fact that the *corrales de comedias* found protection—not only in the form of royal and aristocratic patrons but also as a result of their relationships with Tridentine charitable lay piety examined in the previous chapters. In Spain and colonial Latin America, where playhouses developed financial connections to lay brotherhoods, hospitals, orphanages, and other institutions of good works, there was more antitheatrical sentiment. But ironically, it was ultimately less effective in the long term than its English counterpart because, even as Spanish opponents of the stage complained frequently that theater created a diseased and overly feminine body politic, it was theater itself that funded many efforts to care for the public of Spanish subjects in its global empire.

One of the key differences between the Renaissance theaters that developed in England and Spain heightened this issue. While women were not typically allowed on the stages of the commercial playhouses of early modern London, Bristol, or Dublin, they played prominent roles on those of Madrid, Seville, Mexico City, and Puebla. In 1580 and again in 1586 the Council of Castile issued decrees that banned women from public performance on the stage. However, acting companies, audiences, and authorities alike seem to have ignored the edict. From the last decade of the sixteenth century on, women in the Spanish Empire used the developing theater business to pursue careers as actresses, troupe directors, playwrights, and food sellers. The highly visible presence of women, as opposed to boy actors, on the Spanish stage provided greater verisimilitude, but this helped to give rise to authorities' and antitheatricalists' anxieties about theater. Women were also more generally present at the *corrales*—although the compartmentalization of the Spanish theaters at least theoretically segregated them from the men of lower social ranks in the audiences. Meanwhile, sick and destitute women sought care and assistance in hospitals, such as Madrid's Hospital de la Pasión, which the theaters helped to fund.

Opposition to the performance of drama had deeply rooted foundations in Western philosophical thought and religious writings. Early modern polemical authors drew on currents of antitheatricality that dated back to antiquity. For instance, Stephen Gosson "cited over twenty-five Greek and Roman writers in support of his objections to the stage. He relied on stalwarts such as Plato for the foundations of his attack, and employed colourful snippets of Ovid, Homer, Plutarch, and Virgil for illustrative anecdotes and examples" in his work *The School for Abuse,* first printed in 1579.[2] Another important source for antitheatrical writers living in early modern Europe was the writings of the early Church fathers, who had abhorred "the degenerate tastes of the time" including "unashamedly realistic" acting and "the grossest of indecencies in jest and gesture."[3] Anthony Munday drew on the work of Salvian, the fifth-century Christian author of *De gubernatione Dei,* translating some of Salvian's writings into English and appending his own to *A Second and Third Blast of Retreat from Plays and Theatres.* Pedro de Guzmán, the author of *Los bienes del honesto trabajo y los daños de la ociosidad en ocho discursos,* proclaimed in the early seventeenth century that learned theologians had universally condemned public spectacles, such as dancing and performed plays, and other diversions, like card games, gladiator games, and bullfighting. He observed that "books, sermons, and extremely learned tracts" had been penned against theater and public spectacles by the likes of "Tertullian, Lactantius, Saint Cyprian, John Chrysostom, [and] Saint Augustine."[4] William Prynne claimed in "The Epistle Dedicatory" of his massive *Histrio-Mastix* that such pastimes had been "condemned in all ages, all places, not onely by (f) councels, (g) Fathers, (h) Divines, (i) Civilians, (k) Canonists, (1) Politicians, and (m) other Christian writers, by (n) divers Pagan Authors of all sorts, and by (o) Mahomet himself; but likewise by (p) Sundry Heathen . . . and by the (q) Statutes of our Kingdome."[5] They were not alone in their use of these exemplary ancients to give their works historical and religious authority, as other early modern polemicists such as Juan de Mariana, Juan de Palafox, and Jaume Albert employed similar rhetorical strategies. In doing so, they sought to demonstrate that public theater had always been evil and to convince their readers that, even if they scoffed at contemporary complaints, they should heed the condemnation of the ancients.

Munday stated in the preface of his antitheatrical tract that he had included Salvian's treatise in addition to his own so that "one of them might showe the abomination of the Theatres in the time present, and the other how odious they have seemed to the godlie in time past, and both allure thee utterlie to forbid them, if thou be a Magistrate of power, and to auoide them more than anie pestilence, be thou whosoever."[6] Munday used Salvian to reinforce his own position that the theater was "but the drifts of Satan, which he vseth to blind our eies withal, the more easily to carie us from the obedience of GOD." However, in spite of his severe tone, Munday was pragmatic enough to argue that if the theaters were to stay open that they should at least be reformed. He especially wanted a ban on performances on the Sabbath.[7] Although Munday's desire for a ban on Sunday performances eventually was instituted in the 1580s and was reconfirmed by Royal Proclamation in May of 1603, his hopes for a long-term ban on commercial performances would take much longer. In fact, by then, Munday no longer hoped for it: after 1580 he began to write plays for performance.

I would suggest that Munday's change of heart reflects a more general historical trend. There were no new, printed polemics opposing the stage in England during the first two decades of the seventeenth century. It was during this period that Bristol's Wine Street Playhouse became the setting for most performances in that provincial English port city. Meanwhile in the Irish possessions of the English crown, private performances for nobles made up the majority of theatrical activity. During the 1630s, the playhouse in Werburgh Street evoked criticisms, but these were more laments about the limited audience and its lack of appreciation and taste than they were antitheatrical rants. In other words, timing is everything, and while there may have been some readers of antitheatrical tracts in late sixteenth-century Ireland, there was not much public theater to oppose there at the time.

English antitheatrical sentiment had dwindled in the first decades of the seventeenth century but gained a bit of new momentum in London during the 1630s. Numerous theaters had been constructed in the metropolis since the 1560s—although not all remained open for the entire period. Playgoing continued to be a popular pastime. These developments may have given a sense of desperation to a new generation of antitheatricalists, such as William Prynne, who had stronger puritanical leanings. Prynne's work *Histrio-Mastix,* published in 1633, is the most infamous English diatribe against the early modern theater. He argued in "The Epistle Dedicatory" of *Histrio-Mastix* that his book had to be long in order to counterbalance the influence of "Players, Play-bookes, Play-haunters, and Play-houses still increasing" in seventeenth-century London. Prynne found a particular source of frustration in the remodeling of The Fortune and The Red Bull and in the building of the newest performance venue, the Salisbury Court playhouse at Whitefriars. He bemoaned that "even in vitious Nero his raigne there were but (b) three standing Theatres in Pagan Rome."[8]

The idolatrous and formative nature of public drama disturbed Prynne. Although this idolatry had pagan origins, Prynne also feared that contemporary stage plays evoked and would bring back "popery."[9] Consequently, his loathing of graven images permeated his other concerns about representation. Prynne also believed that the playhouses—those "sugured poysoned potions of the Divell"—were schools of sin and vice, inspiring imitation in the members of the audience.[10] He attacked the stage for the types of representations that took place on it. According to his line of thought, depictions of sinful activities like murder and rape instilled loose morals in audiences and compelled playgoers to leave the theaters and behave badly. Even if plays were not so corrupting as to cause strings of murders, thefts, and the constant cross-dressing of Englishmen everywhere, the performance of sinning onstage should nonetheless have caused Christians to "feare and tremble." Certainly, they had no place in the godly society for which Prynne prayed.[11]

The polemicist pronounced the "damnable odiousnesse" of playgoing as one of the most "unlawful of pastimes," and in holding this opinion, he knew he was not alone, as he drew on a variety of ancient sources for his lengthy diatribe, including "the very best of Pagans." In his lengthy diatribe against dancing, he noted that wise pagans, such as Seneca and Statius, had also "abundantly condemned all mixt, lascivious, accurate, amorous dancing," and he also listed other ancient critics. Drawing on the Roman historian Sallust, he reinforced his argument that dancing was an infamous activity. Prynne also cited the Latin pagan author Macrobius, who had claimed that "skill in dancing was reputed infamous and a badge of dishonesty among the Romanes" to further drive home his point about the evils that took place on the stages of London.[12]

Such alleged evils also took place in the Spanish *corrales*. One of the most influential opponents of the stage there was the Jesuit, Juan de Mariana.[13] In *De spectaculis*, one of the treatises that comprised his *Tractatus VII*, published in 1609, Mariana examined the legitimacy of numerous forms of public diversion, taking up the issues of not only theater and music, but also the circus, the running of bulls, bullfights, and prostitution. In the first chapter of *De spectaculis* he outlined the history of public spectacles, observing that "spectacle is nothing but a publically instituted sport to delight the public." As an anti-Molinist Jesuit and an heir of Ignatius Loyola's "charismatic masculinity" and affective piety, Mariana distrusted things that delighted the senses because they could mislead a man's observations and "inflame" his senses as the "lewd movements and gestures" of actors and actresses allegedly did.[14] Such anxieties were heavily gendered, as such forms of Jesuit piety celebrated clerical celibacy. Ulrike Strasser has argued that the Jesuits extolled a paternalistic and cooperative masculinity and that one of the defining features of Jesuit life was "the regular practice of self-examination under the guidance of a more spiritually advanced man."[15] In *De spectaculis* Mariana invited his readers to be guided, to reflect on their playgoing habits, and to reform them.

Mariana demonstrated his erudition, as well as his spiritual advancement, and addressed a learned audience by writing in Latin and grounding his work in historical sources. Not only did his frequent references to ancient philosophers and early church fathers satisfy the humanist expectations of his educated readers, they also assisted him in tying his arguments against the theater to older critiques, which compellingly demonstrated public theater's propensity for bringing about the ruin of powerful polities. In order to set up his definitions of the genres of entertainment, which he essentially divided into two types of spectacles—scenics and gymnastics—Mariana drew on the works of the ancient theologians, such as Tertullian, Cassiodorus, Salvian, and Basil. He also referred to the writings of pagan authors, like Seneca, and to the great early medieval Spanish author, Isidore of Seville, to elaborate on his typology of entertainments.[16] Observing that sensual pleasures of the flesh and the pursuit of such pleasures as could be found at the playhouse reflected negatively on the spirit and soul of a man, Mariana reminded his readers of Basil's teachings on virginity and their ability to give one a tranquil mind that was better suited for the contemplation of godly things.[17]

Mariana thought that the very nature of performed drama delighted an audience and was therefore dangerous to the soul because the pleasure of spectacle trapped the average member of an audience in a cycle of sinful appetite, stripping him little by little of reason and honesty. He contended that spending too much time at the playhouse triggered the baser instincts in men and unleashed uncontrollable lusts and passions.[18] Playgoing caused men to degenerate in their condition and nature. Mariana feared the presence of actresses further provoked wantonness and corruption in the hearts of susceptible men and women in the audiences of the *corrales*. Such corruption led to weakness; such weakness could lead to the downfall of Spain, to a kingdom stripped of her overseas holdings and ravaged by her enemies.

Pedro de Guzmán, who cited his spiritually advanced fellow Jesuit, Juan de Mariana, also pointed out that Saint Augustine and Saint Isidore, "using almost the exact same words," had decried public theater and traced the decline of Rome to the Romans' use of theater to placate their gods, who "were demons."[19] Similarly, the Jesuit priest Juan Ferrer (1558–1636) devoted several chapters of his work *Tratado de las comedias* to exploring the ways that early church fathers had treated theater and public spectacles in their writing. Another Jesuit, Jaume Albert, claimed in a printed sermon of 1629 that going to the *corrales de comedias* had a number of pernicious effects on audiences and sought in his tract to show that the public theater was a social "plague" and "the ruin of the Republic."[20] Drawing upon Tertullian's admonitions about the damage such entertainments could cause, he suggested that theater was not only dangerous to the soul but could even be deadly. Albert resorted to scare tactics. Using one of Tertullian's colorful tales about two women who were punished by God for attending a theatrical performance, he reminded his readers that playgoing had the potential to result in demonic possession or in such fatal misfortunes as attracting hobgoblins and terrible phantasms that could scare a person to death by suddenly appearing in the night and "making threatening feints at her with a burial shroud, causing her to die five days later."[21] Along these same lines, his sermon also drew upon Salvian's claim that theater's evil besmirched not only the players, but the spectators as well.[22] Salvian, Albert, and Munday all contended that the Romans had become so addicted to spectacle that they were incapable of being cured by catastrophic waves of devastating, barbarian invasions sent down as punishment from heaven for their love of theaters and gladiator games.

The antitheatrical Bishop Palafox of Puebla de los Angeles believed that Spanish society had been and should continue to be organized according to a hierarchical structure provided by belief in divine, canon, royal, and natural law.[23] In his view, balance and godly order could be more fully extended to Spain's Atlantic realms through the more thorough application of these legal strictures. Accordingly, Palafox urged not only a program of clerical secularization, which would reorder the sacred geography of Spain's American dominions, but also more austere sacral choreographies of ritual that would eliminate superfluous distractions from the performance of true piety. As previously discussed, his reform efforts also included attacks on the playgoing practices of his parishioners. In his 1645 *Discurso en favor de cierto religioso de vida ejemplar,* Palafox drew on Tertullian, Saint Cyprian, John Chrysostom, Salvian, and Saint Augustine. Despite his general animosity toward the Jesuits, he shared common ground with Jesuit antitheatrical writers like Mariana, Guzmán, and Albert in his rhetorical use of the ancients, including his retelling of Tertullian's cautionary tale of demonic possession.[24]

Although opposition to the theater in England had not disappeared entirely from printed sermons, like those of William Holbrooke, or from the pulpits of certain parishes, the publishing of antitheatrical tracts waned in England during the final years of the sixteenth century and the first three decades of the seventeenth century. This was not the case in Spain, where antitheatrical writers continued to produce tracts at frequent intervals. For antitheatrical polemicists and some reformers, continued attendance at the *corrales de comedias* was a sure sign that Spain was opening itself up to further weakness, continued scandal, and emasculating ruin. Such frequent outpourings of vitriol resulted not only from military losses, inflation, and losses of treasure to pirates and privateers, but also from the routine visibility of theater in Spanish daily life that had resulted from the playhouses' links with the charitable giving that flourished as part of the outpouring of Counter Reformation piety among laypeople as well as clergy. For those who loathed it, theater was inescapable.

Even if it is worth remembering that it is "misguided to take the obstreperous comments of biased theatre haters and often paranoid civic authorities at face value," these prejudiced opponents of the early modern playhouses may have had a point about how tempting attending plays could be, as the example of Antonio González, discussed at the beginning of the first chapter, and the following case suggest. In 1655, while the court was at Aranjuez, Philip IV reminded his company of guards and servants of an order from the previous decade that "he had repeated on various occasions." The king instructed the captains of the guard to sternly remind their men that neither they nor any of his servants "were exempt from paying at the doors of the [playhouses] when they went to see the [performances]" and that doing so defrauded the hospitals.[25] Clearly the desire to be entertained could at times provoke poor job performance and even a lack of charity.

González and the members of the king's guard were not the only ones mesmerized by dramatic performance. Twenty-five years before chastising his soldiers, Philip IV had an affair with the celebrated actress María Inés Calderón. She gave birth to the king's son, who was initially called Juan de la tierra, in 1629. Important nobles, like the Duke of Osuna and Rodrigo Calderón, gave large sums of money to individual actresses and maintained private boxes at the public theaters. And although noblemen (and noblewomen) had more leisure time and money to spend at the *corrales*, they were not the only ones to do so.

This continued attendance of all sectors of Spanish society, including many clergymen, along with the patronage of nobles, and the continued connection of the playhouses to charitable works, frustrated opponents of the theater in the Spanish Atlantic. As we have seen from numerous incidents at the theaters, women also made up members of the audience. For antitheatricalists, the damage to the body politic, made weaker and more feminine with every staging of a play, far outweighed the social good provided to individuals in hospitals and orphanages. The actresses who violated norms of female enclosure and seductively attracted audiences compounded polemicists' fears about destabilized masculinity. And this gave rise to the trope of the diseased and corrupt body of the state that resulted from society's overexposure to theater.

The highly visible presence of women on the stage—and to a lesser extent as playgoers—further heightened gendered opposition to the *corrales*. Actresses frequently performed in the costumes of women who ranked more highly than they did in early modern society. Worse still, from the perspective of disturbed polemicists, actresses also appeared onstage in male garb. Antitheatrical authors bemoaned actresses' sensuous and seductive qualities. In 1598 Lupercio Leonardo de Argensola ranted that "one noble of this realm got so tangled up in a love affair with a hussy of an actress that he not only set her up in a house, but he publicly—and with notable scandal—gave her a place in his household and gifts of gold plate and he embroidered her dresses, and his servants waited on her and respected her as if she were his legitimate wife." This besotted noble, who allegedly had even taken on womanly activities like embroidering, was then further cuckolded by the ungrateful recipient of his affection, who forced him to endure fits of jealousy as she received similar attentions from other men.[26] Argensola was a former playwright who had written tragedies in the classical humanist style, and had been edged out of the business by the rise of the three-act *comedia*. Therefore, he might have had firsthand knowledge of actresses and performances to draw from, but he was also disgruntled and had an axe to grind.

One did not have to be a failed playwright to think that the most harmful aspects of theater included the presence of beautiful women on the stage and in attendance at the *corrales de comedias*. According to the Jesuit Pedro de Guzmán, these women who "*came to be seen*" were "dressed up, painted, made up with kohl, lovely, [and] elegant." This was how they seduced and weakened men. They were like—as was the theater itself—the serpent Scitale, the fabulous mythical beast who killed her prey by stunning it into near-motionlessness with her dazzling scales. For Guzmán, the dangers that the theater presented were feminine, and women were not far removed metaphorically from beasts. Indeed this was the very same species of beast that had caused the fall of man and was now, at least according to opponents of the stage, bringing sickness, death, and decline to Spain. The Jesuit warned his readers that the "gilded and glittery scales of this beautiful serpent, of the Comedia, enchant the ear, delight the sight and the senses, [and] rob the heart" of playgoers.[27] Antitheatrical writers like Argensola, Guzmán, and Albert equated theater with unworldly, ungodly, and unmanly forces.

Undoubtedly such complaints were exaggerated, but they occasionally gained traction with some officials. Lawmakers attempted to prevent women from behaving like the "hussy of an actress" described by Argensola. They decreed that women in acting companies had to be the wife or daughter of a man in the acting companies to which they belonged.[28] They also frequently attempted to legally circumscribe women's costumes—namely, they sought to prevent women from appearing onstage in breeches that showed off their shapely calves. For reformers, this seemed especially necessary since so many early modern Spanish plays involved the heroine cross-dressing for part of the performance. Although the regular intervals with which the Council of Castile issued sumptuary laws for the theater perhaps implies their ineffectiveness, they do indicate that polemicists' fears of free and seductive women struck a chord with reform-minded judges and other officials.[29]

For Jaume Albert, the dangers of the playhouse included immodesty, extravagant dress, and lascivious dancing. Albert, like the rhetorician and fourth-century convert to Christianity, Lactantius, whose writings he also drew upon, fretted that going to plays made men behave like women and caused them to go about "with studied gestures and dress, so that they seem like whores."[30] He argued that the "perverse" art of public drama robbed the soul of the "precious balsam of honesty" and created a world turned upside down—possibly because too many men had lost their virility and piety. Theater provoked all sorts of bad behaviors: "in servants, insolence; in female servants, rudeness; in students, excesses of behavior; in married couples, coldness and little faithfulness, to the point of impudent rapaciousness!"[31]

Antitheatricalists in the Spanish Atlantic World equated theater with women behaving badly, with men behaving like women, and with unworldly and ungodly forces that entered the diseased and weakened bodies of subjects of the universal Spanish monarchy. Because female bodies were supposedly more porous, they were more prone to demonic penetration. Opponents of the stage feared that men would take on womanly characteristics that would have corporeal effects for them individually and for the body politic as a whole. Womanliness equated with sickness.

Lupercio Leonardo de Argensola claimed in a *memorial* directed to Philip II that "the [disgusting] worms that the *comedia* breeds are men who live in concubinage, gluttons, thieves, [and] pimps of their wives," leaving the reader struck with the image of the playhouse giving birth to a stillborn body politic already decaying into a rank and maggot-eaten corpse.[32] His association of social decline with a degenerative and effeminizing disease was a thread picked up by other opponents of the stage. Lupercio's brother Bartholemé's treatise, *De cómo se remediarán los vicios de la Corte y que no acuda a ella tanta gente inútil,* written in 1600, urged a wholesale reformation of Spanish society. He lumped theater in with other allegedly excessive and emasculating luxuries that had spread moral sickness and malaise throughout Spain's realms. Plays, along with ridiculous fashions, gambling, and other vices, should be shunned by manly Spaniards and all respectable women in order that "the whole body politic of the Republic be cured."[33]

Pedro de Guzmán explicitly deemed theater a sickness and a poison, claiming that all of the seeming beauty, grace, wit, and elegance of performances was in reality demonic dishonesty. For Guzmán, Scitale had stunned the state into submission and the *comedia's* poison then penetrated the body politic. "All of this entering by the eyes and by the ears is fire, is poison, is venom, is subtle corrosive sublimate that injures the heart of the person watching."[34] He claimed that the public theater was not only a school for vice, where audiences allegedly watched plays about such scandalous topics as the love lives of prostitutes, but also "a cathedra of pestilence and the plague of the city."[35]

According to polemicists and reformers, the state was sick. One of the causes of such illness was excessive luxury, which these writers frequently equated with extravagant dress, sumptuous eating, and indulging in sensual pleasures, such as attending the theater. Antitheatrical polemicists' arguments overlapped with those being made by more general reformers in the seventeenth century. For example, Alonso Carranzai was not primarily concerned with prohibiting plays. Nonetheless, he not only blamed the fashionable mode of dress, the *guardainfante,* for a number of women's health problems, including hip pain and miscarriages, but he also blamed actors and actresses—in concert with the devil and other "slavish and idle people"—for introducing these fads. To make matters worse, they were dressing above their rank and further undermining the integrity and health of the Spanish monarchy while doing so. Playgoing had essentially caused the state to degenerate into a woman who miscarried her children.[36]

Many of Bishop Juan de Palafox's arguments against the theater in Puebla and beyond were the rather standard ones that we have seen—

comedias awakened sensual appetites, stupefied and tricked women, taught men and women how to sin, and poisoned the soul. He also called theater "the plague of the republic, the fire of virtue, the fuel of sensuality, the devil's court, the consistory of vice, the schoolroom of the most scandalous of sins."[37] Since Palafox's primary audience in this tract was his fellow clergymen, he needed to respond to the arguments used by proponents of the theater and their charitable funds: namely, *comedias* had been allowed for their potentially civilizing influence and that even clergymen attended them, watching from their own designated section of some of Spain's and Mexico's playhouses. The bishop likened the playhouse to a "bishop's throne of pestilence" and the sickness was contagious.[38] If the sacerdotal subjects of the Spanish crown wanted to create a truly angelic republic in Puebla, one of the first steps was to stop attending plays.

To further this argument, which he expanded in *Epístola exortatoria a los curas y bēneficiados de la Puebla de los Ángeles,* Palafox played the orthodoxy card. He observed that although there were plenty of defenders of the theater, such tolerance was dangerous to the state: "the synagogue is permitted in Oran and in all other parts the judaizar is justly burnt."[39] He equated the theater with not only sin and demons like Belial but also with what clerics would have viewed as terrible spiritual sicknesses: heresy, apostasy, and false conversions. Readers might have recalled that the Mexican Inquisition had condemned heretics and practitioners of Jewish belief and turned them over to the secular authorities to be burnt at the stake, and that attending the playhouse could put their souls in similar jeopardy.

Early modern people took appearances seriously, and policed their communities' bodily performances of rank, religion, and sex. Dressing as someone of a different rank or gender was a transgression of social norms and sumptuary laws. On the stage this typically took place within legal constraints, but still led some to fear that the "self could easily be made into anything because it has no inherent nature."[40] Such beliefs crossed national and confessional lines as well as the ocean. Although the presence of women on the stage and the specific social contexts of theater in cities throughout Spain's global realms shaped polemicists' particular anxieties, English opponents of the stage also shared their more general fears about the alleged social ills caused by destabilized gender norms. For English opponents of the stage in London, where antitheatrical sentiment was most prominent since it was a response to a more visible presence of theatrical activity in daily life, concerns centered on the appearance of femininity.

Gosson, Munday, and Prynne condemned cross-dressing and ambiguous gender roles on the stage. Like their Spanish counterparts, they believed that theater could mentally, physically, and possibly even biologically turn males into females. In the English case, antitheatrical polemicists feared that it was the outward trappings of clothing rather than the presence of actresses that stunted the nation's virility. First, this occurred in boy actors, whose not yet fully formed bodies and minds were deemed to be more impressionable, and then in the men in the audiences who gazed upon them.

Take, for example, William Prynne's assessment of the "discommendable" practice of using boy actors to play the roles of women. In *Histrio-Mastix* he countered the claims of those who argued that it was better for men actors to appear onstage in the roles of women than for women to perform by contending that "it is no good argument to say, Adultery is worse then simple Fornication." He claimed that while actresses represented "temptation to whoredome, and adultery," boy actors who donned women's clothing violated natural law.[41] The puritan polemicist reminded his readers of Tertullian's observation "'that no kinde of rayment as he could find was accursed of God, but womens apparell worn by men." Such transvestitism was abominable because it aroused "filthy lusts, both in the Actors and Spectators . . . [and] likewise instigates them to selfe-pollution . . . and to that unnaturall Sodomiticall sinne of uncleanesse." Prynne, like a number of contemporary Spanish polemicists and reformers, extended his argument to place blame on the practices of players for what he viewed as disastrously sinful forays into fashion and hairstyles for Englishmen and women. He bemoaned men who had "metamorphosed into women in their deformed frizled lockes and hair" and women who had "growne so farre past shame, past modesty, grace and nature, as to clip their hair like men with lockes and foretops, and to make this Whorish cut, the very guise and fashion of the times."[42]

Although historians can point to relatively few instances when women or men seem to have believed that they had biologically changed into the other sex, certainly some transvestitism took place offstage as well.[43] In spite of confessional differences, early modern antitheatrical polemicists in Catholic Spain and Protestant England shared fears about this practice as well as some overlapping views about appropriate gender roles, based on a one-sex model of the human body. These understandings, along with humanist conceptions of early Christian opposition to plays, shaped their antitheatricality. That is not to say religious differences did not matter: where Catholics feared theater's demonic nature, Protestants feared its demonic *and* popish nature—which they held to be the same thing. Spanish Catholics feared the presence of women, some of them wearing men's garb on the stage. English Protestants feared the presence of women in the audiences and those who appeared to be women through their costume. In both cases, they believed that theater undermined pious forms of masculinity.

Opponents of the stage saw the playhouse as the immoral and all-too-public center of a dangerous debate between right and wrong—between godly, masculine health and demonic, womanish disease—taking place in the public realm. They hoped to sway public opinion with their arguments. Such views gained some traction as civil war, revolt, and revolution framed policy-making in Catholic Spain and Protestant England during the middle decades of the seventeenth century. These years were fraught with wars, meteorological disasters, plagues, floods, and famines.[44] Many feared that the end of the world was close at hand. In such times, luxuries and pastimes like theater made convenient targets for scapegoating and reform.

Yet even as Spanish antitheatricalists continued to write and as reformers sought to cure the state and to purge behaviors they deemed weak, unmanly, and immoral, the *corrales de comedias* remained open.[45] As the 1640s began, the commercial theaters of Spain continued to operate and attract audiences. Urban dwellers still attended plays not only in Madrid and Seville but also in many other cities on both sides of the Atlantic on a regular basis. Similarly, at least three of London's public playhouses and three of its six private theaters continued to function and draw playgoers. Theatrical activity seems to have continued even in the wake of rising prices, revolts in Portugal and Catalonia, war in Scotland, armed rebellion in Ireland, floods, and outbreaks of the plague that all contributed to a general sense of decline and disaster. It was only extreme political crisis that changed this pattern.

In the spring of 1640, London began to experience increasingly polarized political activity. Although Parliament met only briefly, its closure by King Charles I brought pressing problems into clear view: the unpopularity of the war against the Scots, the resentment of Charles's advisers, and the depletion of the treasury. When what would become known as the Long Parliament was called on 3 November 1640, the work of constitutional change and reform of abuses began. Parliamentarians began to debate the place of the stage. On 26 January 1642 Sir Edward Partridge proposed that the Lord Chamberlain should move that Charles I suppress all theater performances. Although Partridge attended conformist services, he was an observer of the puritan Sabbath, kept a religious household, and had worked with the nonconformist faction in Sandwich.[46] He encouraged the closure of the playhouses because of the "times of calamity in Ireland and the distractions in this kingdom." However, Mr. Edmund Waller, a wealthy poet, and Mr. John Pym, who had been involved in the loan resistance movement and in the agitation in calling for the parliament, opposed the motion. Waller and Pym claimed that it would hurt the trade of actors and playwrights. For the time being, the Long Parliament laid the motion aside, but the issue resurfaced several months later.[47] On the 31 August 1642 the Long Parliament, after celebrating a public fast and hearing two sermons—neither of which seem to have made any explicit reference to public theater—formulated the order that "all Stage Plays may be put down during this Time of Distractions."[48] Meanwhile, the Werburgh Street Theater in Dublin had already closed and been turned to military purposes, and the actors who had been contracted to work there had fled.

When Parliament proclaimed, "Publike Sports do not well agree with Publike Calamities, nor Publike Stage-playes with the Seasons of Humiliation," many of its members probably intended for this ban on performance to be temporary. However, this first prohibition gave opponents of the stage what they wanted—if not for the reasons that they wanted it. The 1642 proclamation was furthered by repeated ordinances in October of 1647 and February of 1648. The ordinance of 1648 decreed that "all Stage-players and Players of Interludes and common Playes, are hereby declared to be, and are, and shall be taken to be Rogues."[49] Initially, this second set of bans was not stringently enforced, but raids by soldiers in 1649 led to the imprisonment of actors. Over the next few years more zealous enforcers of the law stripped the interiors of playhouses and demolished the Blackfriars Theatre.[50]

It is worth noting, however, that lawful drama did not completely disappear from England during this period either. Mark Bayer has recently argued that magistrates allowed some specific performances at the Red Bull during the Civil War because the actors directed part of the admission fees collected toward poor rates. In fact, he compellingly suggests authorities allowed the Red Bull's continued existence because of its charitable connections with the wider community.[51] In 1653 Cromwell allowed the position of the Master of the Revels to be revived. William Davenant, who had managed the Cockpit Theatre prior to the Civil War and had written masques for the English court, received permission to stage plays commercially during the period of the Protectorate. Davenant, however, was careful to avoid certain topics and put on performances that promoted patriotic English feeling. By staging works like *The Cruelty of the Spaniards in Peru* he avoided political controversy at home and further promoted the anti-Spanish sentiment—this is perhaps not surprising since England and Spain were once again at war in 1658 when the performance occurred.[52]

Meanwhile, during the 1640s Philip IV faced revolts in Portugal and in Catalonia as well as a serious dynastic crisis. The queen consort Isabel of Bourbon died on 6 October 1644. Closing the public theaters for a brief period for royal mourning or during an outbreak of disease was routine, and certainly the queen's death was the primary catalyst for closing the *corrales de comedias* in Castile in 1644. After the brief closure, they reopened. On 5 August 1645, Philip IV decreed that the price of admission to the theaters should be increased by 25 percent. These price increases were likely in part due to inflation, but they were also meant to help fund the frontier hospitals—and thus aid the soldiers who were fighting to put down the rebellions in Catalonia and Portugal—as well as to further aid city hospitals.[53]

In spite of these attempts to increase the charitable capacities of the *corrales,* the king felt God was punishing him, as financial problems, foreign wars, rebellious subjects, and the deaths of family members continued to plague his reign, inspiring him to give more credence to the antitheatricalists' notion that plays were the "plague of the republic." In a letter written on 7 March 1646 to one of his spiritual advisors, the Franciscan nun and mystic María de Ágreda, Philip IV declared, "I clearly see that my sins, even the most minor of them, deserve greater penance."[54] He confided to her that he had truly recognized the need for reforming his kingdoms, noting, in a way that is again suggestive of the links between dress, appearances, and concerns about the theater, that "orders had been given to regulate the clothing of women and of men and for the performance of *comedias* to be ceased." Ágreda replied that although she was "very poor and weak" her "gratitude was immense."[55]

Ágreda was far from weak—after all, she purportedly bilocated to the New World—but this rhetorical strategy seems to have worked.[56] On 28 March 1646 her gratitude increased when the Council of Castile recommended that the performances of *comedias* be suspended indefinitely, and the king acted in accordance with its advice. This was a decision that impacted other parts of Spain as well, as the order extended to Aragón. Duarte Fernández Álvarez de Toledo, the Viceroy of Valencia, wrote the king in late May of 1646 just to be sure that "the order to cease all performances of plays" that had been dispatched "also included these kingdoms." He also noted that "here they have already begun to discuss how the hospitals might be compensated for this loss of funds."[57] The death of Balthasar Carlos, the prince and heir of Philip IV, on 9 October 1646, undoubtedly further prolonged the closures of the *corrales.* His death left the Spanish Empire without a prince and heir, and Spaniards in a prolonged state of mourning. Even the performances of *autos sacramentales* during festivals like Corpus Christi initially ceased, as the archival records of city governments in Madrid, Seville, and other cities demonstrate. Compare, for example, the records of the commission for the Corpus festival in Seville in the years 1644 (prior to the death of Isabel of Bourbon in October) and then in 1646 and 1647 when theatrical performances had been banned. Acting companies were commissioned and paid for their services in the 1644 Corpus Christi celebrations. In 1646 and 1647 there is no documentation to support the hiring of or paying of directors, actors, and artisans for the staging of religious one-act plays as part of the festive activities.[58]

However, Philip IV's resolve to avoid the sins brought on by dramatic performances soon began to falter. At the end of 1647 the king had masques presented at court to celebrate the birthday of his niece and new wife, Mariana of Austria. The performance of *autos sacramentales* on feast days resumed, and in 1648 Philip IV ordered the Council of Castile to reexamine the issue of the propriety of the theater closures. Before reconsidering the qualities and characteristics of plays, the Council reminded the king that some earlier reports on the subject had concluded that the crown's subjects needed some way to alleviate their cares, and that a portion of "the admission fees were for the maintenance and support of the hospitals and the care and rearing of orphans and foundlings of this court and other cities."[59] While the king hesitated and the Council deliberated, the hospitals mounted pressure. Petitions and letters came from the administrators of hospitals in numerous cities, citing the "very great necessity and poverty" of patients in cities like Seville.[60] Administrators stressed that "things have been deteriorating so much and the needs of the parishioners have been increasing."[61] The city fathers of Valencia petitioned in August of 1650 to be given the rights, authority, and licenses to put on performances to aid the General Hospital of Valencia because "the benefits that would proceed from them would be very significant and provide for the said hospital."[62]

In 1651 the commercial playhouses of Spain officially reopened, some were renovated, and performances resumed. This took place in spite of the continued admonitions of opponents of the stage such as Luis Crespí de Borja, a Valencian doctor and theologian who spent a number of years in Rome and later became the bishop of Orihuela. He claimed that the theater had both pagan and demonic origins and that, even though audiences comprised of learned men and some clergymen misguidedly attended them, plays were execrable. In a tract that he wrote in 1649 in response to the issue of whether or not the *corrales de comedias* should be reopened, he reminded his audience that plays were the cause of "immodesty in dress, insolence in women, dishonesty in dealings, licentiousness in dances and interludes, [and] libidinousness in love."[63] Sermonizing that it was sacrilegious to tie the profane and indecent entertainment of the Spanish playhouses to the charitable works of city hospitals, orphanages, and houses of recovery for reformed prostitutes, he compared those who claimed this legitimated theater and made it a social good to Christ's betrayer Judas. In the hopes of destroying the one argument that defenders of the playhouse had used to win royal, civil, and even some ecclesiastical authorities to their side, the Valencian theologian declared that "one is not justified in sinning to assist the poor, nor should one tell even a white lie to help an innocent."[64] This argument was not so dissimilar to that made almost eighty years earlier in Barcelona by the Christian humanist Diego Pérez de Valdivia. He had noted that due to the "large number of widows, elderly, infirm, honest beggars, [and the] great necessity" in early modern Spain there were numerous proponents of the playhouses that provided charity to hospitals and convalescence houses. However, according to Pérez de Valdivia, this argument held little weight because of "how small" the amounts of alms provided by the theaters were.[65] Such claims were perhaps significant exaggerations—even white lies—as the proceeds from the theaters actually provided quite substantive sums to the hospitals.[66]

Therefore, in the Spanish Atlantic World, the situation developed rather differently than it did in the Anglo Atlantic; despite the publication of even more antitheatrical discourses in the seventeenth century, the Spanish theaters reopened more swiftly. This was in large part due to the relationship between the *corrales de comedias*, the hospitals, and the municipal governments throughout the Spanish Empire. In spite of admonishments from antitheatrical polemicists who claimed that the sins of acting on the stage and attending the theater created a diseased and emasculated state and could not be balanced by the charitable works funded by admission fees, the responses of city fathers and the royal government were ultimately ambivalent at best and pro-theater at worst, from the perspective of opponents of the stage. As Guzmán had observed some decades before, the early modern playhouses of Spain had defenders and protectors "of which there were many, and not a few, nor were they of little authority."[67] These authorities realized that hospitals needed money to care for their patients, and this trumped the claims of writers like Mariana, Guzmán, Palafox, and Crespí de Borja that banning theater would cure the diseased body politic. Indeed, hospital administrators perhaps needed these funds even more in the mid-seventeenth century than usual in many cities of Spain due to the disasters of war, famine, and flood that characterized this period. In the case of Puebla, even the presence of an antitheatrical bishop could not put an end to the successfully integrated theater.

In England and Ireland, the theaters reopened for quite different reasons—largely, monarchical and military prerogative with much less concern for theater's charitable benefit to institutions of public health and welfare. Upon the return of monarchy to England after a long exile in Paris, King Charles II authorized the formation of two acting companies in Westminster. Under the influence of continental trends, which also influenced the structure and plot of written dramas, the Restoration theaters legally allowed the presence of women on the stage. While Spanish lawmakers increasingly sought to prevent female performers from wearing breeches onstage, English playgoers were progressively more able to see the legs of famous actresses like Eleanor Gwyn. Nicknamed Nell, this famous performer—like Maria Calderón had half a century before—drew the attention of the monarch and became his mistress. The Restoration theater helped to create a new generation of opponents of the stage. Similar concerns developed in Dublin, where actresses began to perform in 1662. One historian has contended that the growing association of actresses and female playwrights with prostitution limited the opportunities for women to write for the theater there. Consequently, acting companies rarely performed plays written by women in Dublin during the last decades of the seventeenth century.[68] Actresses, though, would continue to face the vitriol of polemicists in the Anglo Atlantic. Such opponents included Jeremy Collier, who asked the rhetorical question: "For can one die of an easier disease than diversion?"[69] Hospital administrators throughout the realms of the Spanish monarchy knew the answer to this question even if antitheatrical polemicists still did not.

Conclusion

The previous chapter devoted a great deal of attention to those who opposed the stage for various reasons. These antitheatrical authors feared the stage's ability to influence behavior, and indeed some proponents of plays made that same argument—albeit one that reached different conclusions about the instructive qualities of theater. Some, such as the English poet, courtier, and soldier Philip Sidney, believed that plays and poetry could serve to educate and instill virtue. In his *Apology for Poetry,* Sidney contended that, while the philosopher could only educate those who were already learned, the poet could help to educate all members of society by moving them to virtue and right behavior. While Sidney acknowledged that many playwrights did not live up to this potential, he still believed that the "right use of Comedy will (I think) by nobody be blamed, and much less the high and excellent Tragedy, that openeth the greatest wounds, and showeth forth the ulcers that are covered with tissue. . . . that with stirring the affects of admiration and commiseration, teacheth the uncertainty of this world, and upon how weak foundations gilden roofs are builded."[1]

An Apology for Poetry is a work of literary theory that contains a similar argument made by Spanish opponents and proponents of the playhouse: theater served as a mirror to early modern society.[2] For those who feared its power, the mirror showed the grotesquely feminine and diseased body politic of a society in decay. For those who believed in its power as a mechanism of social good and urban propriety, theater had the potential to move and possibly reform those in the audience. It was both sides of this complex issue, as well as the plight of the hospitals, that the Council of Castile weighed in the balance while considering reopening the playhouses in 1648. As we have seen, theater may have often fallen short of its incredible potential either to teach morality or to tempt into sinfulness, but it was an influential institution of urban life—occasionally inspiring violence in the streets, spreading fashions and news, and inciting conflict between competing authorities.

During the early modern period, it was nowhere more influential than it was in the Spanish Atlantic World. No other European national theater—not the English, the French, the German, or the Dutch—matched that of Spain in terms of output of plays, and no other European theater was transported to and adapted to American colonies to the same degree at this point in history. Since some Spanish playwrights were born in or spent time in these overseas viceroyalties, and since they and others wrote about New World events and incorporated characters who were *indios* and *indianos,* this became truly an Atlantic World theater phenomenon. In both Castile and colonial Mexico commercial drama intersected with issues of charity and public health to significant degrees.

This asymmetrical comparison of the commercial theaters of early modern Spain and England has demonstrated that they shared similar trajectories in many ways: the emergence of licensed acting companies, the thriving commercial drama of their most urbanized, metropolitan centers, and the patronage of monarchs and nobles, and, eventually, the transatlantic nature of colonial drama. Yet there were significant differences in these theater histories, too. Women appeared onstage much earlier and more frequently directed the actors performing onstage in the Spanish Empire. Theater became linked to municipal governments through charitable giving, and this relationship created a space for commercial theater to become a part of daily life in Spanish cities, not just in Castile, the heart of Spain, but also in the Americas. This relationship connected Spanish commercial drama to charitable giving and to questions of public health and social order in ways that it did not in English cities. In Mexico City, for example, early theatrical performances actually took place in the physical space of the hospital itself. Although there were some obstacles and plenty of problems, the financial reality of this symbiotic relationship meant that social work and public health in the Spanish Atlantic relied on the productivity and popularity of commercial drama. This system persisted there into the nineteenth century. Such a link between charitable care and commercial drama never developed as fully in the English system in spite of early legislation to encourage such a connection in London and the charitable undertakings of Nicholas Woolfe in Bristol.

The charitable function of playhouses throughout the universal Spanish monarchy helped to legitimize and popularize theater. The *corrales* of Madrid, Seville, Mexico City, Puebla de los Angeles, and other cities not examined in this book were centrally located in what contemporaries considered to be respectable neighborhoods. Although these theaters were generally compartmentalized, with private boxes for the nobles who could afford to rent them (thus providing more money to the hospitals), and segregated by gender and to some extent occupation with the *cazuela* and *tertulia,* their audiences engaged in a theatrical public that was participatory. The result was the largest theatrical output of the Renaissance, and theater treated the public to entertainment and health care on both sides of the Spanish Atlantic. In other words, a key difference between the public theater of Spain and that of England was the earlier and more developed role that commercial drama took on in provincial and colonial cities—both important centers of empire and quieter towns—in the kingdoms of the Spanish monarchy.

The *corrales* treated the public of spectators to two hours of entertainment in the inn-yard theaters as they provided essential financial assistance to the hospitals of Spanish cities. They provided a trade for many actors, actresses, directors, and playwrights. The *corrales* also enabled other economic opportunities for food vendors, carpenters, and municipal and corporate bodies. For these reasons, authorities generally viewed theater with more ambivalence than outright animosity, even if they were not outright "friends of seeing farces" like Don Antonio González, Rodrigo Calderon, or the Marquis of Cerralvo.[3] "*Al fin y al cabo,*" as the Spanish playwrights and the actors who delivered their lines would say at the close of the performance, the centrality of the Spanish theater in urban daily life and its connection to assisting the poor and diseased patients of the hospitals expanded the real and discursive spaces in which theater entertained, influenced, and treated the public.

NOTES

INTRODUCTION

1. Victor Dixon, *En busca del fénix: quince estudios sobre Lope de Vega y su teatro* (Madrid: Iberoamericana, 2013), 93.

2. Ibid., 105.

3. Claudia Parodi, "Lope y Calderón en Náhuatl: Teatro Indianizado," in Ignacio Arellano y J. A. Rodríguez Garrido, eds., *El teatro en la hispanoamérica colonial* (Pamplona: Editorial Iberoamericana, 2008), 99–117.

4. James Shapiro, ed., *Shakespeare in America: An Anthology from the Revolution to Now* (New York: Library of America, 2014).

5. Andrew Gurr, *The Shakespearean Stage 1574–1642* (Cambridge: Cambridge University Press, 2006), 9.

6. J. E. Varey and N. D. Shergold, *Teatros y Comedias en Madrid: 1600–1650: Estudio y Documentos* (London: Tamesis, 1971), 57.

7. Melveena McKendrick, *Theatre in Spain 1490–1700* (Cambridge: Cambridge University Press, 1989), 49.

8. Joaquin de Entrambasaguas, *Lope de Vega y su tiempo* (Barcelona: Teide, 1962), 254.

9. S. M. Imamuddin, *Muslim Spain 711–1492 A.D.: A Sociological Study* (Leiden: Brill Academic Press, 1997), 220–29.

10. Michele Clouse, *Medicine, Government, and Public Health in Philip II's Spain: Shared Interest, Competing Authorities* (Burlington: Ashgate, 2011).

11. Carmen Sanz Ayán y Bernardo J. García García, *Teatros y comediantes en el Madrid de Felipe II* (Madrid: Editorial Complutense, 2000).

12. Varey and Shergold, *Teatros y Comedias en Madrid*; J. E. Varey and N. D. Shergold, *Los Arriendos de Los Corrales de Comedias de Madrid: 1587–1719* (London: Tamesis, 1987); Charles Davis and J. E. Varey, *Los corrales de comedias y los hospitales de Madrid: 1574–1615* (London: Tamesis, 1997); Charles Davis and J. E. Varey, *Los corrales de comedias y los hospitales de Madrid: 1615–1849* (London: Tamesis, 1997).

13. Steven Mullaney, *The Place of the Stage: License, Play, and Power in Renaissance England* (Chicago: University of Chicago Press, 1988), 72; Michael MacDonald, *Mystical*

Bedlam: Madness, Anxiety and Healing in Seventeenth-Century England (Cambridge: Cambridge University Press, 1983).

14. Kenneth Jackson, *Separate Theaters: Bethlem ("Bedlam") Hospital and the Shakespearean Stage* (Newark: University of Delaware Press, 2005).

15. José Antonio Maravall, *La cultura del barroco: análisis de una estructura histórica* (Barcelona: Ariel, 1980).

16. José María Díez Borque, *Sociedad y teatro en la España de Lope de Vega* (Barcelona: Casa Editorial, S.A., 1978), 140–47.

17. See, for example, Edward Wilson, "Nuevos Documentos Sobre Las Controversias Teatrales, 1650–1681," in *Actas del Segundo Congreso Internacional de Hispanista* (Nimega: Instituto Español de la Universidad de Nimega, 1967), 155–70; J. H. Elliott, "Self Perception and Decline in Early Seventeenth-Century Spain," *Past & Present* 74 (1977): 41–61; Elizabeth Lehfeldt, "Ideal Men: Masculinity and Decline in Seventeenth Century Spain," *Renaissance Quarterly* 61, no. 2 (2008): 463–94.

18. Jodi Campbell, *Monarchy, Political Culture, and Drama in Seventeenth-Century Madrid: Theater of Negotiation* (Burlington: Ashgate, 2006).

19. See, for example, Mullaney, *The Place of the Stage,* which for a long time defined the social as well as the spatial place of the theater and still exerts great influence over the field; Anthony Dawson and Paul Yachnin, eds., *The Culture of Playgoing in Shakespeare's England: A Collaborative Debate* (Cambridge: Cambridge University Press, 2001); and Andrew Gurr, *Playgoing in Shakespeare's London* (Cambridge: Cambridge University Press, 2004).

20. Paul Yachnin, *Stage-wrights: Shakespeare, Jonson, Middleton, and the Making of Theatrical Value* (Philadelphia: University of Pennsylvania Press, 1997); and Mark Bayer, *Theatre, Community, and Civic Engagement in Jacobean London* (Iowa City: University of Iowa Press, 2011).

21. E. K. Chambers, *The Elizabethan Stage* (Oxford: Clarendon Press, 1924), 5 vols.

22. Richard Dutton, *Mastering the Revels: The Regulation and Censorship of Renaissance English Drama* (Iowa City: University of Iowa Press, 1991); and Richard Dutton, *Licensing, Censorship and Authorship in Early Modern England: Buggeswords* (New York: Palgrave, 2000).

23. Margot Heinemann, *Puritanism and Theatre: Thomas Middleton and Opposition Drama under the Early Stuarts* (Cambridge: Cambridge University Press, 1980).

24. Walter Cohen, *Drama of a Nation: Public Theater in Renaissance England and Spain* (Ithaca, NY: Cornell University Press, 1985); John Loftis, *Renaissance Drama in England and Spain: Topical Allusion and History Plays* (Princeton: Princeton University Press, 1987), 4; Ivan Cañadas, *Public Theatres of Golden Age Madrid and Tudor-Stuart London: Class, Gender, and Festive Community* (Burlington: Ashgate, 2005).

25. Margaret R. Greer, "A Tale of Three Cities: The Place of the Theatre in Early Modern Madrid, Paris and London," *Bulletin of Hispanic Studies* 77 (2000): 398–401.

26. Adam Versényi, *Theatre in Latin America: Religion, Politics, and Culture from Cortes to the 1980s* (Cambridge: Cambridge University Press, 1993).

CHAPTER ONE

1. Hispanic Society of America (hereafter HSA), Altamira, II-7-22, 24 iii 1586.

2. HSA, Altamira, II-7-29, 21 viii 1586. Unless otherwise noted, all translations are mine.

3. Walter Cohen, *Drama of a Nation: Public Theater in Renaissance England and Spain* (Ithaca, NY: Cornell University Press, 1985); and Jean Howard, *Theater of a City: The Places of London Comedy, 1598–1642* (Philadelphia: University of Pennsylvania Press, 2007), 2.

4. David Ringrose, "The Impact of a New Capital City: Madrid, Toledo, and New Castile, 1560–1660," *Journal of Economic History* 33, no. 4 (December 1973): 761–91. These population statistics are adapted from Friedrich Edelmayer, *Philipp II. Die Biographie enes Weltherrschers* (Stuttgart: Kohlhammer, 2009), 118–19.

5. Beatriz Blasco Esquivias, *iAgua Va! La higiene urbana en Madrid (1561–1761)* (Madrid: Caja Madrid, 1998), 35.

6. Melveena McKendrick, *Woman and Society in the Spanish Drama of the Golden Age: A Study of the Mujer Varonil* (Cambridge: Cambridge University Press, 1974), 34.

7. María José del Río Barredo, *Madrid, Urbs Regia: La capital ceremonial de la Monarquía Católica* (Madrid: Marcial Pons, 2000), 7.

8. Jane Albrecht, *The Playgoing Public of Madrid in the Time of Tirso de Molina* (New Orleans: University Press of the South, 2001).

9. Carmen Sanz Ayán and Bernardo García García, *Teatros y comediantes en el Madrid de Felipe II* (Madrid: Editorial Complutense, 2000), 58.

10. Teresa Huguet-Termes, "Madrid Hospitals and Welfare in the Context of the Hapsburg Empire," *Medical History Supplement* 29 (2009): 70.

11. See Jon Arrizabalaga, Andrew Cunningham, and Ole Peter Grell, *Health Care and Poor Relief in Counter-Reformation Europe* (New York: Routledge, 2005); John Patrick Donnelly and Michael W. Maher, *Confraternities and Catholic Reform in Italy, France, and Spain* (Kirksville, MO: Truman State University Press, 1999); Maureen Flynn, *Sacred Charities: Confraternities and Social Welfare in Spain, 1400–1700* (Ithaca, NY: Cornell University Press, 1989); John Henderson, *The Renaissance Hospital: Healing the Body and Healing the Soul* (New Haven: Yale University Press, 2006); and Valentina Tikoff, "Gender and Juvenile Charity, Tradition and Reform: Assistance for Young People in Eighteenth-Century Seville," *Eighteenth-Century Studies* 41, no. 3 (2008): 307–35.

12. Miguel Ángel García Sánchez, "Mujeres pobres y sociabilidad en el Madrid moderno: el Hospital de la Pasión, 1565–1700," *Torre de los lujanes* 52 (2004): 206.

13. Charles Davis and J. E. Varey, *Los corrales de comedias y los hospitales de Madrid, 1574–1615: estudio y documentos* (London: Tamesis, 1997), 89–90.

14. Sanz Ayán and García García, *Teatros y comediantes*, 5.

15. Davis and Varey, *Los corrales de comedias y los hospitales de Madrid, 1574–1615*, 97.

16. N. D. Shergold, "Ganassa and the 'Commedia dell'arte' in Sixteenth-Century Spain," *The Modern Language Review* 51, no. 3 (July 1956): 359–68.

17. Sanz Ayán and García García, *Teatros y comediantes*, 9.

18. Davis and Varey, *Los corrales de comedias y los hospitales de Madrid*, 117–18.

19. Archivo Regional de la Comunidad de Madrid (hereafter ARM), Signatura 5310, Leg. 4, 24 iv 1584.

20. Margaret R. Greer, "A Tale of Three Cities: The Place of the Theatre in Early Modern Madrid, Paris and London," *Bulletin of Hispanic Studies* 77, no. 1 (2000): 395.

21. Ibid. See also Sanz Ayán and García García, *Teatros y comediantes*, 15–18.

22. See Rachael Ball, "Wine, Water, and *Aloja:* Consuming Interests in the Theater During the Reign of Philip IV," *Comedia Performance* 10, no. 1 (Spring 2013), 59–92; and J. E. Varey and N. D. Shergold, *Los Arriendos de Los Corrales de Comedias de Madrid: 1587–1719* (London: Tamesis, 1987), 67.

23. John J. Allen, *The Reconstruction of a Spanish Golden Age Playhouse: El Corral del Príncipe (1583–1744)* (Gainesville: University of Florida Press, 1983), 5.

24. Georgina Dopico Black, *Perfect Wives, Other Women: Adultery and Inquisition in Early Modern Spain* (Durham, NC: Duke University Press, 2001).

25. Hugo Rennert, "Review of *Obras de Lope de Vega* by Emilio Cotalero y Mori," *Modern Language Review* 14, no. 4 (1919): 439–51.

26. N. D. Shergold and J. E. Varey, *Genealogía, Origen y Noticias de los comediantes de España* (London: Tamesis, 1985), 407.

27. J. E. Varey and N. D. Shergold, *Teatros y Comedias en Madrid: 1600–1650: Estudio y Documentos* (London: Tamesis, 1971), 57.

28. AHN, Consejo de Castilla, Leg. 7051, No. 16, 5 x 1590.

29. Charles Davis and J. E. Varey, *Actividad teatral en la región de Madrid según los protocolos de Juan García de Albertos, 1634–1660* (London: Tamesis, 2003), 1:24.

30. BNE, Mss 12917, fol. 47, undated. See also José Subira, *El gremio de representantes españoles y la cofradía de nuestra señora de la novena* (Madrid: CSIC, 1960), 18.

31. Teresa Ferrer Valls, *Diccionario biográfico de actores del teatro clásico español (DICAT): Edición digital* (Kassel: Edition Reichenberger, 2008), "La fundación de la Cofradía de la Novena," Folio 14r.

32. Teresa Huguet-Termes, "Madrid Hospitals and Welfare in the Context of the Hapsburg Empire," *Medical History Supplement* 29 (2009): 64–85.

33. In the early seventeenth century a loaf of bread cost around 34 *maravedís*.

34. Carmen Sanz Ayán and Bernardo García García, *Teatros y comediantes*, 71.

35. Ibid.

36. See J. E. Varey and N. D. Shergold, *Los arriendos de los corrales de comedias de Madrid*, 67–68. Also see Ball, "Water, Wine, and Aloja."

37. ARM, Signatura 5083, Leg. 8, 15 iv 1610.

38. Archivo de la Villa de Madrid (hereafter AMM), Sección 2, Leg. 475, No. 2, undated.

39. See, for example, the audit accounts of the Hospital de la Pasión from 1613. ARM, Signatura 8483, Carpeta 1.

40. ARM, Signatura 5347, Leg. 5, 11 iv 1615.

41. AMM, Sección Secretaría, Libros de Actas, Tomo 33, fol. 181r, undated.

42. Davis and Varey, *Los corrales de comedias y los hospitales de Madrid,* 84–85.

43. ARM, Signatura 5083, Leg. 32, 30 ix 1633.

44. See McKendrick, *Theatre in Spain,* 178; and Davis and Varey, *Los corrales de comedias y los hospitales de Madrid,* 159. The same year, construction began on the Coliseo at the Buen Retiro. The Coliseo was simultaneously a court theater and a public playhouse and opened for performances two years later on 4 February 1640.

45. AMM, Signatura 4, Leg. 52, No. 131, 24 ix 1632.

46. Ibid.

47. Ángel González Palencia, *Noticias de Madrid, 1621–1627* (Madrid: Sección de Cultura e Información Artes Graficas Municipales, 1942), 59–60.

48. Ibid.

49. J. E. Varey y N. D. Shergold, *Los arriendos de los corrales de comedias de Madrid: 1587–1719* (London: Tamesis, 1987), 93.

50. Archivo del Palacio Real, Buen Retiro, 11744, Expediente 18, 24 i 1648.

51. Teresa Ferrer Valls, *Diccionario biográfico,* "La fundación de la Cofradía de la Novena," Folio 17r.

52. Pilar Huelga Criado, *En la raya de Portugal: solidaridad y tensiones en la comunidad judeoconversa* (Salamanca: Ediciones Universidad de Salamanca, 1994), 113.

53. AMM, Signatura 2, Leg. 468, No. 9, 14 x 1644.

54. Ibid., 13 ii, 1645.

55. Miguel Angel Garcia Sanchez, *Análisis sociológico de la pobreza en Madrid, 1578–1650* (PhD diss., Universidad Complutense de Madrid, 2004), 108–10.

56. Esquivias, *¡Agua Va!,* 85; and Robert Jütte, *Poverty and Deviance in Early Modern Europe* (Cambridge: Cambridge University Press, 1994), 174.

57. ARM, Sección Visitas, Signatura 8483, Carpeta 2, fol. 4r–5r.

58. Teresa Huguet-Termes, "Madrid Hospitals and Welfare in the Context of the Hapsburg Empire," *Medical History Supplement* 29 (2009): 81.

59. ARM, Sección Visitas, Signatura 8483, Carpeta 1, fol. 26r–27v.

60. ARM, Sección Visitas, Signatura 8483, Carpeta 1, fol. 1.

61. ARM, Sección Visitas, Signatura 8483, Carpeta 1, fol. 30. This particular set of documents corresponds to June through September of 1613, two years before the shift in the administration of the hospitals.

62. ARM, Sección Visitas, Signatura 8483, Carpeta 1, fol. 41r–v.

63. See, for example, ARM, Sección Visitas, Signatura 5169, Carpeta 1, No. 76/17, 134r.

64. Gregorio de Aldana y Arellano, *Los hospitales reales, general, y passion de esta Corte; con sus convalencias, obligaciones, salario, su govierno politico, y assistencia, rentas que gozan, con la quenta y razon de lo que gastaron el año passado de 1665* (Madrid, 1666), 11.

65. Ibid., 26.

66. Leonardo Galdiano y Croy, *Breve tratado de los hospitales y casas de recogimiento de esta Corte . . .* (Madrid, 1677), 15.

67. Ibid., 4–5 and 15.

68. Ibid., 6–7.

69. Quoted in Alan Somerset, "Cultural Poetics, or Historical Prose? The Places of the Stage," in *Medieval and Renaissance Drama in England,* ed. John Pitcher (Fairleigh, PA: Dickinson University Press, 1999), 11:42.

70. Andrew Gurr, *The Shakespearean Stage, 1574–1642* (Cambridge: Cambridge University Press, 2006), 20.

71. Michael Shapiro, *Children of the Revels: The Boy Companies of Shakespeare's Time and Their Plays* (New York: Columbia University Press, 1977).

72. Joseph Black, ed., *The Martin Marprelate Tracts: A Modernized and Annotated Edition* (Cambridge: Cambridge University Press, 2008), xvi.

73. Richard Dutton, "The Revels Office and the Boy Companies, 1600–1613: New Perspectives," *English Literary Renaissance* 32, no. 2 (2002): 325.

74. Peter Thomson, *Shakespeare's Theatre* (New York: Routledge, 1983).

75. Alan Somerset, "Cultural Poetics or Historical Prose?," 42–43.

76. Melissa Aaron, *Global Economics: A History of the Theater Business, the Chamberlain's/King's Men, and Their Plays, 1599–1642* (Newark: University of Delaware Press, 2005), 31–33.

77. Mark Bayer, *Theatre, Community, and Civic Engagement in Jacobean London* (Iowa City: University of Iowa Press, 2011).

78. Howard, *Theater of a City,* 93.

79. Paul Slack, "Hospitals, Workhouses, and the Relief of the Poor in Early Modern London," in *Health Care and Poor Relief in Protestant Europe, 1500–1700,* ed. Ole Peter Grell and Andrew Cunningham (London: Routledge, 1997), 234–51. See also Paul Slack, *From Reformation to Improvement: Public Welfare in Early Modern England* (Oxford: Clarendon Press, 1999).

80. A. L. Beier, "Social Problems in Elizabethan London," *Journal of Interdisciplinary History* 9, no. 2 (Autumn 1978): 203–21.

81. Claire S. Schen, "Constructing the Poor in Early Seventeenth-Century London," *Albion* 32, no. 3 (Autumn 2000): 450–63.

82. *An example for all those that make no conscience of swearing and forswearing shewing Gods heauy iudgement vpon a maid-seruant in London, who forswore her selfe, and now lies rotting in S. Bartholomewes Hospitall in Smithfield, where many resort daily to see her. To the tune of Aime not too high* (London: G. Purslow for J. Wright, c. 1625). EEBO.

83. See for example Thomas Vicary, *A profitable treatise of the anatomie of mans body: compyled by that excellent chirurgion, M. Thomas Vicary esquire, seriaunt chirurgion to king Henry the eyght, to king Edward the. vj. to Queene Mary, and to our most gracious Soueraigne Lady Queene Elizabeth, and also cheefe chirurgion of S. Bartholomewes Hospital. Which work is newly reuyued, corrected, and published by the chirurgions of the same hospital now beeing* (London: Henry Bamforde, 1577). EEBO.

84. José Antonio Maravall, *La cultura del barroco: análisis de una estructura histórica* (Barcelona: Ariel, 1980); Ruth MacKay, "The Maravall Problem: A Historical Inquiry," *Bulletin of the Comediantes* 65 (2013): 45–56; and Jodi Campbell, *Monarchy, Political Culture, and Drama in Seventeenth-Century Madrid: Theater of Negotiation* (Burlington: Ashgate, 2006).

85. William R. Blue, *Spanish Comedies and Historical Contexts in the 1620s* (University Park: Pennsylvania State University Press, 1996).

86. Tirso de Molina, *Los balcones de Madrid,* Act III, Verses 3177–530, ed. Vern G. Williamsen and J. T. Abraham, http://w3.coh.arizona.edu/projects/comedia/tirso/Balmad.html.

87. Tirso de Molina, *Don Gil de las calzas verdes,* ed. Alonso Zamora Vicente (Madrid: Castalia, 1990), 291.

88. Ibid.

89. Alexander Leggatt has pointed this out in *Citizen Comedy in the Age of Shakespeare* (Toronto: University of Toronto Press, 1973).

90. Charles Barber, ed., *Middleton: A Chaste Maid in Cheapside* (Berkeley: University of California Press, 1969).

91. Howard, *Theater of a City,* 140.

92. Luis Cabrera de Córdoba, *Relaciones de las cosas sucedidas en la corte de España desde 1599 hasta 1614* (Madrid: J. Matin Alegria, 1857), 85.

93. Ibid.

94. Ibid, 87.

95. Thomas Middleton, *A Game at Chess,* ed. T. H. Howard Hill (Manchester: Manchester University Press, 1993). On the Spanish Match, see Glyn Redworth, *The Prince and the Infanta: The Cultural Politics of the Spanish Match* (New Haven: Yale University Press, 2003).

96. Archivo General de Simancas (hereafter AGS), Consejo de Estado, Libro 375, 20 viii 1624. The endorsement shows the letter was received on 3 ix 1624.

97. Geraldo da Vinha, *Carta y relación verdadera del nacimiento, vida y muerte de don Rodrigo Calderón,* 1621, fol. 203v, BNE VC/224/26.

CHAPTER TWO

1. Ramón Menéndez Pidal, ed., *Primera Crónica General de España* (Madrid: Gredos, 1955), 2:768–69.

2. J. H. Elliott, *Spain and Its World 1500–1700* (New Haven & London: Yale University Press, 1989), 9.

3. David Harris Sacks, *Trade, Society, and Politics in Bristol 1500–1640* (London: Garland, 1985), 2:574–75.

4. See Ignacio Navarrete, *Orphans of Petrarch: Poetry and Theory in the Spanish Renaissance* (Berkeley: University of California Press, 1994).

5. Mary Perry, *Crime and Society in Early Modern Seville* (Hanover, NH: University Press of New England, 1980), 19.

6. Alexandra Parma Cook and Noble David Cook, *The Plague Files: Crisis Management in Sixteenth Century Seville* (Baton Rouge: Louisiana State University Press, 2009), 5.

7. Alexander A. Parker, "Notes on the Religious Drama in Medieval Spain and the Origins of the 'Auto Sacramental,'" *Modern Language Review* 30, no. 2 (April 1935): 170–82.

8. On these processions and the competition they engendered, see Susan Webster, *Art and Ritual in Golden Age Spain: Sevillian Confraternities and the Processional Sculpture of Holy Week* (Princeton: Princeton University Press, 1998).

9. Richard Hesler, "A New Look at the Theatre of Lope de Rueda," *Educational Theatre Journal* 16, no. 1 (March 1964): 51.

10. Quoted in José Sánchez Arjona, *El teatro en Sevilla en los siglos XVI y XVII* (Madrid, 1887; repr., Sevilla: Centro Andaluz de Teatro: Padilla Libros, 1990), 43.

11. Richard Hesler, "A New Look at the Theatre of Lope de Rueda," 49; and Hugo Rennert, *The Spanish Stage in the Time of Lope de Vega* (New York: Dover, 1909, 1963).

12. Luis Milán, *Libro Entitulado El Cortesano; Libro de motes de damas y caballeros,* (Madrid, 1874), 411–12.

13. Teresa Ferrer Valls, *La Práctica Escénica Cortesana: de la época del Emperador a la de Felipe III* (London: Tamesis, 1991), 69–70.

14. Archivo Municipal de Sevilla (hereafter AMS), Sección 1, Caja 40, no. 85, fol. 13r.

15. N. D. Shergold, "Ganassa and the 'Commedia dell'arte' in Sixteenth-Century Spain," *Modern Language Review* 51, no. 3 (July 1956): 359–68.

16. AMS, Sección 1, Caja 40, no. 85, fol. 12r.

17. Quoted in Sánchez Arjona, *El teatro en Sevilla,* 84.

18. Casiano Pellicer, *Tratado histórico sobre el origen y progresos de la comedia y del histrionismo en España* (Madrid, 1804), parte primera, 54.

19. J. E. Varey and N. D. Shergold, *Teatros y Comedias en Madrid: 1600–1650: Estudio y Documentos* (London: Tamesis, 1971), 57, 92.

20. Sánchez Arjona, *El teatro en Sevilla,* 83.

21. Piedad Bolaños Donoso, "Nuevas aportaciones documentales sobre el histrionismo sevillano del siglo XVI," in *La Comedia,* ed. Jean Canavaggio (Madrid: Casa de Velázquez, 1995), 135–38.

22. AHPS, Leg. 9220, fol. 1049r–v.

23. AMS, Session Cuarta, Tomo 37, No. 14, 1619.

24. Rennert, *The Spanish Stage,* 51.

25. AMS, Sección XI, Tomo 62, doc. 39. The numbers are comparable to those from slightly earlier periods in Madrid tracked by Bernardo Garcia and Carmen Sanz on the *corrales de comedias* in Madrid.

26. AHPS, Protocolos, Leg. 17812, fol. 289r.

27. AHPS, Protocolos, Leg. 474, fol. 124r–v.

28. AMS, Sección 1, No. 156, 1631. See also Piedad Bolaños Donoso, "Roque de Figueroa y el 'Cuarto' Coliseo Sevillano (1631–1632)," *Hesperia: Anuario de filología hispánica* 9 (2006): 9–38.

29. Rennert, *The Spanish Stage,* 61.

30. Quoted in José Sanchez Arjona, *Noticias referentes á los anales del teatro en Sevilla desde Lope Rueda hasta fines del siglo XVII (Sevilla: El Rasco, 1898),* 250.

31. Daniel Pineda Novo, *El Teatro de Comedias del Corral de la Montería y del Alcazar de Sevilla* (Sevilla: Guadalquivir Ediciones, 2000), 22.

32. Sanchez Arjona, *Noticias,* 281.

33. AHPS Protocolos, Leg. 17811, fol. 576r. This contract was negotiated while the *autor* was in Cáceres and is dated 7 viii 1623.

34. AHPS, Protocolos, Leg. 473, fol. 742v. Seemingly, Figueroa did not meet the terms of the contract, leading to legal difficulties.

35. Bolaños Donoso, "Roque de Figueroa y el 'Cuarto' Coliseo Sevillano," 9–38.

36. AHPS, Leg. 3642, fol. 133r–134r.

37. Agustín de la Granja, "Una carta con indicaciones escénicas para el autor de comedias Roque de Figueroa," *Revista Canadiense de Estudios Hispánicos* 17, no. 2 (Invierno 1993): 383–88.

38. ARM, Signatura 5083, No. 17, fol. 73r–74r.

39. Pineda Novo, *El Teatro de Comedias,* 70.

40. In April of 1632 Roque de Figueroa complained and asked officials to take steps to prevent audiences from evading payment at the entrances of the Montería. See Sánchez Arjona, *Noticias,* 281.

41. Pineda Novo, *El Teatro de Comedias,* 41.

42. Sánchez Arjona, *Noticias,* 283 and 408. Also see Perry, *Crime and Society in Early Modern Seville,* 154.

43. Sánchez Arjona, *Noticias,* 364–65.

44. An undated petition for the payment of 600 *reales* for the cleaning of the gallery where the members of the religious chapters watched the performances held by the Municipal Archive of Sevilla suggests that the city fathers and church leaders frequented the Coliseo. See AMS, Session Cuarta, Tomo 37, No. 21.

45. Sánchez Arjona, *Noticias,* 255–56.

46. Jan Bloemendal, Peter G. F. Eversmann, and Elsa Streitman, eds., *Drama, Performance, and Debate: Theatre and Public Opinion in the Early Modern Period* (Leiden: Brill, 2013), 6–8.

47. Perry, *Crime and Society,* 144–45.

48. Teresa Scott Soufas, *Women's Acts: Plays by Women Dramatists of Spain's Golden Age* (Lexington: University Press of Kentucky, 1996), 133.

49. AMS, Sección 2, Acuerdos, Carpeta 3, Signatura H-657, sin folio, 19 vi 1624.

50. AMS, Sección 2, Acuerdos, Carpeta 20, Signatura H-674, sin folio, 13 vi 1644.

51. AMS, Sección 2, Acuerdos Carpeta 15, H-669, sin folio, 17 vi 1638.

52. Webster, *Art and Ritual in Golden Age Spain,* 151.

53. Maureen M. Flynn, "Charitable Ritual in Late Medieval and Early Modern Spain," *Sixteenth Century Journal* 16, no. 3 (Autumn 1985): 335–48.

54. Webster, *Art and Ritual in Golden Age Spain,* 29.

55. Juan Ignacio Carmona, *El Sistema de Hospitalidad Pública en la Sevilla del Antiguo Régimen* (Sevilla: Diputación Provincial, 1979), 104–05.

56. Juan Ignacio Carmona, "La reunificación de los Hospitales sevillanos," in *Los Hospitales de Sevilla,* ed. Fernando Chueca Goitia (Sevilla: Real Academia Sevillana de Buenas Letras, 1989), 55.

57. Carmona, *El Sistema de Hospitalidad Pública,* Apéndice IV, 489–92. For population estimates in the port city, see Antonio Domínguez Ortíz, *La sociedad española en el si-*

glo XVII (Madrid: CSIC, 1964), 140–41; and Ruth Pike, *Aristocrats and Traders: Sevillan Society in the Sixteenth Century* (Ithaca, NY: Cornell University Press, 1972), 12–13.

58. Perry, *Crime and Society in Early Modern Seville,* 173.

59. Sanchez Arjona, *Noticias,* 334–35.

60. Quoted in Sanchez Arjona, *Noticias,* 47.

61. AHN, Consulta de Viernes, Leg. 7053. 23 × 1593.

62. Copy of an Act dated 10 iv 1614, AMS, Sección XI, Tomo 62, doc. 39.

63. AHPS, Protocolos, Leg. 17812, fol. 289r–v.

64. AGS, Casas y Sitios Reales (Legajos modernos), 270-2-134, undated. This petition addresses the many needs and very great poverty of those given care in the hospital.

65. Ibid.

66. Quoted in Pineda Novo, *El Teatro de Comedias,* 75.

67. Juan Ignacio Carmona, *Crónica Urbana Del Malvivir (S. XIV–XVII): Insalubridad, desamparo, y hambre en Sevilla* (Sevilla: Universidad de Sevilla, 2000), 52.

68. Ibid., 15.

69. Ibid., 110–12.

70. Kristy Wilson Bowers, "Balancing Individual and Communal Needs: Plague and Public Health in Early Modern Seville," *Bulletin of the History of Medicine* 81, no. 2 (2007): 335–58.

71. Antonio Domínguez Ortíz, *Alteraciones andaluzas* (Madrid: Narcea, 1973), 130.

72. James Lee, "'Ye Shall Disturb Noe Man's Right': Oath-Taking and Oath-Breaking in Late Medieval and Early Modern Bristol," *Urban History* 34, no. 1 (2007): 27–38.

73. Mark C. Pilkinton, ed., *Bristol, Records of Early English Drama* (Toronto: University of Toronto Press, 1997), 8:xxiii–xxix. Also see David Harris Sacks, *The Widening Gate: Bristol and the Atlantic Economy, 1450–1700* (Berkeley: University of California Press, 1991), 172–77.

74. Pilkinton, *Bristol,* xxxi–xxxiii.

75. Richard Ferris, *The most dangerous and memorable adventure of Richard Ferris one of the fiue ordinarie messengers of her maiesties chamber, who departed from Tower Wharfe on midsommer day last past* (London: John Wolfe, 1590), 11; and Pilkinton, *Bristol,* 137.

76. Pilkinton, *Bristol,* 203 and 209–10.

77. Ibid., 216.

78. Kathleen Barker, "An Early Seventeenth Century Provincial Playhouse," *Theatre Notebook* 29, no. 2 (1975): 81.

79. Roger Leech, *Topography of Medieval and Early Modern Bristol* (Bristol: Bristol Record Society, 1997), 172–73. See also Barker, "An Early Seventeenth Century Provincial Playhouse," 84. Barker places the closure of the Wine Street Playhouse five years earlier. She contends that it was this transfer of property to new ownership rather than any local action against the theater that resulted in its closure.

80. Mark Pilkinton, "New Information on the Playhouse in Wine Street, Bristol," *Theatre Notebook* 42, no. 2 (1988): 73–74.

81. Pilkinton, *Bristol,* xxxvii and xl.

82. My conversions have been based on John McCusker, *Money and Exchange in Europe and America, 1600–1775* (Chapel Hill: University of North Carolina Press, 1992).

83. Robert Fletcher and Joshua Jones, *Report of Mr. Robert Fletcher presented to the council of the city of Bristol, at a meeting held on the 25th day of February, 1839, and ordered to be printed for the use of the Members of the Council, previously to their taking the same into consideration* (Bristol, 1839), 32–33.

84. Pilkinton, *Bristol*, 205.

85. Ibid., 196.

86. Pilkinton, "New Information on the Playhouse in Wine Street, Bristol," 73–74.

87. Pilkinton, *Bristol*, 176.

88. Sacks, *Trade, Society, and Politics*, 752–57.

89. David Erskine Baker and Stephen Jones, *Biographia Dramatica: Names of the dramas: A–L* (London: Longman, Hurst, Rees, Orme & Brown, 1812), 2:67 and 2:211.

90. Pilkinton, *Bristol*, 215. Also see David Klausner, "The Improvising Vice," in *Improvisation in the Arts of the Middle Ages and Renaissance*, ed. Timothy McGee (Kalamazoo: Western Michigan University Press, 2003), 273–83.

91. Juan de Mal Lara, *Recibimiento que hizo la muy noble y muy leal Ciudad de Sevilla a la C.R.M. del Rey D. Philipe N. S.*, ed. Manuel Bernal Rodríguez (Sevilla: Secretario de Publicaciones, 1992); and Miguel de Cervantes, "Rinconete y Cortadillo," in *Obras Completas 7* (Madrid: Alianza, 1996).

92. Mary Perry, *Gender and Disorder in Early Modern Seville* (Princeton: Princeton University Press, 1990); and Alexandra Parma Cook, "The Women of Early Modern Triana: Life, Death, and Survival Strategies in Seville's Maritime District," in *Women in Port: Gendering Communities, Economies, and Social Networks in Atlantic Port Cities, 1500–1800*, ed. Dougless Catterall and Jodi Campbell (Leiden: Brill, 2012), 41–68.

93. Lope de Vega, *El Arenal de Sevilla*, in *El Perro del Hortelano* (Madrid: Espasa-Calpe, 1977), 139.

94. Ibid.

95. Ibid., 150.

96. Kay E. Weston, "Change and Essence in Lope de Vega's El Arenal de Sevilla," *MLN* 86, no. 2 (March 1971): 216.

CHAPTER THREE

1. Archivo del Ayuntamiento de Distrito Federal (hereafter referred to as ADF), Sección Ayuntamiento de Mexico, Libros de las Actas del Cabildo de Mexico, impresas, Vol. 659a, 34, 16 iv 1626.

2. ADF, Sección Ayuntamiento de Mexico, Actas del Cabildo de Mexico, impresas, Vol. 659a, 90, 25 i 1627.

3. Ibid., 106–07, 9 iv 1627.

4. See Harvey L. Johnson, "Notas Relativas a los Corrales de la Ciudad de México 1626–1641," *Revista Iberoamericana* 3, no. 5 (1941): 133–38.

5. Douglas Shaw, "Thomas Wentworth and Monarchical Ritual in Early Modern Ireland," *Historical Journal* 49, no. 2 (June 2006): 331–55.

6. See Hugo Hernán Ramírez, *Fiesta, espectáculo y teatralidad en el México de los conquistadores* (Madrid: Iberoamericana, 2009).

7. Diego Durán, *Historia de las Indias de Nueva España e Islas de la Tierra Firme* (México: Consejo Nacional para la Cultura y las Artes, 1995), 1:224–25.

8. Durán, *Historia,* 2:13.

9. Ibid., 199.

10. Ibid., 200–01.

11. Adam Versényi, *Theatre in Latin America: Religion, Politics, and Culture from Cortés to the 1980s* (Cambridge: Cambridge University Press, 1993), 1–6.

12. Fernando Horcasitas, Miguel León Portilla, Sten María, and Germán Viveros, eds., *Teatro Nahuatl I: Epocas Novahispana y Moderna* (México: Universidad Nacional de Autónoma, 2004), 545.

13. Louise M. Burkhart, *The Slippery Earth: Nahau-Christian Moral Dialogue in Sixteenth-Century Mexico* (Tucson: University of Arizona Press, 1989), 21.

14. Patricia Lopes Don, "Franciscans, Indian Sorcerers, and the Inquisition in New Spain, 1536–1543," *Journal of World History* 17, no. 1 (March 2006): 27–49.

15. Rodolfo Usigli, *México in the Theater,* trans. Wilder P. Scott (Jackson: University of Mississippi Press, 1976), 27.

16. Fernando Horcasitas, ed., *Teatro Náhuatl: Épocas Novohispana y Moderna* (México: Universidad Nacional Autónoma de México, 2004), 611–18.

17. Louise M. Burkhart, *Aztecs on Stage: Religious Theater in Colonial Mexico* (Norman: University of Oklahoma Press, 2011), 18.

18. Fray Bartolomé de las Casas, *Apologética Historia Sumaria,* Tomo I, Libro III, Capitulo LXIV (México: Universidad de México Instituto de Investigaciones Históricas, 1967), 331–37.

19. See Jonathan Israel, *Race, Class, and Politics in Colonial Mexico, 1610–1660* (Oxford: Oxford University Press, 1976).

20. Usigli, *Mexico in the Theater,* 35.

21. Pedro Moya de Contreras, *Cinco cartas* (Madrid: Ediciones José Porrúa Turanzas, 1962), 101.

22. AGI, Audiencia de Mexico, 19, No. 150, 9 ix 1574.

23. Margaret Greer, "La caza sacro-política: de *El bosque divino* de González de Eslava a Calderón," in *El teatro en la hispanoamérica colonial,* ed. Ignacio Arellano y J. A. Rodríguez Garrido (Pamplona: Editorial Iberoamericana, 2008), 86.

24. Pedro Moya de Contreras, *Cinco cartas,* 106. Moya claimed the playwright spent seventeen days in jail. Stafford Poole, *Pedro Moya de Contreras: Catholic Reform and Royal Power in New Spain 1571–1591* (Norman: University of Oklahoma Press, 2011), 49–53.

25. AGI, Consejo de Indias, Patronato, 182, R. 48, 10 xii 1574.

26. Ibid.

27. Pedro Moya de Contreras, *Cinco cartas,* 104.

28. Usigli, *Mexico in the Theater,* 37.

29. Irving A. Leonard, "A Shipment of Comedias to the Indies," *Hispanic Review* 2, no. 1 (January 1934): 39–50.

30. AGI, Mexico 118, Petition of Gonzalo de Riancho and Francisco de Léon, fol. 2r and 4v.

31. Ibid., fol. 1r.

32. Ibid., fol. 2r.

33. Ibid., fol. 2v.

34. AGI, Mexico 118, Petition of Gonzalo de Riancho and Francisco de Léon, fol. 7v–8r.

35. Raquel Chang-Rodriguez, *Historia de la literatura mexicana: desde sus orígenes hasta nuestros días* (México: Siglo XXI, 2002), 2:211.

36. In 1589 Villalobos sought to obtain the contract to stage the corpus performances but lost out to Gonzalo de Riancho, who undercut him by 500 pesos. See J. Luís Rocamora, *El Teatro en La América Colonial* (Buenos Aires: Editorial Huarpes, 1947), 304–05.

37. Arias de Villalobos, *Canto intitulado mercurio* (Mexico, 1620, 1907), 273 [microfiche].

38. Bernardo de Balbuena, *La grandeza Mexicana,* ed. José Carlos González Boixo (Roma: Bulzoni Editiore, 1988), 43.

39. Ibid., 78.

40. ADF, Ayuntamiento de Mexico, Actas del Cabildo de Mexico, impresas, Vol. 643a, 183.

41. ADF, Ayuntamiento de Mexico, Actas del Cabildo de Mexico, impresas, Vol. 646a, 283, undated document.

42. Vera Candiani, *Dreaming of Dry Land: Environmental Transformation in Colonial Mexico City* (Stanford: Stanford University Press, 2014), 27.

43. ADF, Ayuntamiento de Mexico, Actas del Cabildo, impresas, Vol. 648a, 296, 1612.

44. Boletin del AGN, Tomo XV, N. 1, 112, cited in Schilling, 16.

45. AGI, Audiencia de Mexico, 27. No. 62, not foliated. The decree from Philip III is dated 1 iii 1605.

46. Hildburg Schilling, *Teatro Profano en la Nueva España* (Mexico: Universidad Nacional Autonoma de Mexico, 1958), 129.

47. AGI, Sección Audiencia de Mexico, 26. No. 34, not foliated, 20 x 1604.

48. Ibid.

49. AGI, Audiencia de Mexico, 27. No. 62, fol. 2r, 17 xii 1608.

50. AGI, Audiencia de Mexico, 27. No. 62a, fol. 1r.

51. Schilling, *Teatro Profano,* 76–78.

52. AGI, Audiencia de Mexico, 29. No. 58, fol. 1.

53. ADF, Ayuntamiento de Mexico, Actas del Cabildo, impresas, Vol. 652a, 276, undated.

54. Cited by Harvey L. Johnson, "Notas Relativas a los Corrales de la Ciudad de Mexico 1626–1641," *Revista Iberoamericana* 3, no. 5 (1941): 136.

55. Vera Candiani, "The Desagüe Reconsidered: Environmental Dimensions of Class Conflict in Colonial Mexico," *Hispanic American Historical Review* 92, no. 1 (2012): 6.

56. Louisa Hoberman, "Bureaucracy and Disaster: Mexico City and the Flood of 1629," *Journal of Latin American Studies* 6, no. 2 (November 1974): 212.

57. Candiani, "The Desagüe Reconsidered," 14–15.

58. Archivo General de la Nación (México) (hereafter AGN), Hist. 467, fol. 3.

59. ADF, Ayuntamiento de Mexico, Actas del Cabildo, impresas, Vol. 660a, 231, 15 iv 1630.

60. ADF, Ayuntamiento de Mexico, Actas del Cabildo, impresas, Vol. 664a, 112.

61. AGN, Sección: Reales Cedulas, Vol. 49, Exp. 449, fol. 359r, 27 xi 1642.

62. AGN, Hist. 467, fol. 22–23. Also see Schilling, *Teatro Profano*, 26–27. See AGI, Indiferente General, 453, L.A19, fol. 51v–52r.

63. ADF, Ayuntamiento de Mexico, Actas del Cabildo, impresas, Vol. 661a, 112.

64. ADF, Ayuntamiento de Mexico, Actas del Cabildo, impresas, Vol. 664a, 201, 28 iv 1642.

65. AGN, Reales Cedulas (Duplicadas), Vol. 14, Exp. 764, fol. 479, 3 vii 1649; and AGN, Reales Cedulas Duplicadas, Vol. 14, Exp. 764, fol. 479–80, 12 viii 1649.

66. Manuel Romero de Terreros, *Gregorio M. De Guijo, Diario, 1648-1664,* Vol. 1 (Mexico City: Editorial Porrua, S.A., 1952), 108.

67. Alan Fletcher, *Drama, Performance, and Polity in Pre-Cromwellian Ireland* (Toronto: University of Toronto Press, 2000), 30.

68. Christopher Morash, *A History of the Irish Theatre, 1601–2000* (Cambridge: Cambridge University Press, 2002), 2–3.

69. Jessica Winston, "Expanding the Political Nation: 'Gorboduc' at the Inns of Court and Succession Revisited," *Early Theatre* 8, no. 1 (2005): 15.

70. Raymond Galespie, ed., *The Proctor's Accounts of Peter Lewis, 1564–65* (Ann Arbor, MI: Four Courts Press, 1996), 86.

71. Edict of the Irish Parliament, 12 January 1560, fol. 135, cited in Fletcher, *Drama, Performance and Polity,* 433, n.189.

72. Nicholas Canny, *Making Ireland British: 1580–1650* (Oxford: Oxford University Press, 2003), 275.

73. Douglas Shaw, "Thomas Wentworth and Monarchical Ritual in Early Modern Ireland," *Historical Journal* 49, no. 2 (2006): 331–55.

74. Fletcher, *Drama, Performance, and Polity,* 263; and Richard Dutton, "The St. Werburgh Street Theater, Dublin," in *Localizing Caroline Drama: Politics and Economics of the Early Modern English State, 1625–1642,* ed. Adam Zucker and Alan Farmer (Gordonsville: Palgrave Macmillan, 2006), 131–32.

75. See Christopher Morash, *A History of the Irish Theatre, 1601–2000* (Cambridge: Cambridge University Press, 2002); and Allan H. Stevenson, "James Shirley and the Actors at the First Irish Theatre," *Modern Philology* 40, no. 2 (1942): 147–60.

76. Justine Williams, "The Irish Plays of James Shirley, 1636–1640" (PhD diss., University of Warwick, 2010).

77. Morash, *History of the Irish Theatre,* 19; and Dutton, "The St. Werburgh Street Theater, Dublin," 129–55.

78. Fletcher, *Drama, Performance, and Polity,* 274.

79. Henry Burnell, *Landgartha* (Dublin, 1641), G2r, Early English Books Online.

80. Catherine M. Shaw, "*Landgartha* and the Irish Dilemma," *Eire-Ireland* 13, no. 1 (1978): 26–39.

81. Burnell, *Landgartha,* frontispiece.

82. John Adamson, *The Noble Revolt: The Overthrow of Charles I* (London: Weidenfeld and Nicolson, 2007), 57–59.

83. Morash, *A History of the Irish Theatre,* 13.

84. R. A. Butlin, "The Population of Dublin in the Late Seventeenth Century," *Irish Geography* 5, no. 2 (1966): 51–66.

85. Irving A. Leonard, "A Shipment of Comedias to the Indies," *Hispanic Review* 2, no. 1 (January 1934): 39–50; and Carlos Alberto Gonzalez Sanchez, *Los mundos del libro: medios de difusión de la cultura occidental en las Indias de los siglo XVI y XVII* (Sevilla: Universidad de Sevilla, 1999).

86. ADF, Sección Ayuntamiento de Mexico, Libros de las Actas del Cabildo de Mexico, printed Vol. 659a, 34, 16 iv 1626.

87. Amy Fuller, *Between Two Worlds: The Autos Sacramentales of Sor Juana Inés de la Cruz* (Cambridge: MHRA, 2015), 4.

88. Antonio Castro Leal, in *Juan Ruiz de Alarcón, su vida y su obra* (México: Ediciones Cuadernos Americanos, 1943), 29.

89. See Leonardo Dilillo, "Moral Purpose in Ruiz de Alarcón's 'La verdad sospechosa,'" *Hispania* 56 (April 1973): 257.

90. Alfred Coester, *The Literary History of Spanish America* (New York: Macmillan, 1921).

91. Juan Ruiz de Alarcón, "El semejante a sí mismo," Jornada I, Biblioteca Virtual Miguel de Cervantes, http://213.0.4.19/servlet/SirveObras/89148401093469473465679/index.htm.

92. Ibid.

93. Ibid.

94. S. Griswold Morley and Courtney Bruerton, *Cronología de las comedias de Lope de Vega* (Madrid: Gredos, 1968), 370.

95. Victor Dixon, "Lope de Vega and America: *The New World* and *Arauco Tamed,*" *Renaissance Studies* 6, no. 3–4 (September 1992): 259.

96. Benjamin Keen, *The Aztec Image in Western Thought* (New Brunswick: Rutgers University Press, 1990), 180.

97. AGN, Hist. 467, fol. 3, cited by Schilling, 22.

CHAPTER FOUR

1. Archivo del Ayuntamiento de Puebla (hereafter AAP), Actas del Cabildo de Puebla, Libro 19, fol. 85f, 25 ii 1639.

2. AAP, Actas del Cabildo de Puebla, Libro 19, fol. 43f, 5 ii 1639.

3. Miguel Ángel Cuenya Mateos and Carlos Contreras Cruz, *Puebla de los Ángeles: historia de una ciudad novohispana, aspectos sociales, económicos y demográficos* (Puebla: Universidad Autónoma de Puebla, 2007), 112; Jay Kinsbruner, *The Colonial Spanish-American City: Urban Life in the Age of Atlantic Capitalism* (Austin: University of Texas Press, 2005), 30; Ira Rosenwaike, *Population History of New York City* (Syracuse, NY: Syracuse University Press, 1972), 8; Evarts Boutell Greene and Virginia Draper Harrington, *American Population before the Federal Census of 1790* (New York: Genealogical Publishing, 1932, 1981), 153.

4. Frances Ramos, *Identity, Ritual, and Power in Colonial Puebla* (Tucson: University of Arizona Press, 2012), 5.

5. Guy Thomson, *Puebla de los Angeles, Industry and Society in a Mexican City, 1700–1850* (Boulder, CO: Westview Press, 1989); Julia L. Hirschburg, "Social Experiment in New Spain: A Prosopographical Study of the Early Settlement at Puebla de los Angeles," *Hispanic American Historical Review* 59 (1979): 1–33; Nancy Fee, "La Entrada Angelopolitana: Ritual and Myth in the Viceregal Entry in Puebla de Los Angeles," *The Americas* 52, no. 3 (January 1996): 283–320; and Tatiana Seijas, *Asian Slaves in Colonial Mexico: From Chinos to Indians* (New York: Cambridge University Press, 2014).

6. Sonya Lipsett Rivera, "Water and Bureaucracy in Colonial Puebla de Los Angeles," *Journal of Latin American Studies* 25, no. 1 (1993): 27.

7. Nancy Fee, "La Entrada Angelopolitana," 283–320.

8. See Jan Bazant, "The Evolution of the Textile Industry of Puebla, 1544–1585," *Comparative Studies of Society and History* 7 (The Hague: Mouton, 1964), 57–69; and Sonya Lipsett Rivera, "Water and Bureaucracy," 25–44.

9. Jonathan Israel, "Mexico and the General Crisis of the Seventeenth Century," *Past & Present* 63 (May 1974): 36.

10. Ramos, *Identity, Ritual, and Power in Colonial Puebla.*

11. Felicia Hardison Londré and Daniel J. Watermeier, *The History of North American Theatre From Pre-Columbian Times to the Present* (New York: Continuum, 1998), 53.

12. Harvey L. Johnson, *El Teatro Colonial en Puebla (Primer Siglo)* (Puebla: Secretaría de Cultura, 2002), 13.

13. AAP, Actas del Cabildo de Puebla, Libro 11, fol. 115f, mayo 1582.

14. AAP, Actas del Cabildo de Puebla, Libro 13, fol. 107v, 12 v 1600.

15. AAP, Actas del Cabildo de Puebla, Libro 13, fol. 188f, 12 iv 1600.

16. Quoted in Hildburg. Schilling, *Teatro Profano en la Nueva España* (México: Universidad Nacional Autónoma de México, 1958), 33–34.

17. Quoted in Harvey L. Johnson, *El Teatro Colonial en Puebla (Primer Siglo),* 19–20.

18. AAP, Actas del Cabildo de Puebla, Libro 15, fols. 60f and 104f.

19. Schilling, *Teatro Profano,* 34.

20. Israel, "Mexico and the General Crisis," 49.

21. AAP, Actas del Cabildo de Puebla, Libro 15, fol. 146v, undated.

22. Ida Altman, *Transatlantic Ties in the Spanish Empire: Brihuega, Spain, and Puebla, Mexico, 1560–1620* (Stanford: Stanford University Press, 2000), 175. She observes that Melgarejo arrived, exclaiming "peace, peace."

23. AGN, General de Parte, Volumen 8 No. 9/Exp 9 (11), 1 xi 1640.

24. AGN, General de Parte, Volumen 8 No. 9/Exp 9 (11), 1 xi 1640. For conversion between pesos and maravedís, see C. H. Herring, "Ledgers of the Royal Treasury," *Hispanic American Historical Review* 2, no. 2 (1919): 173–87.

25. Schilling, *Teatro Profano*, 132.

26. Quoted in ibid., 117.

27. AAP, Actas del Cabildo de Puebla, Libro 16, fol. 324v, 29 v 1626.

28. AAP, Actas del Cabildo de Puebla, Libro 13, fol. 188f, 12 iv 1600.

29. AAP, Actas del Cabildo de Puebla, Libro 17, fol. 26v, 16 x 1626.

30. Juan Pedro Viqueira Alban, *Propriety and Permissiveness in Bourbon Mexico*, trans. Sonya Lipsett-Rivera and Sergio Rivera Ayala (New York: Rowman & Littlefield, 1999), 33.

31. Ramos, *Identity, Ritual, and Power*, 62–63; Miguel Ángel Cuenya Mateos, *Fiestas y virreyes en la Puebla colonial* (Puebla: Secretaría de Cultura, 1989), 24.

32. Ben Vinson III, "Articulating Space: The Free-Colored Military Establishment in Colonial Mexico from the Conquest to Independence," *Callaloo* 27, no. 1 (2004): 154.

33. A. Robert Lauer, "The Iberian Encounter of America in the Spanish Theater of the Golden Age," *Pacific Coast Philology* 28, no. 1 (September 1993): 32–42.

34. Laura R. Bass and Amanda Wunder, "The Veiled Ladies of the Early Modern Spanish World: Seduction and Scandal in Seville, Madrid, and Lima," *Hispanic Review* 77, no. 1 (2009): 97–144.

35. Sor Juana Ines de la Cruz, *Los empeños de una casa*, ed. Celsa Carmen García Valdes (Barcelona: Promociones y Publicaciones Universitarias, 1989), 51.

36. Sidney Donnell, "From Cross Gender to Generic Closure: Sor Juan Inés de la Cruz's *Los empeños de una casa*," *Revista Canadiense de Estudios Hispánicos* 33, no. 1 (Autumn 2008): 186.

37. Joanne Rappaport, *The Disappearing Mestizo: Configuring Difference in the Colonial New Kingdom of Granada* (Durham, NC: Duke University Press, 2014).

38. Miguel Zugasti, *La "Trilogía de los Pizarros" de Tirso de Molina, Estudio crítico*, (Kassel: Edition Reichenberger, 1993), 1:17–18.

39. Gladys Robalino, "*Amazonas en las Indias:* Mixed Marriages and the Pizarros' Political Project," in *Female Amerindians in Early Modern Spanish Theater*, ed. Gladys Robalino (Lewisburg, PA: Bucknell University Press, 2014), 117.

40. Zugasti, *La "Trilogía de los Pizarros,"* 3:19–22.

41. Louise Fothergill-Payne, "The Pizarro Trilogy and thc Question of History: From *Ars Historica* to New Historicism and Beyond," in *Tirso de Molina: His Originality Then and Now*, ed. Henry W. Sullivan and Raúl A. Galoppe (Ottawa: Dovehouse Editions, 1996), 197.

42. Zugasti, *La "Trilogía de los Pizarros,"* 1:13.

43. Pedro Moya de Contreras, *Cinco cartas (Madrid: Ediciones José Porrúa Turanzas, 1962)*, 106.

44. AAP, Actas del Cabildo de Puebla, Libro 18, fol. 5v.

45. AAP, Actas del Cabildo de Puebla, Libro 18, fol. 6v.

46. AAP, Actas del Cabildo de Puebla, Libro 18, fol. 271v.

47. Rachael Ball, "Water, Wine, and Aloja: Consuming Interests in the *Corrales de Comedias* 1600–1646," *Comedia Performance* 10, no. 1 (2013): 81–82.

48. Schilling, *Teatro Profano*, 37.

49. AAP, Actas del Cabildo de Puebla, Libro 18, fol. 18v and 44r–45r.

50. Schilling, *Teatro Profano*, 72–73.

51. AAP, Actas del Cabildo de Puebla, Libro 17, fol. 331v, 13 iv 1632, and Libro 18, fol. 44f, 19 v 1633.

52. Schilling, *Teatro Profano*, 97.

53. Marina Lamus Obregón, *Geografías del teatro en América Latina: Un relato histórico* (Bogotá: Luna Libros, 2014).

54. Schilling, *Teatro Profano*, 145.

55. AGI, Mexico 118, Petition of Gonzalo de Riancho and Francisco de Léon, fol. 4v.

56. Schilling, *Teatro Profano*, 115.

57. AGN, Reales Cedulas (Duplicadas), Vol. 14, Exp. 764, fol. 479, 3 vii 1649.

58. Ibid., fol. 479–80, 12 viii 1649.

59. Michael Manuel Brescia, "The Cultural Politics of Episcopal Power: Juan de Palafox y Mendoza and Tridentine Catholicism in Seventeenth-Century Puebla de los Angeles, Mexico" (PhD diss., University of Arizona, 2002), 26–37.

60. Juan de Palafox y Mendoza, *Discurso en favor de cierto religioso de vida ejemplar, a quien castigó rigurosamente un prelado superior, porque subió a predicar al púlpito de cierto convento de religiosas, al tiempo y cuando se representaba en él una mal ordenado comedia, de que resultaron muchos daños*, ed. Efraín Castro Morales (Pueblo: Museo Mexicano, 2003), 23–24.

61. AAP, Actas del Cabildo de Puebla, Libro 21, fol. 5v.

62. Ibid., fol. 8v–9f.

63. Emilio Cotarelo y Mori, Bibliografía de las *Controversias sobre la licitud del teatro en España* (Madrid: Biblioteca Nacional, 1904), 495.

64. Richard Hakluyt, *A Discourse on Western Planting*, ed. Charles Dean (Cambridge: John Wilson and Son, 1877), 154.

65. J. H. Elliott, *Empires of the Atlantic World: Britain and Spain in America 1492–1830* (New Haven: Yale University Press, 2006), 36.

66. Richard Kagan, "Urbs and Civitas in Sixteenth- and Seventeenth-Century Spain," in *Envisioning the City: Six Studies in Urban Cartography*, ed. David Buisseret (Chicago: University of Chicago Press, 1998), 75–108.

67. Elliott, *Empires of the Atlantic World*, 41–43.

68. Frederic Gleach, *Powhatan's World and Colonial Virginia: A Conflict of Cultures* (Lincoln: University of Nebraska Press, 1997); and Karen Kupperman, *Indians and English: Facing Off in Early America* (Ithaca, NY: Cornell University Press, 2000).

69. John Grenier, *The First Way of War: American War Making on the Frontier, 1607–1814* (Cambridge: Cambridge University Press, 2005), 21–25.

70. Greene and Harrington, *American Population before the Federal Census of 1790*, 153.

71. See, for example, Jeffrey Richards's chapter on Smith, "Prospero in Virginia," in his book *Theater Enough: American Culture and the Metaphor of the World Stage, 1607–1789*

(Durham, NC: Duke University Press, 1991); and Karen Robertson, "Pocahontas at the Masque," *Signs* 21, no. 3 (1996): 551–83.

72. Odai Johnson, *Absence and Memory in Colonial American Theatre: Fiorelli's Plaster* (New York: Palgrave, 2006), 5.

73. Robert Land, "The First Williamsburg Theater," *William and Mary Quarterly* 5, no. 3 (1948): 363.

74. Odai Johnson, "Working up from Postholes: (Im)Material Witnesses, Evidence, and Narrativity in the Colonial American Theatre," *Theatre Survey* 46, no. 2 (2005): 186.

75. Susanne K. Sherman, *Comedies Useful: A History of the American Theatre in the South, 1775–1812* (Williamsburg, VA: Celeste Press, 1998), 7.

76. "Sarah Hallam," *William and Mary Quarterly* 12, no. 4 (1904): 236.

77. Sherman, *Comedies Useful.*

78. Ibid., 5.

79. Lucy Blandford Pilkinton, "Theatre in Norfolk, Virginia, 1788–1812" (4 vols., PhD diss., University of Michigan, 1993).

80. Elliott, *Empires of the Atlantic World,* xiii–xiv.

CHAPTER FIVE

1. Significant portions of this chapter appear in my article "'Beautiful Serpents' and 'Cathedras of Pestilence': Antitheatrical Traditions, Gendered Decline, and Political Crisis in Early Modern Spain and England," *Sixteenth Century Journal* 43, no. 3 (Autumn 2015): 541–63.

2. Héloïse Sénéchal, "The Antitheatrical Criticism of Stephen Gosson," *Literature Compass* 1, no. 1 (2004): 2.

3. J. C. J. Metford, "The Enemies of the Theatre in the Golden Age," *Bulletin of Hispanic Studies* 28 (1951): 77.

4. Pedro de Guzmán, *Los bienes del honesto trabajo y daños de la ociosidad en ocho discursos* (Madrid: Emprenta Real, 1614), 191.

5. William Prynne, *Histrio-Mastix: The Players Scourge, or the Actors Tragedi,* ed. Peter Davison (New York: Johnson Reprint, 1972), 2–3.

6. Anthony Munday, *A Second and Third Blast of Retreat from Plays and Theatres,* ed. J. W. Binns (New York: Johnson Reprint, 1962), unpaginated preface.

7. Ibid., 86–87 and 119.

8. Prynne, *Histrio-Mastix,* 1–11.

9. Metford, "Enemies of the Theatre," 76–92.

10. Prynne, *Histrio-Mastix,* 1–11.

11. Ibid., 88–90.

12. Ibid., 245.

13. Mariana wrote tracts on numerous subjects. See Herald E. Braun, *Juan de Mariana and Early Modern Spanish Political Thought* (Burlington: Ashgate, 2007), 6–9; Guenter Lewy, *Constitutionalism and Statecraft During the Golden Age of Spain: A Study*

of the Political Philosophy of Juan de Mariana, S.J. (Geneva: Librairie E. Droz, 1960), 28–33.

14. Juan de Mariana, *Ioannis Marianae E Societate Iusu Tractatus VII* Nunc primum in lucem editi (Cologne, 1609), 128. Molinists, named after the Jesuit theologian Luis de Molina, held that God knows everything that would happen even if He acted differently, in addition to knowing everything that does happen and will happen. On Jesuit masculinity, see Ulrika Strasser, "'The First Form and Grace': Ignatius of Loyola and the Reformation of Masculinity," in *Masculinity in the Reformation Era,* ed. Scott H. Hendrix and Susan Karant-Nunn (Kirksville, MO: Truman State University Press, 2008), 45–70.

15. Strasser, "First Form," 48.

16. Mariana, *Tractatus VII,* 129.

17. Ibid., 135.

18. Ibid., 136.

19. Guzmán, *Los bienes,* 264.

20. Jaume Albert, *Circunsión de comedias: sermón contra el abuso dellas predico en San Vicente* (Lerida, 1629), A3, BNE, VE/170/11.

21. Ibid., A5.

22. Jonas Barish, *The Antitheatrical Prejudice* (Berkeley: University of California Press, 1981), 80.

23. Michael Manuel Brescia, "The Cultural Politics of Episcopal Power: Juan de Palafox y Mendoza and Tridentine Catholicism in Seventeenth-Century Puebla de los Angeles, Mexico" (PhD diss., University of Arizona, 2002), 66.

24. Juan de Palafox y Mendoza, *Discurso en favor de cierto religioso de vida ejemplar,* 40–41.

25. BNE, Mss. 20.273/26, *Real Orden para que los soldados de su guardia paguen la entrada en los corrales de comedias.*

26. Quoted in Emilio Cotarelo y Mori, *Bibliografía de las Controversias sobre la licitud del teatro en España* (Madrid: Biblioteca Nacional, 1904), 68.

27. Guzmán, *Los bienes,* 305–11.

28. Cotarelo y Mori, *Bibliografía de las Controversias,* 164.

29. AHN, Sala de Alcaldes de Casa y Corte, Comedias, Libro de gobierno 1.257, fol. 360 and 1.260, fol. 450. See also Ursula Heise, "Transvestitism and the Stage Controversy in England and Spain, 1580–1680," *Theatre Journal* 44 (1992): 357–74.

30. Albert, *Circunsión de comedias,* C2r.

31. Ibid., B1r.

32. Quoted in Cotarelo y Mori, *Bibliografía de las Controversias,* 68.

33. BNE, Mss. 9855, fol. 157r., 1600.

34. Guzmán, *Los bienes,* 301.

35. Ibid., 287.

36. BNE, R/8171(1), fol. 32v., 1636.

37. Juan de Palafox y Mendoza, *Discurso en favor de cierto religioso de vida ejemplar,* 37.

38. Ibid., 39.

39. Juan de Palafox y Mendoza, *Epístola exortatoria a los curas y beneficiados de la Puebla de los Ángeles,* ed. Efraín Castro Morales (Pueblo: Museo Mexicano, 2003), 72.

40. Laura Levine, *Men in Women's Clothing: Anti-theatricality and Effeminization, 1579-1642* (Cambridge: Cambridge University Press, 1994), 17; Laura Levine, "Women in Men's Clothing: Antitheatricality and Effeminization, 1579–1642," *Criticism* 28 (1986): 121–43; Heise, "Transvestitism and the Stage Controversy."

41. Prynne, *Histrio-Mastix*, 215–16 and 199.

42. Prynne, *Histrio-Mastix*, 187, 208, 201, and 220. See also Elizabeth Lehfeldt, "Ideal Men: Masculinity and Decline in Seventeenth Century Spain," *Renaissance Quarterly* 61, no. 2 (2008): 463–94; Saul Martínez Bermejo, "Beyond Luxury: Sumptuary Legislation in 17th-Century Castile," in *Making, Using, and Resisting the Law in European History*, ed. Günther Lottes, Eero Madijainen, and Jón Viðar Sigurðsson (Pisa: Pisa University Press, 2008), 93–108; and Ruth Kennedy, "Certain Phases of the Sumptuary Decrees of 1623 and Their Relation to Tirso's Theatre," *Hispanic Review* 10 (1942): 91–115.

43. Richard Kagan and Abigail Dyer, *Inquisitorial Inquiries: Brief Lives of Secret Jews and Other Heretics* (Baltimore: Johns Hopkins University Press, 2004), 64–87.

44. See, for example, Trevor Aston, *Europe in Crisis, 1560-1660* (New York: Routledge, 1965); Geoffrey Parker, *Global Crisis: War, Climate Change, and Catastrophe in the Seventeenth Century* (New Haven: Yale University Press, 2013); T. K. Rabb, *The Struggle for Stability in Early Modern Europe* (Oxford: Oxford University Press, 1972); I. A. A. Thompson and Bartolomé Yun Casalilla, *The Castilian Crisis of the Seventeenth Century* (Cambridge: Cambridge University Press, 1994); Hugh Trevor-Roper, *The Crisis of the Seventeenth Century: Religion, The Reformation, and Social Change* (Indianapolis: Liberty Fund, 1971).

45. J. H. Elliott, "Self Perception and Decline in Early Seventeenth-Century Spain," *Past & Present* 74 (February 1977): 41–61. Also see Martínez Bermejo, "Beyond Luxury," 93–108; and Lehfeldt, "Ideal Men," 463–94.

46. Mary Frear Keeler, *The Long Parliament, 1640-1641: A Biographical Study of Its Members* (Philadelphia: American Philosophical Society, 1954), 208.

47. Wilson Coates, Anne Young, and Vernon Snow, eds., *The Private Journals of the Long Parliament* (New Haven: Yale University Press, 1982), 1:182.

48. Ibid., 3:328. One of the sermons was printed by parliamentary order. See William Carter, *Israels peace with God, Beniamines overthrow* (London: printed for Giles Calvet, 1642).

49. C. H. Firth and R. S. Rait, *Acts and Ordinances of the Interregnum, 1642-1660* (London: Wyman and Sons, 1911), 26–27 and 1070–72.

50. Janet Clare, *Drama of the English Republic, 1649-1660: Plays and Entertainments* (Manchester: Manchester University Press, 2006), 5–6.

51. Mark Bayer, *Theatre, Community, and Civic Engagement in Jacobean London* (Iowa City: University of Iowa Press, 2011), 209–10.

52. Susan Wiseman, *Drama and Politics in the English Civil War* (Cambridge: Cambridge University Press, 1998), 137–64.

53. AMM, Sección 2, Legajo 468, No. 12, 5 viii 1645.

54. Carlos Seco Serrano, ed., *Cartas de Sor María de Jesús de Ágreda, Biblioteca de Autores Españoles: Epistolario Español* (Madrid: Atlas, 1958), 4:52–53.

55. Ibid. See also J. E. Varey and N. D. Shergold, “Datos históricos sobre los primeros teatros de Madrid: prohibiciones de autos y comedias y sus consecuencias,” *Bulletin Hispanique* 62 (1960): 286–325.

56. Marilyn Fedewa, *María of Ágreda: Mystical Lady in Blue* (Albuquerque: University of New Mexico Press, 2010).

57. Archivo de la Corono de Aragón (hereafter ACA), Secretaria de Valencia, Leg. 725, No. 38, 29 v 1646.

58. AMS, Sección 2, Acuerdos Carpeta 20, Signatura H-674, and AMS, Sección 2, Acuerdos Carpeta 21, Signatura H-675.

59. AMM, Sección 2, Legajo 468, No. 11, 8 x 1648.

60. AGS, Casas y Sitios Reales, Leg. 270, No. 2, fol. 134r.

61. ACA, Secretaria de Valencia, Leg. 725, No. 30, fol. 5, 18 vi 1647.

62. ACA, Secretaria de Valencia, Leg. 729, No. 38, fol. 2, 9 viii 1650.

63. Luis Crespí de Borja, *Respuesta a una consulta, sobre si son licitas las comedias que se usan en España* (Valencia: Bernardo Nogués, 1649), 11–12.

64. Ibid., 36.

65. Pérez de Valdivia's sermon “Plática o lecion de las máscaras” was printed with Fructuoso Bisbe y Vidal, *Tratado de las comedias: en el qual se declara si son licitas: y si hablando en todo rigor seran pecado mortal el representarlas, el verlas y el consentirlas* (Barcelona: Geronymo Margarit, 1618); see 22.

66. Carmen Sanz Ayán and Bernardo García García, *Teatros y comediantes en el Madrid de Felipe II* (Madrid: Editorial Complutense, 2000), 71.

67. Guzmán, *Los bienes*, 329–30.

68. Christopher Morash, *A History of the Irish Theatre, 1601–2000* (Cambridge: Cambridge University Press, 2002), 25.

69. Jeremy Collier, *A Short View of the Immorality and Profaneness of the English Stage; Together with the Sense of Antiquity Upon This Argument* (London: S. Keble, 1698), 162.

CONCLUSION

1. Philip Sidney, *An Apology for Poetry*, ed. R. W. Maslen and Geoffrey Shepherd (Manchester: Manchester University Press, 2002), 92–98.

2. AMM, Sección 2, Leg. 468, No. 11.

3. HSA, Altamira, II-7-29.

BIBLIOGRAPHY

ARCHIVAL COLLECTIONS

Spain

Archivo de la Villa de Madrid (AMM)
Sección Secretaría, Diversiones públicas, Sección 2, Leg. 468, 475
Sección Secretaría, Libros de Acuerdos, Tomo 33, 37, 51
Sección Secretaría, Sección 4, Leg. 52

Archivo del Palacio Real (APR)
Sección de Espectáculos Públicos y Privados, Leg. 661, 666, 671
Secretario de la Cámara, Cuentas, 11744

Archivo General de Indias (AGI)
Indiferente General, 453
México, 26, 27, 118
Patronato, 182

Archivo General de Simancas (AGS)
Casa Real, Casas y Sitios Reales, Leg. 270
Estado S.P. Libro 375

Archivo Histórico Nacional, Madrid (AHN)
Consejo de Castilla, Consultas de viernes
Sala de Alcaldes de Casa y Corte, Comedias, Libros de Gobierno 1.257, 1.260

Archivo Regional de la Comunidad de Madrid (ARM)
Sección Diputación Provincial, Instituciones Benéficas y Asistenciales, Corrales de Comedias, Signaturas 5084, 5310, 5347

Sección Diputación Provincial, Instituciones Benéficas y Asistenciales, Hospital General y de la Pasión, Visitas, Signaturas 5169, 8483

Biblioteca Nacional de España (BNE)
Mss. 7.797: Cuentas del Buen Retiro
Mss. 8.177: Sobre el Coliseo del Buen Retiro
Mss. 9.855: Bartolomé Leonardo de Argensola
Mss. 12.917: Genealogía, origen, y noticias de los comediantes de España
Mss. 12.961/9: Peligro de oír comedias lascivas y asistir a bailes y danzas
Mss. 14.004/5: Papeles referentes al Coliseo del Buen Retiro
Mss. 20.273/26: Real Orden para que los soldados de su guardia paguen la entrada en los corrales de comedias.
R/8171(1): Alonso Carranzai, Discurso contra malos trages y adornos lascivos

Archivo Municipal de Sevilla (AMS) Sección 1, Nos. 40, 156
Sección 2, Acuerdos
Sección 4, Tomo 5, 21, 37
Sección 11, Tomo 62

Archivo de Protocolos de Sevilla (AHPS)
Protocolos Legajos 473, 474, 3642, 922, 17811, 17812

Archivo de la Corono de Aragón (ACA)
Secretaria de Valencia, Legajo 725, 729

México

Archivo General de la Nación (AGN)
General de Parte, Vol. 8, No. 9/Exp. 9
Historia, 467
Reales Cedulas, Vol. 49, Exp. 449
Reales Cedulas (Duplicados), Vol. 14, Exp. 764, Exp. 765

Archivo Histórico del Distrito Federal (ADF)
Ayuntamiento de México, Actas de Cabildo, impresas Vol. 643a–55a, 659a–64a

Archivo Histórico del Palacio Municipal de Puebla/ Archivo del Ayuntamiento de Puebla (AAP)
Actas de Cabildo de Puebla, Libros 11–23

United States

The Hispanic Society of America (HSA)
Altamira, Box II

PUBLISHED PRIMARY SOURCES

Alarcón, Juan Ruiz de. *El semejante a sí mismo.* Biblioteca Virtual Miguel de Cervantes. http://213.0.4.19/servlet/SirveObras/89148401093469473465679/index.htm.

Albert, Jaume. *Circunsión de comedias: sermon contra el abuso dellas predico en San Vicente.* Lérida, 1629.

Aldana y Arellano, Gregorio de. *Los hospitales reales, general, y passion de esta Corte; con sus convalencias, obligaciones, salario, su govierno politico, y assistencia, rentas que gozan, con la quenta y razon de lo que gastaron el año passado de 1665.* Madrid, 1666.

An example for all those that make no conscience of swearing and forswearing shewing Gods heauy iudgement vpon a maid-seruant in London, who forswore her selfe, and now lies rotting in S. Bartholomewes Hospitall in Smithfield, where many resort daily to see her. To the tune of Aime not too high. London: G. Purslow for J. Wright, c. 1625. EEBO.

Balbuena, Bernardo de. *La grandeza Mexicana.* Edited by José Carlos González Boixo. Roma: Bulzoni Editiore, 1988.

Barber, Charles ed. *Middleton: A Chaste Maid in Cheapside.* Berkeley: University of California Press, 1969.

Bisbe y Vidal, Fructuoso. *Tratado de las comedias: en el qual se declara si son licitas: y si hablando en todo rigor seran pecado mortal el representarlas, el verlas y el consentirlas.* Barcelona: Geronymo Margarit, 1618.

Black, Joseph, ed. *The Martin Marprelate Tracts: A Modernized and Annotated Edition.* Cambridge: Cambridge University Press, 2008.

Burnell, Henry. *Landgartha.* Dublin, 1641. Early English Books Online.

Cabrera de Córdoba, Luis. *Relaciones de las cosas sucedidas en la corte de España desde 1599 hasta 1614.* Madrid: J. Matin Alegria, 1857.

Calderón de la Barca, Pedro. *No hay burlas con el amor.* Madrid: Espasa-Calpe, 1962.

———. *El médico de su honra.* Madrid: Clásicos Castalia, 1989.

Carranzai, Alonso. *Discurso contra malos trages y adornos lascivos.* Madrid, 1636.

Carter, William. "Israels peace with God, Beniamines overthrow." London: Printed for Giles Calvert, 1642. EEBO.

Cervantes, Miguel de. "Rinconete y Cortadillo." In *Obras Completas 7*. Madrid: Alianza, 1996.

Coates, Wilson, Anne Young, and Vernon Snow, eds. *The Private Journals of the Long Parliament*. Vol. 1. New Haven: Yale University Press, 1982.

Collier, Jeremy. *A Short View of the Immorality and Profaneness of the English Stage; Together with the Sense of Antiquity Upon This Argument*. London: S. Keble, 1698.

Cotarelo y Mori, Emilio. *Bibliografía de las controversias sobre la licitud del teatro en España*. Madrid: Biblioteca Nacional, 1904.

———. *Comedias de Tirso de Molina*. Vols. I and II. Madrid: Bailly, Bailliere e hijos, Editores, 1906.

Contreras, Pedro Moya de. *Cinco cartas*. Madrid: Ediciones José Porrúa Turanzas, 1962.

Crespí de Borja, Luis. *Respuesta a una consulta, sobre si son licitas las comedias que se usan en España*. Valencia: Bernardo Nogués, 1649.

Cruz, Sor Juana Inés de la. *Los empeños de una casa*. Edited by Celsa Carmen García Valdes. Barcelona: Promociones y Publicaciones Universitarias, 1989.

Davis, Charles, and J. E. Varey. *Actividad Teatral en la región de Madrid según los protocolos de Juan García de Albertos, 1634–1660*. Vols. 1 and 2. London: Tamesis, 2003.

———. *Los Corrales de Comedias y Los Hospitales de Madrid, 1574–1615: Estudio y Documentos*. London: Tamesis, 1997.

———. *Los corrales de comedias y los hospitales de Madrid: 1615–1849*. London: Tamesis, 1997.

Durán, Diego. *Historia de las Indias de Nueva España e Islas de la Tierra Firme*. Vols. 1 and 2. México: Consejo Nacional para la Cultura y las Artes, 1995.

Ferris, Richard. *The most dangerous and memorable adventure of Richard Ferris one of the fiue ordinarie messengers of her maiesties chamber, who departed from Tower Wharfe on midsommer day last past*. London: John Wolfe, 1590.

Fletcher, Robert, and Joshua Jones. *Report of Mr. Robert Fletcher presented to the council of the city of Bristol, at a meeting held on the 25th day of February, 1839, and ordered to be printed for the use of the Members of the Council, previously to their taking the same into consideration*. Bristol, 1839.

Firth, C. H., and R. S. Rait. *Acts and Ordinances of the Interregnum, 1642–1660*. Vol. 1. London: Wyman and Sons, 1911.

Galdiano y Croy, Leonardo. *Breve tratado de los hospitales y casas de recogimiento de esta Corte*. Madrid, 1677.

García Mercadal, J. *España vista por los extranjeros*. Tomo III. Madrid: Biblioteca Nueva, 1918.

González Palencia, Ángel. *Noticias de Madrid, 1621–1627*. Madrid: Sección de Cultura e Información Artes Graficas Municipales, 1942.

Guzmán, Pedro de. *Los bienes del honesto trabajo y daños de la ociosidad en ocho discursos*. Madrid: Emprenta Real, 1614.

Hakluyt, Richard. *A Discourse on Western Planting*. Edited by Charles Dean. Cambridge: John Wilson and Son, 1877.

Jonson, Ben. "On the Famous Voyage." In *Ben Jonson: The Complete Poems*. Edited by George Parfitt. New Haven: Yale University Press, 1975.

Kingsford, Charles Lethbridge, ed. *A Survey of London by John Stow: Reprinted from the text of 1603*. Vol. 1. London: Henry Frowde, 1908.

Las Casas, Bartolomé de. *Apologética Historia Sumaria*. Tomo I, Libro III. México: Instituto de Investigaciones Históricas, 1967.

Mal Lara, Juan de. *Recibimiento que hizo la muy noble y muy leal Ciudad de Sevilla a la C.R.M. del Rey D. Philipe N. S.* Edited by Manuel Bernal Rodríguez. Sevilla: Secretario de Publicaciones, 1992.

Mariana, Juan de. *Ioannis Marianae E Societate Iusu Tractatus VII* Nunc primum in lucem editi. Cologne, 1609.

Menéndez Pidal, Ramón, ed. *Primera Crónica General de España*. Madrid: Gredos, 1955.

Middleton, Thomas. *A Game at Chess*. Edited by T. H. Howard Hill. Manchester: Manchester University Press, 1993.

Milán, Luis. *Libro Entitulado El Cortesano : Libro de motes de damas y caballeros*. Madrid, 1874.

Molina, Tirso de. *El amor médico*. Biblioteca Virtual Miguel de Cervantes. http://www.cervantesvirtual.com/.

———. *Don Gil de las calzas verdes*. Edited by Alonso Zamora Vicente. Madrid: Castalia, 1990.

———. *Los balcones de Madrid*. Electronic Text by Vern G. Williamsen and J. T. Abraham. http://w3.coh.arizona.edu/projects/comedia/tirso/Balmad.html.

Munday, Anthony. *The Death of Robert, Earle of Huntington, Otherwise Called Robin Hood of merrie Sherwodde: with the lamentable tragedy of chaste Matilda, his fair maid Marian, poysoned at Dunmowe by King John*. London: William Leake, 1601.

———. *A Second and Third Blast of Retreat from Plays and Theatres*. Edited by J. W. Binns. New York: Johnson Reprints, 1962.

Palafox y Mendoza, Juan de. *Discurso en favor de cierto religioso de vida ejemplar, a quien castigó rigurosamente un prelado superior, porque subió a predicar al púlpito de cierto convento de religiosas, al tiempo y cuando se representaba en él una mal ordenado comedia, de que resultaron muchos daños.* Edited by Efraín Castro Morales. Pueblo: Museo Mexicano, 2003.

———. *Epístola exortatoria a los curas y beneficiados de la Puebla de los Ángeles.* Edited by Efraín Castro Morales. Pueblo: Museo Mexicano, 2003.

Pilkinton, Mark C., ed. *Bristol, Records of Early English Drama.* Vol. 8. Toronto: University of Toronto Press, 1997.

Plato. *The Republic.* Translated by Paul Shorey. Cambridge, MA: Harvard University Press, 1970.

Prynne, William. *Histrio-Mastix: The Players Scourge, or the Actors Tragedi.* Edited by Peter Davison. New York: Johnson Reprint, 1972.

Romero de Terreros, Manuel, ed. *Gregorio M. De Guijo, Diario, 1648–1664.* Vol. 1. México: Editorial Porrúa, S.A., 1952.

Seco Serrano, Carlos, ed. *Cartas de Sor María de Jesús de Ágreda.* In *Biblioteca de Autores Españoles: Epistolario Español.* Tomo IV. Madrid: Atlas, 1958.

Shergold, N. D., and J. E. Varey. *Genealogía, Origen y Noticias de los comediantes de España.* London: Tamesis, 1985.

Sidney, Philip. *An Apology for Poetry.* Edited by R. W. Maslen and Geoffrey Shepherd. Manchester: Manchester University Press, 2002.

Varey J. E., and N. D. Shergold. *Los Arriendos de Los Corrales de Comedias de Madrid: 1587–1719.* London: Tamesis, 1987.

———. *Teatros y Comedias en Madrid: 1600–1650: Estudio y Documentos.* London: Tamesis, 1971.

Vega, Lope de. *El acero de Madrid.* Edited by Stefano Arata. Madrid: Clásicos Castilia, 2000.

———. *El Arenal de Sevilla.* In *El Perro del Hortelano.* Madrid: Espasa-Calpe, 1977.

———. *El Nuevo mundo descubierto por Cristóbal Colón.* Edited by Robert M. Shannon. New York: Peter Lang, 2001.

Vicary, Thomas. *A profitable treatise of the anatomie of mans body: compyled by that excellent chirurgion, M. Thomas Vicary esquire, seriaunt chirurgion to king Henry the eyght, to king Edward the. vj. to Queene Mary, and to our most gracious Soueraigne Lady Queene Elizabeth, and also cheefe chirurgion of S. Bartholomewes Hospital. Which work is newly reuyued, corrected, and published by the chirurgions of the same hospital now beeing.* London: Henry Bamforde, 1577. EEBO.

Villalobos, Arias de. *Canto intitulado mercurio.* México, 1620, 1907.

Villandrando, Agustín de Rojas. *El Viaje Entretenido.* Edited by Jacques Joset. Madrid: Espasa Calpe, 1977.

Vinha, Geraldo da. *Carta y relación verdadera del nacimiento, vida y muerte de don Rodrigo Calderón.* 1621. BNE VC/224/26.

Zabaleta, Juan. *El Día de fiesta por la mañana y por la tarde.* Edited by Cristóbal Cuevas García. Madrid: Editorial Castalia, 1983.

Zugasti, Miguel. *La "Trilogía de los Pizarros" de Tirso de Molina, Estudio crítico.* Tomos II–IV. Kassel: Edition Reichenberger, 1993.

SECONDARY SOURCES

Aaron, Melissa. *Global Economics: A History of the Theater Business, the Chamberlain's/King's Men, and Their Plays, 1599–1642.* Newark: University of Delaware Press, 2005.

Adamson, John. *The Noble Revolt: The Overthrow of Charles I.* London: Weidenfeld and Nicolson, 2007.

Albrecht, Jane. *The Playgoing Public of Madrid in the Time of Tirso de Molina.* New Orleans: University Press of the South, 2001.

Allen, John J. *The Reconstruction of a Spanish Golden Age Playhouse: El Corral del Príncipe (1583–1744).* Gainesville: University of Florida Press, 1983.

———. "The Reemergence of the Playhouse in the Renaissance: Spain, 1550–1750." In *Theatrical Spaces and Dramatic Places.* Edited by Paul C. Castagno, 27–38. Tuscaloosa: University of Alabama Press, 1996.

Altman, Ida. *Transatlantic Ties in the Spanish Empire: Brihuega, Spain, and Puebla, Mexico, 1560–1620.* Stanford: Stanford University Press, 2000.

Alvarez de Toledo, Cayetana. *Politics and Reform in Spain and Viceregal Mexico: The Life and Thought of Juan de Palafox 1600–1659.* Oxford: Clarendon Press, 2004.

Arellano, Ignacio. *Historia del teatro español del siglo xvii.* Madrid: Cátedra, 2005.

Arellano, Ignacio, and J. A. Rodríguez Garrido, eds. *El teatro en la hispanoamérica colonial.* Pamplona: Editorial Iberoamericana, 2008.

Arrizabalaga, Jon, Andrew Cunningham, and Ole Peter Grell. *Health Care and Poor Relief in Counter-Reformation Europe.* New York: Routledge, 2005.

Aston, Trevor. *Europe in Crisis, 1560–1660.* New York: Routledge, 1965.

Baker, David Erskine, and Stephen Jones. *Biographia Dramatica: Names of the dramas: A–L.* Vol. 2. London: Longman, Hurst, Rees, Orme & Brown, 1812.

Ball, Rachael. "'Beautiful Serpents' and 'Cathedras of Pestilence': Antitheatrical Traditions, Gendered Decline, and Political Crisis in Early Modern Spain and England." *Sixteenth Century Journal* 43, no. 3 (Autumn 2015): 541–63.

———. "Water, Wine, and *Aloja*: Consuming Interests in the *Corrales de Comedias* 1600–1646." *Comedia Performance* 10, no. 1 (Spring 2013): 59–92.

Barish, Jonas. *The Antitheatrical Prejudice.* Berkeley: University of California Press, 1981.

Barker, Kathleen. "An Early Seventeenth Century Provincial Playhouse." *Theatre Notebook* 29, no. 2 (1975): 81–84.

Bass, Laura R., and Amanda Wunder. "The Veiled Ladies of the Early Modern Spanish World: Seduction and Scandal in Seville, Madrid, and Lima." *Hispanic Review* 77, no. 1 (2009): 97–144.

Bayer, Mark. *Theatre, Community, and Civic Engagement in Jacobean London.* Iowa City: University of Iowa Press, 2011.

Bazant, Jan. "The Evolution of the Textile Industry of Puebla, 1544–1585." *Comparative Studies of Society and History* 7: 57–69. The Hague: Mouton, 1964.

Beier, A. L. "Social Problems in Elizabethan London." *Journal of Interdisciplinary History* 9, no. 2 (Autumn 1978): 203–21.

Beier, A. L., and Roger Finlay, eds. *London 1500–1700: The Making of the Metropolis.* London: Longman, 1986.

Bireley, Robert. *The Refashioning of Catholicism, 1450–1700.* Washington: Catholic University of America Press, 1999.

Blasco Esquivias, Beatriz. *¡Agua Va! La higiene urbana en Madrid (1561–1761).* Madrid: Caja Madrid, 1998.

Bloemendal, Jan, Peter G. F. Eversmann, and Elsa Streitman, eds. *Drama, Performance, and Debate: Theatre and Public Opinion in the Early Modern Period.* Leiden: Brill, 2013.

Blue, William R. *Spanish Comedies and Historical Contexts in the 1620s.* University Park: Pennsylvania State University Press, 1996.

Bolaños Donoso, Piedad. "Nuevas aportaciones documentales sobre el histrionismo sevillano del siglo XVI." In *La Comedia.* Edited by Jean Canavaggio, 131–44. Madrid: Casa de Velázquez, 1995.

———. "Roque de Figueroa y el 'Cuarto' Coliseo Sevillano (1631–1632)." *Hesperia: Anuario de filología hispánica* 9 (2006): 9–38.

Bowers, Kristy Wilson. "Balancing Individual and Communal Needs: Plague and Public Health in Early Modern Seville." *Bulletin of the History of Medicine* 81, no. 2 (2007): 335–58.

Boyle, Margaret. *Unruly Women: Performance, Penitence, and Punishment in Early Modern Spain.* Toronto: University of Toronto Press, 2014.

Braun, Herald E. *Juan de Mariana and Early Modern Spanish Political Thought.* Burlington: Ashgate, 2007.

Bravo-Villasante, Carmen. *La Mujer Vestida de Hombre en el Teatro Español (Siglos XVI-XVII)*. Madrid: Revista de Occidente, 1955.

Brescia, Michael Manuel. "The Cultural Politics of Episcopal Power: Juan de Palafox y Mendoza and Tridentine Catholicism in Seventeenth-Century Puebla de los Angeles, Mexico." PhD diss., University of Arizona, 2002.

Burke, Peter. "Popular Culture in Seventeenth Century London." *London Journal* 3 (1977): 143–62.

Burkhart, Louise M. *Aztecs on Stage: Religious Theater in Colonial Mexico*. Norman: University of Oklahoma Press, 2011.

———. *The Slippery Earth: Nahau-Christian Moral Dialogue in Sixteenth-Century Mexico*. Tucson: University of Arizona Press, 1989.

Butler, Martin. *Theatre and Crisis 1632–1642*. Cambridge: Cambridge University Press, 1984.

Butlin, R. A. "The Population of Dublin in the Late Seventeenth Century." *Irish Geography* 5, no. 2 (1966): 51–66.

Campbell, Jodi. *Monarchy, Political Culture, and Drama in Seventeenth-Century Madrid: Theater of Negotiation*. Burlington: Ashgate, 2006.

Cañadas, Ivan. *Public Theatres of Golden Age Madrid and Tudor-Stuart London: Class, Gender, and Festive Community*. Burlington: Ashgate, 2005.

Candiani, Vera. "The Desagüe Reconsidered: Environmental Dimensions of Class Conflict in Colonial Mexico." *Hispanic American Historical Review* 92, no. 1 (2012): 5–39.

———. *Dreaming of Dry Land: Environmental Transformation in Colonial Mexico City*. Stanford: Stanford University Press, 2014.

Canny, Nicholas. *Making Ireland British: 1580–1650*. Oxford: Oxford University Press, 2003.

Carmona, Juan Ignacio. *Crónica Urbana Del Malvivir (S. XIV-XVII): Insalubridad, desamparo, y hambre en Sevilla*. Sevilla: Universidad de Sevilla, 2000.

———. *Enfermedad y sociedad en los primeros tiempos modernos*. Sevilla: Universidad de Sevilla, 2005.

———. "La reunificación de los Hospitales sevillanos." In *Los Hospitales de Sevilla*. Edited by Fernando Chueca Goitia, 53–71. Sevilla: Real Academia Sevillana de Buenas Letras, 1989.

———. *El Sistema de Hospitalidad Pública en la Sevilla del Antiguo Régimen*. Sevilla: Diputación Provincial, 1979.

Castro Leal, Antonio. *Juan Ruiz de Alarcón, su vida y su obra*. México: Ediciones Cuadernos Americanos, 1943.

Chambers, E. K. *The Elizabethan Stage*. Oxford: Clarendon Press, 1924.

Chang-Rodriguez, Raquel. *Historia de la literatura mexicana: desde sus orígenes hasta nuestros días*. Vol. 2. México: Siglo XXI, 2002.

Clare, Janet. *Drama of the English Republic, 1649–1660: Plays and Entertainments*. Manchester: Manchester University Press, 2006.

Clegg, Cyndia Susan. *Press Censorship in Jacobean England*. Cambridge: Cambridge University Press, 2001.

Clouse, Michele. *Medicine, Government, and Public Health in Philip II's Spain: Shared Interest, Competing Authorities*. Burlington: Ashgate, 2011.

Coester, Alfred. *The Literary History of Spanish America*. New York: Macmillan, 1921.

Cohen, Walter. *Drama of a Nation: Public Theater in Renaissance England and Spain*. Ithaca, NY: Cornell University Press, 1985.

Cook, Alexandra Parma. "The Women of Early Modern Triana: Life, Death, and Survival Strategies in Seville's Maritime District." In *Women in Port: Gendering Communities, Economies, and Social Networks in Atlantic Port Cities, 1500–1800*. Edited by Dougless Catterall and Jodi Campbell, 41–68. Leiden: Brill, 2012.

Cook, Alexandra Parma, and Noble David Cook. *The Plague Files: Crisis Management in Sixteenth Century Seville*. Baton Rouge: Louisiana State University Press, 2009.

Cruickshank, William. "The First Edition of *El burlador de Sevilla*." *Hispanic Review* 49 (1981): 443–67.

Cuenya Mateos, Miguel Ángel. *Fiestas y virreyes en la Puebla colonial*. Puebla: Secretaría de Cultura, 1989.

Cuenya Mateos, Miguel Ángel, and Carlos Contreras Cruz. *Puebla de los Ángeles: historia de una ciudad novohispana, aspectos sociales, económicos y demográficos*. Puebla: Universidad Autónoma de Puebla, 2007.

Day, Stuart A. "Performing Mexico." In *Writing and Rewriting National Theatre Histories*. Edited by S. E. Wilmer, 153–73. Iowa City: University of Iowa Press, 2004.

Díez Borque, José María. *Sociedad y teatro en la España de Lope de Vega*. Barcelona: Casa Editorial, S.A., 1978.

Dilillo, Leonardo. "Moral Purpose in Ruiz de Alarcón's 'La verdad sospechosa.'" *Hispania* 56 (April 1973): 254–59.

Dixon, Victor. *En busca del fénix: quince estudios sobre Lope de Vega y su teatro*. Madrid: Iberoamericana, 2013.

———. "Lope de Vega and America: *The New World* and *Arauco Tamed*." *Renaissance Studies* 6, no. 3–4 (September 1992): 249–69.

Domínguez Ortíz, Antonio. *Alteraciones andaluzas*. Madrid: Narcea, 1973.

——. *La sociedad española en el siglo XVII.* Madrid: CSIC, 1964.

Don, Patricia Lopes. "Franciscans, Indian Sorcerers, and the Inquisition in New Spain, 1536–1543." *Journal of World History* 17, no. 1 (March 2006): 27–49.

Donnell, Sidney. "From Cross Gender to Generic Closure: Sor Juan Inés de la Cruz's *Los empeños de una casa.*" *Revista Canadiense de Estudios Hispánicos* 33, no. 1 (Autumn 2008): 177–93.

Donnelly, John Patrick, and Michael W. Maher. *Confraternities and Catholic Reform in Italy, France, and Spain.* Kirksville, MO: Truman State University Press, 1999.

Dopico Black, Georgina. *Perfect Wives, Other Women: Adultery and Inquisition in Early Modern Spain.* Durham, NC: Duke University Press, 2001.

Dutton, Richard. *Licensing, Censorship and Authorship in Early Modern England: Buggeswords.* New York: Palgrave, 2000.

——. *Mastering the Revels: The Regulation and Censorship of English Renaissance Drama.* Iowa City: University of Iowa Press, 1991.

——. "The Revels Office and the Boy Companies, 1600–1613: New Perspectives." *English Literary Renaissance* 32, no. 2 (2002): 324–51.

——. "The St. Werburgh Street Theater, Dublin." In *Localizing Caroline Drama: Politics and Economics of the Early Modern English State, 1625–1642.* Edited by Adam Zucker and Alan Farmer, 129–56. Gordonsville, VA: Palgrave Macmillan, 2006.

"Early Modern Plays Presented in London." Early Modern Drama Database. http://homepage.mac.com/tomdalekeever/date.html.

Edelmayer, Friedrich. *Philipp II. Die Biographie enes Weltherrschers.* Stuttgart: Kohlhammer, 2009.

Elliott, J. H. *Empires of the Atlantic World: Britain and Spain in America 1492–1830.* New Haven: Yale University Press, 2006.

——. "Self Perception and Decline in Early Seventeenth-Century Spain." *Past & Present* 74 (February 1977): 41–61.

——. *Spain and Its World 1500–1700.* New Haven: Yale University Press, 1989.

Entrambasaguas, Joaquin de. *Lope de Vega y su tiempo.* Barcelona: Teide, 1962.

Fedewa, Marilyn. *María of Ágreda: Mystical Lady in Blue.* Albuquerque: University of New Mexico Press, 2010.

Fee, Nancy. "La Entrada Angelopolitana: Ritual and Myth in the Viceregal Entry in Puebla de Los Angeles." *The Americas* 52, no. 3 (January 1996): 283–320.

Ferrer Valls, Teresa. *Diccionario biográfico de actores del teatro clásico español (DICAT): Edición digital.* Kassel: Edition Reichenberger, 2008.

——. *La Práctica Escénica Cortesana: de la época del Emperador a la de Felipe III.* London: Tamesis, 1991.

Fletcher, Alan. *Drama, Performance, and Polity in Pre-Cromwellian Ireland.* Toronto: University of Toronto Press, 2000.

Fletcher, Anthony. *Gender, Sex, and Subordination in England, 1500–1800.* New Haven: Yale University Press, 1995.

Flynn, Maureen M. "Charitable Ritual in Late Medieval and Early Modern Spain." *Sixteenth Century Journal* 16, no. 3 (Autumn 1985): 335–48.

———. *Sacred Charities: Confraternities and Social Welfare in Spain, 1400–1700.* Ithaca, NY: Cornell University Press, 1989.

Fothergill-Payne, Louise. "The Pizarro Trilogy and the Question of History: From *Ars Historica* to New Historicism and Beyond." In *Tirso de Molina: His Originality Then and Now.* Edited by Henry W. Sullivan and Raúl A. Galoppe, 187–205. Ottawa: Dovehouse Editions, 1996.

Fuller, Amy. *Between Two Worlds: The Autos Sacramentales of Sor Juana Inés de la Cruz.* Cambridge: MHRA, 2015.

Galespie, Raymond, ed. *The Proctor's Accounts of Peter Lewis, 1564–65.* Ann Arbor, MI: Four Courts Press, 1996.

García Sánchez, Miguel Ángel. *Análisis sociológico de la pobreza en Madrid, 1578–1650.* PhD diss., Universidad Complutense de Madrid, 2004.

———. "Mujeres pobres y sociabilidad en el Madrid moderno: el Hospital de la Pasión, 1565–1700." *Torre de los lujanes* 52 (2004): 203–32.

Gleach, Frederic. *Powhatan's World and Colonial Virginia: A Conflict of Cultures.* Lincoln: University of Nebraska Press, 1997.

González Sánchez, Carlos Alberto. *Los mundos del libro: medios de difusión de la cultura occidental en las Indias de los siglo XVI y XVII.* Sevilla: Universidad de Sevilla, 1999.

Gordon, Bruce, and Peter Marshall. *The Place of the Dead: Death and Remembrance in Late Medieval and Early Modern Europe.* Cambridge: Cambridge University Press, 2000.

Granja, Agustín de la. "Una carta con indicaciones escénicas para el autor de comedias Roque de Figueroa." *Revista Canadiense de Estudios Hispánicos* 17, no. 2 (1993): 383–88.

Greene, Evarts Boutell, and Virginia Draper Harrington. *American Population before the Federal Census of 1790.* New York: Genealogical Publishing, 1932, 1981.

Greer, Margaret R. *The Play of Power: Mythological Court Dramas of Calderón de la Barca.* Princeton, NJ: Princeton University Press, 1991.

———. "A Tale of Three Cities: The Place of the Theatre in Early Modern Madrid, Paris and London." *Bulletin of Hispanic Studies* 77, no. 1 (2000): 391–419.

Grenier, John. *The First Way of War: American War Making on the Frontier, 1607-1814*. Cambridge: Cambridge University Press, 2005.

Gurr, Andrew. *Playgoing in Shakespeare's London*. Cambridge: Cambridge University Press, 2004.

———. *The Shakespearean Stage, 1574–1642*. Cambridge: Cambridge University Press, 1992, 2006.

Hardison Londré, Felicia, and Daniel J. Watermeier. *The History of North American Theatre From Pre-Columbian Times to the Present*. New York: Continuum, 1998.

Heinemann, Margot. *Puritanism and Theatre: Thomas Middleton and Opposition Drama under the Early Stuarts*. Cambridge: Cambridge University Press, 1980.

Heise, Ursula. "Transvestitism and the Stage Controversy in England and Spain, 1580–1680." *Theatre Journal* 44 (1992): 357–74.

Henderson, John. *The Renaissance Hospital: Healing the Body and Healing the Soul*. New Haven: Yale University Press, 2006.

Herring, C. H. "Ledgers of the Royal Treasury." *Hispanic American Historical Review* 2, no. 2 (1919): 173–87.

Hesler, Richard. "A New Look at the Theatre of Lope de Rueda." *Educational Theatre Journal* 16, no. 1 (March 1964): 47–54.

Hirschburg, Julia L. "Social Experiment in New Spain: A Prosopographical Study of the Early Settlement at Puebla de los Angeles." *Hispanic American Historical Review* 59 (1979): 1–33.

Hoberman, Louisa. "Bureaucracy and Disaster: Mexico City and the Flood of 1629." *Journal of Latin American Studies* 6, no. 2 (November 1974): 211–30.

Horcasitas, Fernando, ed. *Teatro Náhuatl I: Épocas Novohispana y Moderna*. México: Universidad Nacional Autónoma de México, 2004.

Howard, Jean. *Theater of a City: The Places of London Comedy, 1598–1642*. Philadelphia: University of Pennsylvania Press, 2007.

Huelga Criado, Pilar. *En la raya de Portugal: solidaridad y tensiones en la comunidad judeoconversa*. Salamanca: Ediciones Universidad de Salamanca, 1994.

Huguet-Termes, Teresa. "Madrid Hospitals and Welfare in the Context of the Hapsburg Empire." *Medical History Supplement* 29 (2009): 64–85.

Imamuddin, S. M. *Muslim Spain 711-1492 A.D.: A Sociological Study*. Leiden: Brill Academic Press, 1997.

Israel, Jonathan. "Mexico and the General Crisis of the Seventeenth Century." *Past & Present* 63 (May 1974): 33–57.

——. *Race, Class, and Politics in Colonial Mexico, 1610–1660.* Oxford: Oxford University Press, 1976.

Jackson, Kenneth. *Separate Theaters: Bethlem ("Bedlam") Hospital and the Shakespearean Stage.* Newark: University of Delaware Press, 2005.

Johnson, Harvey L. "Notas Relativas a los Corrales de la Ciudad de México 1626–1641." *Revista Iberoamericana* 3, no. 5 (1941): 133–38.

——. *El Teatro Colonial en Puebla (Primer Siglo).* Puebla: Secretaría de Cultura, 2002.

Johnson, Odai. *Absence and Memory in Colonial American Theatre: Fiorelli's Plaster.* New York: Palgrave, 2006.

——. "Working up from Postholes: (Im)Material Witnesses, Evidence, and Narrativity in the Colonial American Theatre." *Theatre Survey* 46, no. 2 (2005): 183–98.

Jütte, Robert. *Poverty and Deviance in Early Modern Europe.* Cambridge: Cambridge University Press, 1994.

Kagan, Richard. *Students and Society in Early Modern Spain.* Baltimore: John Hopkins University Press, 1974.

——. "Urbs and Civitas in Sixteenth- and Seventeenth-Century Spain." In *Envisioning the City: Six Studies in Urban Cartography.* Edited by David Buisseret, 75–108. Chicago: University of Chicago Press, 1998.

Kagan, Richard, and Abigail Dyer. *Inquisitorial Inquiries: Brief Lives of Secret Jews and Other Heretics.* Baltimore: Johns Hopkins University Press, 2004.

Keeler, Mary Frear. *The Long Parliament, 1640–1641: A Biographical Study of Its Members.* Philadelphia: American Philosophical Society, 1954.

Keen, Benjamin. *The Aztec Image in Western Thought.* New Brunswick, NJ: Rutgers University Press, 1990.

Kennedy, Mark. "Charles I and Local Government: The Draining of the East and West Fens." *Albion: A Quarterly Journal Concerned With British Studies* 15, no. 1 (Spring 1983): 19–31.

Kennedy, Ruth L. "Certain Phases of the Sumptuary Decrees of 1623 and Their Relation to Tirso's Theatre." *Hispanic Review* 10 (1942): 91–115.

Klausner, David. "The Improvising Vice." In *Improvisation in the Arts of the Middle Ages and Renaissance.* Edited by Timothy McGee, 273–83. Kalamazoo: Western Michigan University Press, 2003.

Kinsbruner, Jay. *The Colonial Spanish-American City: Urban Life in the Age of Atlantic Capitalism.* Austin: University of Texas Press, 2005.

Kupperman, Karen. *Indians and English: Facing Off in Early America.* Ithaca, NY: Cornell University Press, 2000.

Lamus Obregón, Marina. *Geografías del teatro en América Latina: Un relato histórico.* Bogotá: Luna Libros, 2014.

Land, Robert. "The First Williamsburg Theater." *William and Mary Quarterly* 5, no. 3 (1948): 359–74.

Lauer, A. Robert. "The Iberian Encounter of America in the Spanish Theater of the Golden Age." *Pacific Coast Philology* 28, no. 1 (September 1993): 32–42.

Lee, James. "'Ye Shall Disturb Noe Man's Right': Oath-Taking and Oath-Breaking in Late Medieval and Early Modern Bristol." *Urban History* 34, no. 1 (2007): 27–38.

Leech, Roger. *Topography of Medieval and Early Modern Bristol.* Bristol: Bristol Record Society, 1997.

Leggatt, Alexander. *Citizen Comedy in the Age of Shakespeare.* Toronto: University of Toronto Press, 1973.

Lehfeldt, Elizabeth. "Ideal Men: Masculinity and Decline in Seventeenth Century Spain." *Renaissance Quarterly* 61, no. 2 (2008): 463–94.

Lennon, Colm. "The Changing Face of Dublin, 1550–1750." In *Two Capitals: London and Dublin 1500–1840.* Edited by Peter Clark and Raymond Gillespie, 39–52. Oxford: Oxford University Press, 2001.

Leonard, Irving A. "A Shipment of Comedias to the Indies." *Hispanic Review* 2, no. 1 (January 1934): 39–50.

Levine, Laura. *Men in Women's Clothing: Anti-theatricality and Effeminization, 1579–1642.* Cambridge: Cambridge University Press, 1994.

———. "Women in Men's Clothing: Antitheatricality and Effeminization, 1579–1642." *Criticism* 28 (1986): 121–43.

Lewy, Guenter. *Constitutionalism and Statecraft During the Golden Age of Spain: A Study of the Political Philosophy of Juan de Mariana, S.J.* Geneva: Librairie E. Droz, 1960.

Lipsett-Rivera, Sonya. "Water and Bureaucracy in Colonial Puebla de Los Angeles." *Journal of Latin American Studies* 25, no. 1 (1993): 25–44.

Loftis, John. *Renaissance Drama in England and Spain: Topical Allusion and History Plays.* Princeton, NJ: Princeton University Press, 1987.

MacDonald, Michael. *Mystical Bedlam: Madness, Anxiety and Healing in Seventeenth-Century England.* Cambridge: Cambridge University Press, 1983.

MacKay, Ruth. "The Maravall Problem: A Historical Inquiry." *Bulletin of the Comediantes* 65 (2013): 45–56.

Maravall, José Antonio. *La cultura del barroco: análisis de una estructura histórica.* Barcelona: Ariel, 1980.

———. *Teatro y literatura en la sociedad barroca.* Madrid: Seminarios y Ediciones, 1972.

Martínez Bermejo, Saul. "Beyond Luxury: Sumptuary Legislation in 17th-Century Castile." In *Making, Using, and Resisting the Law in European History.* Edited by Günther Lottes, Eero Madijainen, and Jón Viðar Sigurðsson, 93–108. Pisa: Pisa University Press, 2008.

Mathes, Valerie L. "Enrico Martinez of New Spain." *The Americas* 33, no. 1 (July 1976): 62–77.

McCusker, John. *Money and Exchange in Europe and America, 1600–1775.* Chapel Hill: University of North Carolina Press, 1992.

McKendrick, Melveena. *Theatre in Spain, 1490–1700.* Cambridge: Cambridge University Press, 1989.

———. *Woman and Society in the Spanish Drama of the Golden Age: A Study of the Mujer Varonil.* London: Cambridge University Press, 1974.

Metford, J. C. J. "The Enemies of the Theatre in the Golden Age." *Bulletin of Hispanic Studies* 28 (1951): 76–92.

Morash, Christopher. *A History of the Irish Theatre, 1601–2000.* Cambridge: Cambridge University Press, 2002.

Morley, S. Griswold. "El acero de Madrid." *Hispania Review* 13, no. 2 (April 1945): 166–69.

Morley, S. Griswold, and Courtney Bruerton. *Cronología de las comedias de Lope de Vega.* Madrid: Gredos, 1968.

Muir, Edward. *Ritual in Early Modern Europe: New Approaches to European History.* Cambridge: Cambridge University Press, 2005.

Mullaney, Steven. *The Place of the Stage: License, Play, and Power in Renaissance England.* Chicago: University of Chicago Press, 1988.

Múñoz Jiménez, José Miguel. "El patio de las comedias del Hospital de la Misericordia de Guadalajara." *Wad-al-Hayara: Revista de estudios de Guadalajara* 11 (1984): 239–58.

Navarrete, Ignacio. *Orphans of Petrarch: Poetry and Theory in the Spanish Renaissance.* Berkeley: University of California Press, 1994.

Orgel, Stephen. *Impersonations: The Performance of Gender in Shakespeare's England.* Cambridge: Cambridge University Press, 1996.

Parker, Alexander A. "Notes on the Religious Drama in Medieval Spain and the Origins of the 'Auto Sacramental.'" *Modern Language Review* 30, no. 2 (April 1935): 170–82.

Parker, Geoffrey. *Global Crisis: War, Climate Change, and Catastrophe in the Seventeenth Century.* New Haven: Yale University Press, 2013.

Pellicer, Casiano. *Tratado histórico sobre el origen y progresos de la comedia y del histrionismo en España*. Madrid: 1804.

Pelling, Margaret. *The Common Lot: Sickness, Medical Occupations and the Urban Poor*. London: Longman, 1998.

Pérez Pastor, Cristóbal. *Nuevos datos Acerca del Histrionismo Español en los Siglos XVI y XVII*. Madrid: La Revista Española, 1901.

Perry, Mary. *Crime and Society in Early Modern Seville*. Hanover, NH: University Press of New England, 1980.

———. *Gender and Disorder in Early Modern Seville*. Princeton, NJ: Princeton University Press, 1990.

Pike, Ruth. *Aristocrats and Traders: Sevillan Society in the Sixteenth Century*. Ithaca, NY: Cornell University Press, 1972.

Pilkinton, Lucy Blandford. "Theatre in Norfolk, Virginia, 1788–1812." 4 vols., PhD diss., University of Michigan, 1993.

Pilkinton, Mark. "New Information on the Playhouse in Wine Street, Bristol." *Theatre Notebook* 42, no. 2 (1988): 73-75.

Pineda Novo, Daniel. *El Teatro de Comedias del Corral de la Montería y del Alcazar de Sevilla*. Sevilla: Guadalquivir Ediciones, 2000.

Poole, Stafford. *Pedro Moya de Contreras: Catholic Reform and Royal Power in New Spain 1571–1591*. Norman: University of Oklahoma Press, 2011.

Rabb, T. K. *The Struggle for Stability in Early Modern Europe*. Oxford: Oxford University Press, 1972.

Ramírez, Hugo Hernán. *Fiesta, espectáculo y teatralidad en el México de los conquistadores*. Madrid: Iberoamericana, 2009.

Ramos, Frances. *Identity, Ritual, and Power in Colonial Puebla*. Tucson: University of Arizona Press, 2012.

Rappaport, Joanne. *The Disappearing Mestizo: Configuring Difference in the Colonial New Kingdom of Granada*. Durham, NC: Duke University Press, 2014.

Redworth, Glyn. *The Prince and the Infanta: The Cultural Politics of the Spanish Match*. New Haven: Yale University Press, 2003.

Rennert, Hugo A. *The Life of Lope de Vega 1562–1635*. New York: Benjamin Blom, 1968.

———. "Review of *Obras de Lope de Vega* by Emilio Cotalero y Mori." *Modern Language Review* 14, no. 4 (1919): 439–51.

———. *The Spanish Stage in the Time of Lope de Vega*. New York: Dover, 1963.

Richards, Jeffrey H. *Theater Enough: American Culture and the Metaphor of the World Stage, 1607–1789*. Durham, NC: Duke University Press, 1991.

Ringrose, David. "The Impact of a New Capital City: Madrid, Toledo, and New Castile, 1560–1660." *Journal of Economic History* 33, no. 4 (December 1973): 761–91.

Río Barredo, María José del. *Madrid, urbs regia: la capital ceremonial de la Monarquía Católica.* Madrid: Marcial Pons, 2000.

Robalino, Gladys. "*Amazonas en las Indias:* Mixed Marriages and the Pizarros' Political Project." In *Female Amerindians in Early Modern Spanish Theater.* Edited by Gladys Robalino, 117–40. Lewisburg, PA: Bucknell University Press, 2014.

Robertson, Karen. "Pocahontas at the Masque." *Signs* 21, no. 3 (1996): 551–83.

Rocamora, J. Luís. *El Teatro en La América Colonial.* Buenos Aires: Editorial Huarpes, 1947.

Rosenwaike, Ira. *Population History of New York City.* Syracuse, NY: Syracuse University Press, 1972.

Sacks, David Harris. *Trade, Society, and Politics in Bristol 1500–1640.* London: Garland, 1985.

———. *The Widening Gate: Bristol and the Atlantic Economy, 1450–1700.* Berkeley: University of California Press, 1991.

Sánchez Arjona, José. *Noticias referentes á los anales del teatro en Sevilla desde Lope Rueda hasta fines del siglo XVII.* Sevilla: El Rasco, 1898.

———. *El teatro en Sevilla en los siglos XVI y XVII.* Madrid, 1887; reprint, Sevilla: Centro Andaluz de Teatro: Padilla Libros, 1990.

Sanz Ayán, Carmen, y Bernardo J. García García. *Teatros y comediantes en el Madrid de Felipe II.* Madrid: Editorial Complutense, 2000.

"Sarah Hallam." *William and Mary Quarterly* 12, no. 4 (1904): 236–37.

Schen, Claire S. "Constructing the Poor in Early Seventeenth-Century London." *Albion* 32, no. 3 (Autumn 2000): 450–63.

Schilling, Hildburg. *Teatro Profano en la Nueva España.* México: Universidad Nacional Autónoma de México, 1958.

Seijas, Tatiana. *Asian Slaves in Colonial Mexico: From Chinos to Indians.* New York: Cambridge University Press, 2014.

Sénéchal, Héloïse. "The Antitheatrical Criticism of Stephen Gosson." *Literature Compass* 1, no. 1 (2004): 1–4.

Shapiro, James, ed. *Shakespeare in America: An Anthology from the Revolution to Now.* New York: Library of America, 2014.

Shapiro, Michael. *Children of the Revels: The Boy Companies of Shakespeare's Time and Their Plays.* New York: Columbia University Press, 1977.

Shaw, Catherine. "*Landgartha* and the Irish Dilemma." *Eire-Ireland* 13, no. 1 (1978): 26–39.

Shaw, Douglas. "Thomas Wentworth and Monarchical Ritual in Early Modern Ireland." *Historical Journal* 49, no. 2 (June 2006): 331–55.

Shergold, N. D. "Ganassa and the 'Commedia dell'arte' in Sixteenth-Century Spain." *Modern Language Review* 51, no. 3 (July 1956): 359–68.

———. *A History of the Spanish Stage: From Medieval Times until the End of the Seventeenth Century.* Oxford: Clarendon, 1967.

Sherman, Susanne K. *Comedies Useful: A History of the American Theatre in the South, 1775–1812.* Williamsburg, VA: Celeste Press, 1998.

Slack, Paul. *From Reformation to Improvement: Public Welfare in Early Modern England.* Oxford: Clarendon Press, 1999.

———. "Hospitals, workhouses, and the relief of the poor in early modern London." In *Health Care and Poor Relief in Protestant Europe, 1500–1700.* Edited by Ole Peter Grell and Andrew Cunningham, 234–51. London: Routledge, 1997.

———. *The Impact of Plague in Tudor and Stuart England.* London: Routledge, 1985.

Somerset, Alan. "Cultural Poetics or Historical Prose?: The Places of the Stage." In *Medieval and Renaissance Drama in England.* Vol. 11. Edited by John Pitcher, 34–59. Fairleigh, PA: Dickinson University Press, 1999.

Soufas, Teresa Scott. *Women's Acts: Plays by Women Dramatists of Spain's Golden Age.* Lexington: University Press of Kentucky, 1996.

Stevenson, Allan H. "James Shirley and the Actors at the First Irish Theatre." *Modern Philology* 40, no. 2 (1942): 147–60.

Strasser, Ulrika. "'The First Form and Grace': Ignatius of Loyola and the Reformation of Masculinity." In *Masculinity in the Reformation Era.* Edited by Scott H. Hendrix and Susan Karant-Nunn, 45–70. Kirksville, MO: Truman State University Press, 2008.

Subira, José. *El gremio de representantes españoles y la cofradía de nuestra señora de la novena.* Madrid: CSIC, 1960.

Thompson, I. A. A., and Bartolomé Yun Casalilla, eds. *The Castilian Crisis of the Seventeenth Century.* Cambridge: Cambridge University Press, 1994.

Thompson, Peter E. *The Triumphant Juan Rana: A Gay Actor of the Spanish Golden Age.* Toronto: University of Toronto Press, 2006.

Thomson, Guy. *Puebla de los Angeles, Industry and Society in a Mexican City, 1700–1850.* Boulder, CO: Westview Press, 1989.

Thomson, Peter. *Shakespeare's Theatre.* Boston: Routledge, 1983.

Tikoff, Valentina. "Gender and Juvenile Charity, Tradition and Reform: Assistance for Young People in Eighteenth-Century Seville." *Eighteenth-Century Studies* 41, no. 3 (2008): 307–35.

Trevor-Roper, Hugh. *The Crisis of the Seventeenth Century: Religion, The Reformation, and Social Change.* Indianapolis: Liberty Fund, 1971.

Usigli, Rodolfo. *México in the Theatre.* Translated by Wilder P. Scott. Jackson: University of Mississippi Press, 1976.

Valbuena Briones, Ángel. *Perspectiva critica de los dramas de Calderón.* Madrid: Ediciones Rialp, 1965.

Varey, J. E., and N. D. Shergold. "Datos históricos sobre los primeros teatros de Madrid: prohibiciones de autos y comedias y sus consecuencias." *Bulletin Hispanique* 62 (1960): 286–325.

Versényi, Adam. *Theatre in Latin America: Religion, Politics, and Culture from Cortes to the 1980s.* Cambridge: Cambridge University Press, 1993.

Vinson, Ben III. "Articulating Space: The Free-Colored Military Establishment in Colonial Mexico from the Conquest to Independence." *Callaloo* 27, no. 1 (2004): 150–71.

Viqueira Alban, Juan Pedro. *Propriety and Permissiveness in Bourbon Mexico.* Translated by Sonya Lipsett-Rivera and Sergio Rivera Ayala. New York: Rowman & Littlefield, 1999.

Webster, Susan. *Art and Ritual in Golden Age Spain: Sevillian Confraternities and the Processional Sculpture of Holy Week.* Princeton, NJ: Princeton University Press, 1998.

Weiger, John G. "Lope's Role in the Lope de Vega Myth." *Hispania* 63, no. 4 (December 1980): 658–65.

Weiss, Judith, et al. *Latin American Popular Theatre: The First Five Centuries.* Albuquerque: University of New Mexico Press, 1993.

Weston, Kay E. "Change and Essence in Lope de Vega's El Arenal de Sevilla." *MLN* 86, no. 2 (March 1971): 211–24.

Wickham, Glynne. *Early English Stages: 1300-1660.* Vols. 1–4. London: Routledge and Paul, 1959–1981.

Wickham, Glynne, Herbert Berry, and William Ingram. *English Professional Theatre, 1530-1660.* Cambridge: Cambridge: University Press, 2000.

Wikander, Matthew. *Fangs of Malice: Hypocrisy, Sincerity, & Acting.* Iowa City: University of Iowa Press, 2002.

Williams, Justine. "The Irish Plays of James Shirley, 1636–1640." PhD diss., University of Warwick, 2010.

Williams, Patrick. *The Great Favourite: The Duke of Lerma and the Court and Government of Phillip III of Spain, 1598–1621.* Manchester: Manchester University Press, 2006.

Wilson, Edward. "Nuevos Documentos Sobre Las Controversias Teatrales, 1650–1681." In *Actas del Segundo Congreso Internacional de Hispanista,* 155–70. Nimega: Instituto Español de la Universidad de Nimega, 1967.

Wilson, Margaret. *Tirso de Molina*. Boston: Twayne, 1977.

Winston, Jessica. "Expanding the Political Nation: 'Gorboduc' at the Inns of Court and Succession Revisited." *Early Theatre* 8, no. 1 (2005): 11–34.

Wiseman, Susan. *Drama and Politics in the English Civil War*. Cambridge: Cambridge University Press, 1998.

Wright, Elizabeth R. *Pilgrimage to Patronage: Lope de Vega and the Court of Phillip III, 1598-1621*. Lewisburg, PA: Bucknell University Press, 2001.

Yachnin, Paul. "The Populuxe Theatre." In *The Culture of Playgoing in Shakespeare's England: A Collaborative Debate*. Edited by Anthony B. Dawson and Paul Yachnin, 38–65. Cambridge: Cambridge University Press, 2001.

———. *Stage-wrights: Shakespeare, Jonson, Middleton, and the Making of Theatrical Value*. Philadelphia: University of Pennsylvania Press, 1997.

Zugasti, Miguel. *La "Trilogía de los Pizarros" de Tirso de Molina, Estudio crítico*. Tomo I. Kassel: Edition Reichenberger, 1993.

INDEX